Central Asians
under Russian Rule
A Study in Culture Change

Central Asians
under Russian Rule

A Study in Culture Change

By ELIZABETH E. BACON

With an Introduction
to the Paperback Edition
by Michael M. J. Fischer

Cornell University Press

ITHACA AND LONDON

First published 1966 by Cornell University Press.
Published in the United Kingdom by Cornell University Press Ltd.,
Ely House, 37 Dover Street, London W1X 4AH.

Second printing 1968.
First printing, with a new Introduction, Cornell Paperbacks, 1980.

International Standard Book Number: 0-8014-9211-4 (pbk.)
Library of Congress Catalog Card Number: 66-16739

PRINTED IN THE UNITED STATES OF AMERICA

To the Memory of that Learned and Gracious Scholar

ACADEMICIAN A. N. SAMOILOVICH

Contents

Illustrations

Maps

Introduction to the Paperback Edition

MICHAEL M. J. FISCHER

ANTHROPOLOGICALLY, Soviet Central Asia is fascinating not only for its cultural mosaic (the frontier of Persian, Turkish, and Slavic language areas; the historic meeting ground of Zoroastrianism, Manichaeanism, Buddhism, Judaism, Christianity, shamanism, and Islam), nor only for the rich interplay throughout world history of nomads and settled folk (involving the great westward population movements, from the Scythians in the eighth century B.C. to the Mongols and Uzbeks in the thirteenth to sixteenth centuries; the empires and khanates of Ghenghis Khan's successors; and the great overland trade routes from Europe to China). Today, as well, radical experiments in social engineering make it an important model to juxtapose to other parts of the Islamic world undergoing concerted efforts at rapid modernization.

The Soviet invasion of Afghanistan in December 1979, to support the faltering Marxist coup of 1978, and the 1977–79 Islamic revolution in Iran have catapulted the entire Central Asian region into international attention. These events have raised anew the questions whether the changes brought about in Central Asia over six decades under the Soviet regime are structurally different, more effective, or more humane than those occurring elsewhere.

Field research by Western anthropologists has not been allowed under the Soviet regime, and so accounts of cultural change in Central Asia take on the aspect of a detective story or a great puzzle. One of the best places to start remains Elizabeth Bacon's fifteen-year-old *Central Asians under Russian Rule.*[1] Bacon claims that the changes she describes in Central Asia "follow dynamic principles already observed in other parts of the world." By this she means two kinds of things: what anthropologists used to call "culture change" or "acculturation" (hence her subtitle) in areas such as family structure, religion, language, food, dress, and housing; and perhaps more trenchantly the processes of political economy.

Bacon's account of these latter processes make Russian and then Soviet control over Central Asia seem very similar to the expansion of the "free world" economy into Iran and Afghan-

---

[1] For helpful suggestions and information, I would like to thank Marjorie Mandelstam Balzer, Thomas Barfield, Richard Frye, and Eden Naby. Interestingly, most other general introductions appeared in the mid-1960's: Edward Allworth, ed., *Central Asia: A Century of Russian Rule* (New York: Columbia University Press, 1967); Stephen Dunn and Ethel Dunn, "Soviet Regime and Native Culture in Central Asia and Kazakhstan," *Current Anthropology,* VIII, no. 3 (June 1967), 147–208; Lawrence Krader, *Peoples of Central Asia* (Bloomington: Indiana University Press, 1966); Geoffrey Wheeler, *The Modern History of Soviet Central Asia* (London: Weidenfeld and Nicholson, 1964); and an abridged reprint of Eugene Schuyler's 1876 classic, *Turkestan* (New York: Praeger, 1966).

Slightly more specific but equally basic introductions to the history of the area include: Alexandre Bennigsen, and Chantel Lemercier-Quelquejay, *Islam in the Soviet Union* (New York: Praeger, 1967); Seymour Becker, *Russia's Protectorates in Central Asia* (Cambridge: Harvard University Press, 1968); Richard Pierce, *Russian Central Asia 1867–1917* (Berkeley: University of California Press, 1960); Richard Pipes, *The Formation of the Soviet Union: Communism and Nationalism 1917–23* (Cambridge: Harvard University Press, 1964); and Serge A. Zenkovsky, *Pan-Turkism and Islam in Russia* (Cambridge: Harvard University Press, 1967).

More recently published are Jeremy Azrael, ed., *Soviet Nationality Policies and Practices* (New York: Praeger, 1978); and William O. McCagg, Jr., and Brian D. Silver, eds., *Soviet Asian Ethnic Frontiers* (New York: Pergamon, 1979).

istan and elsewhere: the introduction of private property leading to the rich becoming landlords of former tribal lands;
redistribution of agricultural land to peasants encountering problems with credit and indebtedness; inability of governments to
sedentarize nomads satisfactorily by force and the governments'
rediscovery of nomadism as an efficient pastoral strategy; subor-
dination of peripheral regions to capital centers first by unequal
mercantile exchange rates (initially Tatar merchants backed
by Russia, then Russian merchants), then by imposition of cash
taxation (which among the Kazak nomads amounted to a re-
gressive tax since it was imposed on each tent rather than by
herd size), and expansion of industrial crops (cotton) at the
expense of local food production; use of women's liberation as
a means of destroying local autonomy and political alliance
structures; use of linguistic policies to reduce regional autonomy;
increase of Islamic identification and rhetoric as a counter to cen-
tralizing secular and alien control; and use of ethnicity as a
dynamic sorting device derived from adaptation to geographic
and cultural niches (rather than as simple primordial identities).
Soviet theoreticians have debated about whether the nineteenth-
century Russian domination of Central Asia was simple colonialism (and therefore the anti-Russian movements are to be seen
as progressive liberation movements), or whether the Russian
hegemony is to be seen as progressive, a lifting of backward
neighbors and preparation for contemporary Soviet socialism.

For anthropologists, the task of describing cultural change is
more ambitious than such political evaluations. The strength of
anthropological writing is in searching out the organic interconnections among cultural elements. Although Bacon spent only
a few weeks in Central Asia, in Alma Ata, in 1934, she uses her
field experiences in Iran and Afghanistan to convey a sense of
these organic interrelations among the various cultural and social
features of the region—features that in other accounts all too
often become lifeless ethnographic catalogues, statistical com-

pendia, or political chronologies. From a contemporary perspective, Bacon's effort seems somewhat hampered by her training and her Russian sources. Early American anthropology was concerned with recording the dying cultures of the Amerindians and with their acculturation to white culture. Russian ethnography, some of it descriptively first rate, was framed in evolutionary theory, which saw the Kirghiz, for instance, who had a less hierarchical political structure than the Kazaks, as therefore more primitive. Both traditions looked for survivals as clues to past stages of society and culture. By the 1930's and 1940's concern began to turn to "functionalism," the attempt to describe living cultures as organic wholes: cultures did not die but were reworked and transformed.

Bacon's text is an instructive period piece, theoretically a transitional work, struggling toward a modern appreciation of transformation. It is in fact ironic that a major strength of anthropology—the search for functional interconnections among cultural and social features—should lead Bacon into some of the weaker portions of her description: the seemingly ahistorical portraits of a primordial past of nomadic and oasis cultures before the arrival of the Russians. As should be clear from her references to ancient and medieval events, and from the series of political economy processes cited above, this "ahistoricism" stems not from a denial of historical change, but from an attempt to paint a synchronic picture that might serve as a base line to measure change. The solution would seem to lie in incorporating historical change into all descriptions of organic interrelation. When Bacon turns to the Russian and Soviet periods, with equal irony her account includes a clear historical dynamic but suffers from a less sophisticated concern with interrelating the parts of a culture. This lack of concern is even made explicit in the curious sentences on pages 157–58 where she turns away from discussing industry and modern irrigation schemes, preferring to search out cultural "survivals." But "survivals" ought not to be mere ethnographic curiosities. What is fascinating about cultural cohesion is the way survivals are recycled and utilized in contemporary settings.

Over the past fifteen years there has been progress both in anthropological approach and in our understanding of Central Asia. There have been continuing ethnographic and sociological reports from Soviet scholars as well as a few on-site studies by Westerners.[2] In addition there have been several full-scale anthropological studies of Central Asian ethnic groups conducted not in Soviet Central Asia but across the border in Iran and Afghanistan: Kirghiz émigrés in the Pamirs, Arab migrants from Bukhara in Qataghan and Badakhshan, Uzbek refugees from the Fergana Valley in Kunduz, Iranian Turkomans, and living Central Asian musical traditions in northern Afghanistan.[3] Aspects of Central Asian culture have also been illuminated by studies elsewhere of similar institutions such as shamanism and traditional ethnopsychiatry, urban and bazaar organization, agricultural organization, nomadism, and religion.[4] But no one has yet

[2] Stephen and Ethel Dunn, in particular, have translated a series of Russian articles: see their *Introduction to Soviet Ethnography* (Berkeley: Highgate Road Social Science Research Station, 1974); see also the journal *Soviet Anthropology and Archeology*. Among the rare on-site investigations by Westerners is William Medlin, William Cave, and Finley Carpenter, *Education and Development in Central Asia: A Case Study on Social Change in Uzbekistan* (Leiden: E. J. Brill, 1971).

[3] M. Nazif Mohib Shahrani, *The Kirghiz and Wakhi of Afghanistan* (Seattle: University of Washington Press, 1980); Thomas J. Barfield, *The Central Asian Arabs: Pastoral Nomadism in Transition* (tentative title; Austin: University of Texas Press, 1981 forthcoming); Audrey Shalinsky, "Central Asian Emigrés in Afghanistan: Social Dynamics of Identity Creation" (Ph.D. diss., Harvard University, 1979); William Irons, *The Yomut Turkmen: A Study of Social Organization among a Central Asian Turkic Speaking Population,* University of Michigan Museum of Anthropology Papers, no. 58 (Ann Arbor, 1975); Mark Slobin, *Music in the Culture of Northern Afghanistan* (Tucson: University of Arizona Press, 1976).

[4] Of particular theoretical interest in exploring the dynamics of curing cults such as shamanism are: Gholam Hossein Sa'idi's *Al-e Hava* ("Inhabitants of the Air," English translation being prepared by Kaveh Safa-

synthesized these new studies and approaches with the further social changes of the past decade and a half in Central Asia.

Among these changes are the continued rapid demographic increase of Central Asians, their continued refusal to migrate either to large cities or to labor-hungry Russia and Siberia (causing industry to be brought rather to them), and hints of increasing ethnic and cultural consciousness and competition with Russians for upper-level jobs. In the decade 1959–69, while the overall Soviet Union growth rate was 16 percent, that of the Muslim population was 42 percent. In the following decade, 1969–79, the Muslim population grew from 35 to 43 million, including the following Central Asian increases: Uzbeks in-

---

Isfahani of the Department of Anthropology, University of Chicago), a study of the zar cults of the Persian Gulf; Vincent Crapanzano's *The Hamadsha* (Berkeley: University of California Press, 1973), a study of the psychological ambivalences exploited by a Sufi curing cult among the urban poor of Mekness in Morocco; Loring Danforth's "The Anastanaria" (Ph.D. diss., Princeton University, 1978); and Stephen Durrant's "The Nishan Shaman Caught in Cultural Contradiction," *Signs,* V, no. 2 (Winter 1979). A superb study of illness idioms and medical traditions which are relevant to Central Asia is available in Byron Good's "The Heart of What's the Matter" (Ph.D. diss., University of Chicago, 1976); and the article by the same title in *Culture, Medicine and Psychiatry,* I, no. 1 (1977).

Important new studies on urban and bazaar organization which might provide a research base line for the older and presumably comparable Central Asian cities such as Merv, Bukhara, Samarkand, Tashkent, and Khiva include: Michael E. Bonine, "Yazd and Its Hinterland: A Central Place System of Dominance in the Central Iranian Plateau" (Ph.D. diss., University of Texas, 1975); Pierre Centlivres, *Un bazar d'Asie Centrale: Forme et organisation du bazar de Tashqurghan (Afghanistan)* (Neuchâtel: University of Neuchâtel, 1970); C. J. Charpentier, *Bazaar-e Tashqurghan: Ethnographical Studies in an Afghan Traditional Bazaar,* Studia Ethnographica Upsaliensia, no. 36 (Upsala, 1972); Vincent Costello, "The Industrial Structure of a Traditional Iranian City (Kashan)," *Tijdschrift voor Economische en Sociale Geografie,* LXIV, no. 2 (1973); Paul English, *City and Village in Iran: Settlement and Economy in the Kirman Basin* (Madison: University of Wisconsin Press, 1966); M. M. J. Fischer, "Zoroastrian Iran between Myth and Praxis" (Yazd, Iran) (Ph.D. diss., University of Chicago, 1973); M. J. Fry, *The Afghan Economy* (Leiden: E. J. Brill, 1974); Mary-Jo DelVecchio Good, "Social Hierarchy and Social Change in a Provincial Iranian Town" (Maragheh) (Ph.D.

creased by 36 percent to 12.5 million; Tajiks by 36 percent to 2.9 million; Kazaks by 24 percent to 6.6 million; Turkomans by 33 percent to 2 million; Kirghiz by 31 percent to 1.9 million. If these figures are broken down by age structure, the contrast with the Russians is dramatic: while the Russian and Ukrainian populations are aging, half the Central Asian populations are under the age of fifteen. Increasingly, the cohort of young men available to the army are rural non-Slavic recruits; eventually this may mean increasing numbers of non-Slavic officers or conflict over their exclusion, although for the time being few Central Asians voluntarily choose military careers.

Analysts have already sensed such conflict in the technocratic and party elite, called "scientific workers" in Soviet studies.[5] In

---

diss., Harvard University 1977); Howard Rotblat, "Stability and Change in an Iranian Provincial Bazaar" (Ph.D. diss., University of Chicago, 1972); see also the bibliography prepared by Michael Bonine, "Urbanization and City Structure in Contemporary Iran and Afghanistan," Council of Planning Librarians Exchange Bibliography no. 875 (September 1975). Systematic work on periodic markets has been done by Keith Thorpe (University of Durham) around Rasht, and by Thomas Thompson (University of Texas) around Sari in Iran, both unfortunately still unpublished; a good description of marketing hierarchies, however, may be found in Slobin.

On traditional agricultural organization, see particularly Javad Safinejad's *Boneh* (Tehran: University of Tehran Press, 1977), and Ann Lambton's still unsurpassed *Landlord and Peasant in Persia* (Oxford: Oxford University Press, 1953).

On nomadism, there now have been full-scale studies of the Shahsavand Lurs, Bakhtiari, Basseri, Qashqa'i, Boir Ahmad, Komachi, Turkomans in Iran, and of Kirghiz, Arabs, and Pathans in Afghanistan. For a bibliography of the Iranian studies, see M. M. J. Fischer, "Persian Society: Transformation and Strain," in H. Amirsadeghi and R. W. Ferrier, eds., *Twentieth Century Iran* (London: Heinemann, 1977).

On religious dynamics, see particularly Robert Canfield, *Faction and Conversion in a Plural Society: Religious Alignments in the Hindu Kush,* University of Michigan Museum of Anthropology Papers, no. 50 (Ann Arbor, 1973).

[5] Jeremy Azrael and Steven Burg, "Political Participation and Ethnic Conflict in Soviet Central Asia" (Paper delivered at the Conference on Soviet Central Asia: Trends and Changes, sponsored by the International Communication Agency, Washington, D.C., 1978).

Uzbekistan, for instance, the most populous of the Central Asian republics, affirmative action to bring natives into the governing structure (*korenizatsiia* or nativization) has raised the percentage of native "scientific workers" from 14 percent in 1947 to 48 percent in 1975 (from 568 to 14,821 persons). As economic growth slows after a period of rapid expansion, competition is increasing, with natives in high positions preventing the upward mobility of Europeans and attempting to replace Russians with native Central Asians. There have also been anti-Russian riots for the first time since the 1920's in towns such as Tashkent, Dushanbe, Groznyi, and Ordzhonikidze.

One analyst suggests that clan and tribal affiliations are still sufficiently psychologically important that they give to local communist and governmental organizations "a curious and unexpected 'familial' (mafia-type) character."[6] This together with the underground Sufi brotherhoods and the reemergence of cultural pride (*mirasism,* from *miras,* "patrimony") asserted through rehabilitation of Arabic, Turkish, and Persian literature and philosophy provides an anti-Slavic nexus difficult for Russians or the Soviet secret police to infiltrate and control. The conflict of these ethnic identity processes with Soviet goals of cultural rapprochement (*sblizheniye*) and fusion (*sliyaniye*) is by no means a conflict unique to the Soviet Union, nor are the efforts of the Russians to maintain hegemony at the expense of these same goals.

Let us see if we can clarify some of the above themes and issues by direct reference to the three categories into which Bacon divides her essay: pastoralism, oases, culture.

PASTORALISM

One of the best parts of Bacon's essay is her opening survey of the relation between the geography of the Tien Shan–Pamir

[6] Alexandre Bennigsen, "The Nature of Ethnic Consciousness in Soviet Central Asia" (Paper delivered at the Conference on Soviet Central Asia:

mountain chains, the irrigated valleys, and the steppe, on the one hand, and of the several ethnic groups, with their variated pastoral and agricultural economic strategies, on the other. A clear visualization of this relation makes sense of what otherwise for the novice would seem a jumble of complicated facts. Indeed the increasing sophistication of pastoralist studies since 1965 depends upon such visualization. The sharp division between pastoralists and agriculturalists, popular earlier in the century, has continued to come under attack, as has the romantic notion of self-sufficient and independent nomads. Increasingly, studies have supported Owen Lattimore's aphorism, "the only pure nomad is a poor nomad,"[7] and have investigated the changing interrelation between economic strategies and political organization.

Take first Bacon's casual summary of migration routes of Central Asian nomads as varying from short transhumance (moving up and down a mountain) to thousand-mile migrations to Siberia. An important technique for refining this account would be to map ecological niches and show exactly where the different groups moved. The result would demonstrate a tighter interaction between nomads and settled folk than Bacon allows. The technique has been used effectively, for example, in Thomas Barfield's study of the Central Asian "Arabs," one of the minor ethnic groups mentioned by Bacon, who now reside primarily in northern Afghanistan.

In the nineteenth century, the Arabs were a major sheep-herding group for the Bukhara meat market. Although they were to be found around Balkh, Maimana, and the Karakul (Qaisari river) basin, they were located mainly in the rich Zarafshan Valley, exploiting a niche between the detribalized Uzbek and

---

Trends and Changes, sponsored by the International Communication Agency, Washington, D.C., 1978).

[7] *Inner Asian Frontiers of China* (New York: American Geographical Society, 1940), p. 522.

Tajik farmers of the lowlands and the mountain Tajiks. In the 1870's the valley was conquered by the Russians, who in 1872, after a drought year and during a second year of bad harvests, insisted on changing the taxation system from in-kind payments to cash payments. Immobile farmers had to suffer, but mobile shepherds could simply leave, and the Arabs did. They moved into northern Afghanistan, to a vacant ecological niche similar to the one they had left: in the lowlands of Qataghan they found Uzbek farmers who raised a few animals but did not migrate far with them; and in the mountains of Badakshan there were Tajik farmers who also raised a few animals, limited by the need to provide stall feed during the winters. Both areas were depopulated, the lowlands because of malaria, the highlands because of raiding and attempts by a ruler of the Kunduz khanate in the 1830's to resettle highlanders in the malarial lowlands, where they promptly died. The only problem with this new environment for the Arabs was that it was an economic backwater, and so they continued to market their animals in Bukhara well into the Soviet period, until the border was closed. In the 1930's and 1940's the malarial swamps were drained and became a rich rice- and cotton-producing area, a development in which the Arabs participated either directly (by claiming land) or by utilizing cotton hull from the local mill as feed for their animals.

The concern with marketing or exchange of pastoral products leads to questions about Bacon's description of the Kazaks, the archetypical horse-raising nomads of the Central Asian steppe. Bacon says that most families had fifteen to thirty mares to produce *kumiss* (fermented milk), but the rich might have up to three thousand horses. What does one do with three thousand horses? How are they herded, and what does this mean for the political structure? Are these mostly mares for the production of kumiss? In an almost throwaway line, Bacon admits that sheep were the prime economic livestock, but that horses were the focus of cultural elaboration: one rode everywhere, races were a major entertainment (and mode of flirting between boys and girls), there were celebrations at first foalings and first kumiss making of the season, a chief's death might be celebrated with a sacrificial meal of his horse, and so on. It turns out, of course, that horses (geldings) were sold not only to city folk, but in larger numbers as military mounts and as draught animals. In the pre-Russian days these mounts were sold to the several khanates and petty political contenders; later they were sold to the Russians. In 1892 the Russians bought nine thousand horses in Turgai *oblast* for distribution as farm animals in Europe, and another forty thousand were purchased in 1899. Horse meat is also eaten, especially a sausage made with coriander called *basterma*.

The inequity in herd size (and the shepherding politico-economic structure it implies) may already have had to do with other political processes. Bacon notes that as pasturage was curtailed for the Kazaks because of Russian peasant colonization of the steppe, the Russians became more concerned to deal with tribal leaders who could control their followers. At first the attempts to work through tribal leaders did not work well because tribesmen did not obey; as time went on, or rather as pasture became more curtailed, such political organization became possible; richer and stronger men began to monopolize territory and convert others into clients and subordinates. One form of this process has been most clearly described for the Lurs of western Iran by Jacob Black, where under forcible sedentarization the rich seized the best and the most land and were able to preserve some of their animals, and when renomadization was allowed, it was they who were able to field flocks. They became capitalists with holdings in both agricultural land and animals, with a series of sharecroppers and shepherds working for them. Similar processes have been described for the group of Kirghiz who moved from the Soviet Union to the Pamirs of Afghanistan.

There, trapped into a limited pasture area by the closing of the Afghan–Soviet border, a large proportion of the animals came to be held and controlled by the khan and given out on contract in a patronage system to his followers. As a result, despite the egalitarian ideology of the tribe, it in fact operates in a highly inegalitarian system."[8]

Again, one would like to ask similar questions about the Turkoman, whom Bacon describes as warlike raiders. The slave markets of Khiva, Merv, and Bukhara were supplied by the Turkoman raiding Persia. Slaves were used in agriculture, and Bacon makes the highly interesting suggestion that when slavery was abolished, one unintended consequence was to increase the share of female labor in agriculture. One would like to know more about the economics of the slave trade and the modes of control exercised. Even the Kazaks used slaves to cultivate for them.

It is when Bacon attempts to describe a primordial "traditional" past (not to deny historical change, but to establish a base from which to measure contemporary change[9]), that her account seems to become inadvertently romanticized. When she turns to historical change under the Russians and then the Soviet Union, her picture becomes much more dynamic: the reduction in pasture due to Russian colonization, the increase in tribal hierarchy, the 1916 labor conscription that caused 300,000 Kazaks and Kirghiz to flee to China, the programs of sedentarization and collectivization in the 1920's, the large reduction in Kazak population (a decline of 900,000 in the last half of

[8] Jacob Black, "Tyranny as a Strategy for Survival in an 'Egalitarian Society': Luri Facts versus an Anthropological Mystique," *Man,* VII (1972), 614–34; Jacob Black-Michaud, "The Economics of Oppression" (Ph.D. diss., University of London, 1976); Shahrani. Since the Soviet invasion, the Kirghiz have fled to Pakistan.

[9] "One would expect any study of culture change to begin with a characterization of the traditional cultures, the base which is subject to change." So Bacon asserts in a scathing attack on the Dunns' 1967 survey, in *Current Anthropology,* VIII, no. 3 (June 1967), 196.

the twenties), the massive reduction in livestock (from 27.2 million sheep to 2 million, and from 4 million horses to 200,000), the 1953 "virgin lands" program to convert northern Kazakstan into wheat land, and finally the gradual readmission of nomadic pastoralism, and acknowledgment that it could be an efficient economic strategy, with a return to some 30 million sheep in 1962 and one million horses.

OASES

The cities of Central Asia once were the cultural center of the Perso-Islamic civilization. Bukhara—the name apparently comes from *vihara,* a Buddhist monastery—under the Samanids of the ninth and tenth centuries was host to the great poets Rudaki, Daqiqi, and Firdausi, to the scientist al-Biruni, the philosopher Ibn Sina (Avicenha), and the copyist of the first Arabic geometry al-Khwarazmi (who seems to have copied the much older Hebrew *Mishna Hamidot,* which in turn possibly came to Khazaria from China). Richard Frye, in a delightful little book describing Bukhara in its greatness, suggests that the cultural flowering that created a New Persian literature was in fact also a successful attempt to save Islam, to release it from its Arab background, and make it a richer, more adaptable, and universal culture.[10] That Firdausi could create the great national epic of Iran, the *Shahnameh,* fusing Iran's Zoroastrian and Islamic heritage, bespoke a new expansive consciousness of the unity of Iran and its history. The Samanid court, modeled on both the courts of the caliphs in Baghdad and the pre-Islamic Sassanian courts of Iran, became a center of Hanafi law, for a brief time welcomed neoplatonist Ismailis (Ibn Sina's father was an Ismaili), and gradually oversaw a social change in military and rural organization. The old landed nobility gradually moved into the cities, and were replaced by Turkish generals who were

[10] *Bukhara: The Medieval Achievement* (Norman: University of Oklahoma Press, 1965).

given land grants. The army became a slave army like that of the caliphs, rather than a noble cavalry like the pre-Islamic military.

After the fall of the Samanids, the feudalization process continued; the new dynasties were Turkish, and gradually Bukhara became the southern outpost of a Turkish cultural area, rather than the northern edge of a Persian one. By the sixteenth century further major changes had occurred: the rise of the European sea powers shifted the major intercontinental trade routes away from the overland caravans, leaving Central Asia out of the mainstream of commerce; Persia had become Shi'a, while Central Asia remained dominantly Sunni; and the Turkification process had intensified with the thirteenth-century Mongol conquests and the movement south in the sixteenth century of the Uzbeks to establish Uzbek khanates in Kokand, Bukhara, and Khiva. Cultural orientations looked toward Ottoman Turkey and Moghul India rather than the Arab and Persian world.

The oasis cities were based on irrigation agriculture and long-distance trade. Irrigation systems—particularly the underground channels called *kariz* in Central Asia—were expensive and often required royal or mercantile investment. Bukhara had the Zarafshan River, but Khiva depended on six canals 70 to 100 kilometers long. Many of these systems of irrigation fell into disrepair as the rise of the sea trade deprived Central Asia of its previous mercantile centrality. Nonetheless, Bukhara between 1827 and 1837 exported to Russia cotton, silk, dyes, and fruits valuing far more than the imports of pottery, hardware, sugar, and manufactured goods it received in return. The market system of course was not only long distance, but also served the productive regions around the cities through a series of periodic markets: Merv had major markets on Sunday and Thursday, Tashkent on Wednesday, Karshi on Tuesday, Shaar-Kitab on Thursday; the slave bazaar in Bukhara was on Saturday mornings.

Since 1965 there have been a series of systematic studies of such oasis cities in Iran and Afghanistan to learn how production is controlled or co-ordinated by urban elites, how the bazaar provides credit and market mechanisms where newer banking and central planning operations do not reach, and above all how traditional social organizations and affiliations are adapted and utilized under novel conditions. Comparison of outwardly similar towns can show quite different internal organization: Yazd and Kirman, for instance, are about the same size, the former growing more rapidly since it has a poorer agricultural hinterland, modern textile industries to absorb labor, and a more open entrepreneurial structure. A comparison of the two bazaars provides an index: Yazd has a fourth more retail establishments than Kirman but almost two and a half times as many wholesalers. Paul English described Kirman in the 1960's as based on three productive resources—sheep, land, and carpet weaving— all tightly controlled by a small elite. Carpet weaving in particular was organized on a putting-out system in the villages, keeping larger populations in place than could be fed by village agriculture.[11] In Qazvin, Howard Rotblat found that people squeezed off the land were absorbed into the bazaar. Other studies have analyzed how the bazaar operates a social system tightly controlled by a credit system dominated by the great merchants; how governments try to use guilds for taxation, price regulation, and political control; and how ethnic specialization occurs.

These and other descriptions of the systematic economic and social structures of oasis cities and their transformation in modern times have yet to be done for Soviet Central Asia. Bacon instead attempts to illuminate a common cultural pattern composed of remnants of various cultural inputs: Iranian customs such as the ceremony in which brides circle or jump bonfires; women's ritual feasts and pilgrimages; the Persian New Year celebrations;

[11] Robert Dillon, "Carpet Capitalism and Craft Involution in Kirman, Iran" (Ph.D. diss., Columbia University, 1976).

the attention to guild patron saints; the tradition of Sufi brotherhoods; cotton and silk textile crafts; Central Asian polo played with a goat's carcass (*baïga*), and so on. Of these, the more interesting are the craft organizations, the Sufi brotherhoods, and women's religion.

Each craft in Central Asia has a patron saint: Noah for carpenters, David for metalworkers, Ali for underground-canal diggers, among others. Pierre Centlivres gives a full list for Tashqurqan in northern Afghanistan. The Russian ethnographer V. Snesarev (1974) notes that not only do these practices continue but new occupations find themselves appropriate saints: thus truckdrivers have adopted David. Snesarov describes ceremonies taking place each Thursday night (the eve of the day of worship) in which fires are lighted for the spirits of deceased master craftsmen and the charters of the craft may be read. There are also gift-giving ceremonies when an apprentice is graduated to master.[12]

Bacon mentions the Sufi brotherhoods only in passing, to say that Bukhara once had sixty orders (or, more likely, lodges) and that in the past they helped stir up anti-Russian feelings. A number of Sufi orders existed in Central Asia: Chistiya, Qadiriya, and Naqshebandiya. The story of the nineteenth-century revival of the Naqshebandiya (an order founded in Bukhara in the fourteenth century), its quiet spreading of literacy and modernist ideas, would be well worth investigation, particularly if, as Alexandre Bennigsen says, the Sufi brotherhoods continue today to maintain a network of clandestine Koranic schools, places of prayer, and shrines of *sheikhs* martyred in anti-Russian activities, and are "spectacularly and uncompromisingly hostile to the Soviet regime."[13]

[12] V. Snesarev, "On Some Causes of the Persistence of Religio-Customary Survivals among the Khorezm Uzbeks," in S. and E. Dunn, eds., *Introduction to Soviet Ethnography,* I, pp. 215–38.

[13] Bennigsen, 1978. In 1898 a holy war was led by Naqshebandiya leader Ishan Muhammad Ali Khalifa Sabir Sufiev in Andizhan in the Fergana

Shrines are also a focus of women's religious organization: Snesarev acknowledges the continuing existence of *momos* (mid-wives) who play important roles in the several ceremonies after childbirth (placement in the cradle, first clothes, first haircut), female dervishes, and female shamans. Bacon mentions women's ritual feasts for Bibi Seshambeh (Lady Tuesday) and the "Lady Solver of Problems"; these rituals in the Iranian town of Yazd have been described in detail.[14]

The existence of these traditions, of various ethnic groups in the cities, and of the patterns of informal structure within government and Party agencies described by Bennigsen as familial or mafia-like should give a sense of the complexity of urban organization, and a sense that what is often dismissed by Soviet ethnographers (and Bacon) as mere customs and survivals may have vital functions and can serve the informed observer as important social indices. As already mentioned, of the two key sets of economic changes—irrigation and industry—Bacon has little to say, asserting that Soviet writers give ample coverage to these achievements and that she is more "concerned with trying to discover the type and degree of 'survivals'—those facets of traditional culture that have managed to persist" (p. 158). But it is not as survivals that such customs are of interest; rather one would like to understand how they are integrated and give modern cooperatives and bureaucracies cultural depth. Furthermore the agricultural projects—great canals, such as the six-hundred-mile canal from the Amu Darya to Ashkhabad—while successful in raising output, have raised similar ecological concerns as irrigation projects in other arid areas (the Aral Sea has

---

Valley. During the establishment of Soviet control, while some Naqshebandiya were co-opted or co-operated with the Bolsheviks, Naqshebandiya *sheikh* Uzun Haj founded the Emirate of Daghestan-Chechniya (1918–20); he died in 1921 and his tomb remains one of the most popular shrines in the Caucasus. In Afghanistan, the Naqshebandiya leading family, the Mujadidi, helped overthrow Amir Amanullah in 1929.

[14] Fischer, 1973.

dropped six feet, there are worries that leakage is causing formation of marshes and salinization), and one wonders if there are similar social problems. Central Asia produces nearly half the rice, over two-thirds of the cotton, and a quarter of the vegetables and melons of the Soviet Union. In addition, there would seem to be interesting social problems of adaptation in industry as well, given the indications of an oversupply of labor, a refusal of women to become workers, the necessity to bring industry to small towns, and the reluctance of labor to migrate to jobs or urban high-rise apartments. (The original industrial labor force in Central Asia is composed of Europeans brought there during World War Two, when industry was shifted away from the German front.)

CULTURE

The reorganization of a culture is a very complex affair, involving interventions in family life, religion, education, language, authority and sex-role patterns, folklore, and traditional psychotherapies.

What appears as merely a progressive set of goals to liberate women, Gregory Massell has recently argued,[15] was in Central Asia a far more ambitious effort to undermine traditional culture so that it could be reorganized. Central Asia, communist theoreticians worried, had no revolutionary working class at the time of the revolution. Attempts to liquidate traditional local elites backfired: instead of ungluing society and making it pliable to new leadership, they increased solidarity and resistance to Russian outsiders. Women, it was argued, could play a dual role: their liberation, by attacking the basic fabric of family and kinship, might make society pliable; and women, as a segregated, exploited, degraded class under the traditional regime, might

[15] Gregory J. Massell, *The Surrogate Proletariat: Moslem Women and Revolutionary Strategies in Soviet Central Asia 1919–1929* (Princeton: Princeton University Press, 1974).

serve as a surrogate proletariat and revolutionary force. Attempts were made to organize Central Asian women. The example of Ataturk's reforms in Turkey helped spur action, since the Soviets could not allow themselves to be outpaced in revolution. Laws were passed against "crimes based on custom" (payment and acceptance of bride price, forced marriage, giving of a minor girl in marriage, polygamy, levirate, vendetta). In 1927 a vigorous campaign against the veil was launched. There was a violent reaction including riots in which thousands of lives were lost (eight hundred women died between May 27 and December 28, and more than that number of men); unveiled women were harassed, divorced, raped, killed, and mutilated; homes of communist activists were burned; girls were harassed on their way to school; women who had been given land were refused credit to make use of the land. Native officials, even communists, evaded the rules, often hiring Tatar or Kirghiz women to stand in for their wives in public unveilings. Eventually the campaign was toned down.

Religion, of course, was also under attack: all religious schools were closed between 1917 and 1941. Two *medressehs* or religious seminaries have been allowed to reopen: one in Bukhara and one in Tashkent. Officially sanctioned clerics are organized under state Boards of Muslim Spiritual Direction. The one for Central Asia and Kazakstan is headquartered in Tashkent and presided over by a Hanafi Grand Mufti, Ziauddin Babakhanov. In recent years there has been some easing of pressure, and more mosques are being built again. But behind the official facade are not only the clandestine Sufi brotherhoods, women's religion, and shrine pilgrimage, but the human and sometimes amusing compromises and conflicts reminiscent of Giovanni Guareschi's Italian communist Catholics in the Don Camillo series of comic novels: the officials in the twenties who hired stand-in wives to unveil not once but on repeated public occasions; the seclusion of wives of Party and government leaders (seclusion after all is a status symbol as well as a symbol of religiosity); the insistence of the most hardened atheist to be buried with religious rites in segregated Muslim cemeteries; vendetta threats made indirectly so as to avoid the law but to protect one's honor; and so on.

In 1951–54 there was an official purge of epic poetry of the Central Asian nationalities: they were condemned for feudal content, glorification of wars of aggression, reactionary ideology, Muslim fanaticism, and obstruction to friendship among peoples.[16] It was a campaign analogous to the purges of Muslim modernists (*Jadidi*) in 1917–20 and the so-called "national communists" in 1928–38 as bourgeois nationalists and deviationists. (The national communists had suggested that Soviet Central Asians should be the springboard and model of development for the Islamic world, and should aid their brothers. The Russians, however, wished to reserve the role of elder brother to the Third World, and not allow independent leadership roles to Central Asians.) Since the death of Stalin, there has been a rehabilitation of some at least of the Arabic, Persian, and Turkic literature and philosophy previously banned.

The Soviets divided Central Asia into republics on the basis of dialect: Uzbekistan, Kazakistan, Tajikistan, Turkmenia, and Kirghizia. This move was opposed in the teens by the early Muslim communists and again in the twenties by the national communists, who under the leadership of Tatar intellectuals would have preferred a united Turkistan. Not only language but also alphabet reforms were used to divide the Central Asians and reorganize them into new entities. First a modified Arabic script was introduced in 1923, in 1928 a Latin script, and finally in 1940 a Cyrillic script. The Latin script had the effect of cut-

[16] Bennigsen and Lemercier-Quelquejay. On the epics themselves, see Nora Chadwick and V. Zhirmunsky, *Oral Epics of Central Asia* (Cambridge: Cambridge University Press, 1969). There are now two easily accessible translations of *The Book of Dede Korkut*, one by G. Lewis (Baltimore: Penguin Books, 1974), and one by F. Sümer, A. Uysal, and W. Walker (Austin: University of Texas Press, 1972).

ting off the new generation from its heritage in the Arabic script and from communication with the Islamic world. It has been alleged that a reason for changing from the Latin script to the Cyrillic was to discourage easy communication with Turkey, which almost simultaneously introduced a somewhat different Latin script. Cyrillic would encourage a greater facility in learning Russian. Both the Latin and Cyrillic scripts were modified differently for each of the Central Asian dialects, so as to further impede communication among them, alleged opponents of the move.

These interventions in the liberation of women, religion, literature, and language are obvious and openly political. More subtle and interesting changes may also be taking place in psychology and cognitive organization. A pioneering study by A. R. Luria was done in Central Asia to investigate how literacy and cooperative work organization might be changing styles of reasoning.[17] Folktales in the past were treated as mere ethnographic curiosities, but today are being given attention as ways of exploring styles of conflict resolutions and modes of reasoning. A study in Herat, Afghanistan, shows how storytellers may use animal tales to work out alternative options to conflicts that are currently being disputed in the community, and how different storytellers may systematically structure their tales realistically or abstractly.[18]

Traditional curing procedures still in use, such as shamanism, of which V. Basilov has given a brief account,[19] ought to be another area of renewed contemporary interest. Contemporary Western doctors acknowledge that while they are unsurpassed in treating biomedical diseases, the psychology of illness is often

[17] A. R. Luria, *Cognitive Development: Its Cultural and Social Foundations* (Cambridge: Harvard University Press, 1976).

[18] Margaret Mills, "Oral Narrative in Afghanistan" (Ph.D. diss., Harvard University, 1978).

[19] V. Basilov, "Shamanism in Central Asia," *IXth International Congress of Anthropological and Ethnological Sciences* (Chicago, 1973).

handled better by traditional curers, and in fact a large proportion of visits to doctors in the West are for nonbiomedical problems. There are now three or four superb studies of curing rites
in the Middle East. Gholam Hossein Sa'idi has provided both
case materials and descriptions of symptomatologies and matched
curing procedures for zar cult cures along the Persian Gulf. Cures
involve "plays" in which the possessing spirit is called by finding
the proper tune, the curer goes into a trance, the spirit demands
gifts, and the patient is required to follow certain taboos. The
patient is not so much returned to a status quo ante, but is given
a spiritual drama with which to merge his inchoate anxieties,
which can be manipulated by the curer, and which afterward
provides the patient with an ongoing involvement in a cult sup-
port-structure. Vincent Crapanzano has explored the anxieties
and ambivalences coded and manipulated in the Hamadsha
curing cult of Morocco; and Loring Danforth has performed a
similar analysis for the Anastanari in Greece. Byron Good has
provided an account of the semantics of illness discourse in Iran
as well as the several traditions of medicine a patient may en-
counter in the search for care and health.

Finally, Audrey Shalinsky's study of Uzbek émigrés in Kunduz
explores the transfer of culture between generations: fathers who
think the past is important but personal and so do not teach it
to their children; children who are caught up in the current
modernization ideology; and grandchildren who are interested
in an almost lost culture. What Shalinsky describes is a well-
known immigrant process, but one wonders if similar dynamics
are not involved where traditional culture is under pressure and
is in fact undergoing rapid change.

CONCLUSIONS

The issues raised in the previous pages are intended partly to
update, partly to suggest, further reading, but also partly to pose
an interesting dilemma in past anthropological writing which

contemporary anthropology is learning to transcend. A major strength of anthropological research and writing is the searching out of interconnections between cultural and social elements. This fails if the account is allowed to become ahistorical. When done well, it gives accounts of change a richness and cultural depth rarely found in political or economic histories. This is not merely an aesthetic accomplishment, but can inform social and political judgment about the present and future. The informal familial or mafia-like structures within the Party or bureaucracy, the use of traditional marriage rules and alliances, the role of folk medicine and women's religion, adherence to Sufi brotherhoods, and so on are not mere ethnographic curiosities or survivals. Central Asia, after all, is a population of real people, not an organizational chart from a Russian civics book or an input-output chart from a planning ministry. If the Po Valley is inhabited by Catholic communists struggling with the contradictions of that reality, so too there must be Central Asians who read the Turkic epic poem *Dede Korkut,* swear by Lenin, and quote Rumi, the master poet of mystical philosophy. Until someone produces a new synthesis, Bacon's *Central Asians under Russian Rule* will remain a basic starting point for appreciating this culturally deep and rich complexity.

M.M.J.F.

Cambridge, Massachusetts

Preface

DURING the academic year 1933–1934, the author had the rare opportunity of residing in the Soviet Union and traveling in Kazakstan under the joint auspices of Yale University and the U.S.S.R. Academy of Sciences. Because of the long friendship and professional collaboration between Franz Boas of Columbia University and Waldemar Bogoras, dean of Russian anthropologists, a letter from Boas' great student, Edward Sapir of Yale University, opened doors usually closed to foreign social scientists. The author received a welcome far beyond the due of a beginning graduate student. During the winter spent in Leningrad, an office was provided in the domed edifice on the Neva where the Academy of Sciences was born. There, in the Museum of Anthropology and Ethnography, she had the opportunity to associate daily with Russian anthropologists. The great Turkologist, Academician A. N. Samoilovich, then Director of the Orientological Institute and President of the Kazakstan Branch of the Academy of Sciences, most graciously made available the resources of the library of the Orientological Institute, which contained the most extensive Central Asian collection in the world. Even more, he arranged for the writer to join a complex expedition in Kazakstan during the summer of 1934.

As it happened, the complex expedition was canceled in favor of a mineralogical expedition to the Hungry Steppe, a region with scant population. There was thus no chance to do an ethnographic field study of the Kazaks as planned, but the writer spent some weeks in Alma Ata. Through the courtesy of S. J. Asfendiarov, the Kazak Vice-President of the Kazakstan Branch of the Academy of Sciences, it was possible to talk with many Kazaks, some men of the older generation, others youths fresh from the steppe studying in the pedagogical institute.

There was also the opportunity to observe. It cannot be said that in Leningrad the author lived just like a Russian; as a visiting scholar she enjoyed many privileges normally accorded only to the most distinguished Russian scientists. She was able to live among Russians, however, and to make many friends. In this way she learned something of Russian culture and of the workings of the Soviet system. In Alma Ata she could observe many things: the physical appearance of a Russian colonial town; draught camels tethered within a block of the new post office, modern in architectural style; a suburb of yurts on the outskirts of town; lordly Kazak males almost hiding diminutive donkey mounts while their women trudged behind; the absence of visible response when the muezzin made his call to prayer from the minaret of the mosque; and the enthusiastic faces of Kazak students when talking of their new opportunities for education.

The leisurely trip to and from Alma Ata, by railroad and river boat, also offered many opportunities for observation. In May the steppe beyond Orenburg was green with young grass and strewn with tulips. At the northern edge of the Aral Sea the grass was brown and sparse, and Kazaks, who in that region still rejected collectivization, offered handspun woolen yarn for sale to passengers on the train. At one lonely stop without visible habitation rose a single tree; leaning against the trunk, facing away from the train and ignoring it, sat a Kazak playing a *kobyz* (a stringed instrument). From the Turk-Sib railroad, several tombs of khans or saints were seen rising like abandoned fortresses; and a Kazak government official, a fellow traveler on the train, gave advice on the most important attraction in Semipalatinsk—a Hereford bull imported by the Soviet government for breeding. The passage of the river boat down the Irtysh from Semipalatinsk to Omsk was an event that brought all the villagers to the river bank at every stop. In the assembled family groups, many women of Russian physiognomy were seen with Kazak men and with children displaying a range of mixed traits.

After 1934, the fates decreed that the author should not revisit Russian Central Asia, and for some years it was difficult to obtain Soviet publications in the United States. After World War II, when Soviet ethnographic publications became more readily available, this writer began to wonder what had been happening in Central Asia since her visit. To undertake the present comparative study, one should ideally have done extensive field research in Russian Central Asia both in the 1930's and recently. One should have read all the relevant ethnographic publications and have diligently followed events in Central Asian newspapers, periodicals, and other publications. The ideal was not possible. She has not had access to all relevant ethnographic publications, and she has relied on English-language summaries for pertinent Soviet newspaper reports. In 1934 the oases of Turkistan were closed to foreign travelers; for this reason, the author has never seen them except in photographs. Nevertheless, she has done field work in Iran and Afghanistan, where cultures are strikingly similar to those of the oases. Knowledge of Persian culture, and of Tajikicized culture in Afghanistan, has provided a base for understanding the oasis cultures of Russian Turkistan, just as research on the latter area has given new insights into the Tajikicized cultures of Afghanistan. Despite lacunae in available data, the project seemed worth undertaking. The author entered on it out of curiosity and without bias, to discover what had happened to the cultures of Central Asia under the Soviet regime. She was at first surprised at some of the findings but was gratified to learn that culture change in Central Asia follows dynamic principles already observed in other parts of the world.

When writing about Central Asia, an author is faced with special transliteration problems. Turkic, Persian, and Arabic scholars all have their own systems of transliteration; indeed, there are often alternative scholarly systems to choose from. Beyond this, dialectal differences offer a special hazard for one seeking linguistic accuracy, and a further problem arises when non-Russian terms have been filtered through the Russian. Under such circumstances, the author believes that when addressing a general audience there are distinct advantages in avoiding scholarly systems of transliteration. The general reader is likely to be bewildered by diacritical marks and the language scholar to be annoyed if the system he favors has not been employed. Except for adopting an American system for transliterating Russian which avoids diacritical marks, the author has been intentionally unsystematic. Instead, she has followed the principle that foreign terms should be presented in the form most likely to be recognized by the general reader. This principle has on occasion led to forms that would startle the purist. For example, *kalym,* the term employed for bride price, does not belong to the dialect of any of the peoples discussed in the present volume.[1] But it long ago became established in Russian ethnographic literature and was taken over by American and European ethnographers. For this reason, it will be more readily recognized by the anthropologist reader than would more accurate transliterations of the Kazak and Uzbek terms for bride price.

The author has, however, given some attention to phonetics in the transliteration of Tajik terms. Most Tajik words have been presented in a form that should be recognizable to the reader familiar with Persian. But in Central Asian Tajik, the phoneme usually transliterated by *ā* in standard Persian is pronounced in a way represented by linguists as an "open *o*." Since Central Asian Tajik shares this phonetic idiosyncracy with the speech of eastern Iran and Afghanistan, it seemed worth indicating the pronunciation. In words where this phoneme occurs, *o* is used instead of *ā,* but the standard Persian transliteration is offered in parentheses on the first appearance of the word. It is hoped that by this double system readers familiar with standard Persian will recognize the word, while those particularly interested in Tajik culture will receive a special message by reading *o* as an "open *o*."

I am grateful to the American Council of Learned Societies and the Wenner-Gren Foundation for Anthropological Research for grants-in-aid which made this research feasible.

ELIZABETH E. BACON

New York City
November 1965

Central Asians
under Russian Rule
A Study in Culture Change

I

The Land
and the People

CENTRAL ASIA, as its name implies, lies at the heart of the Eurasian continent. Remote from the seas that fringe the vast continental mass, it is an arid land of grasslands, desert, and plains, habitable only by those who know where to find water and channel it to their needs. Yet from prehistoric times its almost treeless expanses have provided a corridor for the movement of ideas and peoples between East and West, North and South. While many of the peoples who entered the area passed on to Europe or southern Asia, some remained in Central Asia and adopted the way of life that early became established there. As early as the fourth millennium B.C., village settlements like those on the Iranian Plateau began to appear along the southern foothills of Central Asia at points where mountain torrents met the plains and spread out to water the arid but fertile lands along their banks. As skill in digging and controlling irrigation channels increased, cultivators built villages along the middle courses of those rivers which flowed out into the plains, and beside streams in high valleys of the mountains where the waters had their source. In time, a chain of oasis towns, set amid gardens, orchards, and fields of grain, extended like a finger across southern Central Asia from the delta of the Amu Darya (the

1

Oxus River of the ancients) south of the Aral Sea to Lob Nor
on the borders of China. In the second century B.C., Chinese
exploration led to the opening of caravan routes that linked
China with India and the West. This new commerce brought
increased prosperity to traders and craftsmen in the oasis
towns along the way.

North of this oasis belt were grassy steppes more suitable
for pasturage than for cultivation. In these grasslands there
developed, around 1000 B.C., a special way of life, that of
pastoral nomadism. The townspeople in the south had do-
mesticated animals—sheep, goats, cattle, horses, asses, and
camels—but the whole life of the northern nomads was centered around their animals, particularly the horses which
gave them a special mobility. They moved their portable
dwellings from pasture to pasture according to season; milk
products and flesh nourished them; and the skins, wool, and
bones of their animals furnished materials for shelter, clothing, and equipment. These pastoral nomads lived by and for
their animals, independent of the sedentary cultivators of
the river valleys.

When nomads came near oasis towns and villages, however,
they were ready enough to use the grains and craft goods produced by their sedentary neighbors. Moreover, when they
were pushed out of their territory by stronger tribes or lost
their livestock through pestilence or severe winters, families
and tribal fragments took refuge on the fringes of the oases,
planting a few crops or hiring out as workers on the land.
Though hoping to return to a fully pastoral way of life, they
were often unable to achieve this. Thus, between the zone of
town dwellers who lived by cultivation, crafts, and trade, and
the grasslands dominated by pastoral nomads, there was always a margin of seminomads whose way of life was transitional between the steppe and the sown. Depending on the
vicissitudes of history, the boundary between steppe and

2

sown shifted back and forth. Sometimes towns, following the rivers, crept out into the steppe. At other periods, nomads swooped into the oases, destroying not only towns but the irrigation systems which made town life possible. Despite these marginal fluctuations, however, the basic patterns of the two cultures, sedentary and nomadic, persisted for some three millenniums. With intensive cultivation and constant care of the irrigation systems, the oases could support a dense sedentary population. The grasslands and deserts were best suited to stockbreeding. To find grazing for the animals required a regular seasonal movement from pasture to pasture, and the population was necessarily sparse.

While these two patterns of life—the nomadic and the oasis village-dwelling—endured over the centuries, many different peoples flowed into Central Asia, either pausing for a few decades or centuries before moving on, or remaining to blend with the earlier population. In the sixth century B.C., the Greek historian, Herodotus, described the pastoral nomads of his time. North of the Black Sea were the Royal Scythians; far east of these, astride the Sir Darya just east of the Aral Sea, were the Massagetae. Beyond them, also along the Sir Darya, were the Sacae. South of these tribal territories were the fortified towns and villages of oasis-dwellers. Along the middle course of the Amu Darya was the Persian satrapy of Bactria, with its capital at Balkh in what is now northern Afghanistan. When Alexander the Great invaded this region in 329–327 B.C., the Bactrians had fields of rice, a crop requiring intensive irrigation. Maracanda (the present Samarkand) was among the fortified towns he encountered, and the Sogdians, who dwelt in the plains between the Amu Darya and the Sir Darya—"the land between the rivers"—also had fortified places.[1]

For many centuries, nomadic tribes posed a serious threat to the settled village-dwellers. In the third century B.C., one of Alexander's Seleucid successors built long walls around Merv to protect the oasis from nomads, and in the middle of the second century nomads erupted into Bactria. These several nomadic tribes, often referred to collectively as "Scythians," seem to have been mostly Iranian-speaking, or at least of Indo-European speech, and entered the ken of history through Greek and Persian documents. The next group of nomads were first reported on the borders of China. The Yüeh-chih, pushed westward by the Hiung-nu in the second century B.C., settled in Bactria and early in the Christian era established the Kushan Empire which encouraged trade and travel between China and India. Close on the heels of the Yüeh-chih came the Huns, who pushed rapidly through toward Europe, and the Ephthalite Huns, who conquered the Sogdians in the fifth century A.D. and invaded India.

It was around the sixth century A.D. that Turkic tribes began to sweep into western Central Asia. The Pechenegs established a territory between the Ural and Volga rivers from which some were driven westward in the ninth century by the Oghuz. Many of these latter, in turn, pressed south and west into Iran, Afghanistan, and Turkey. After the Oghuz came the Kipchak tribal confederation, which survives only as the name of segments of several tribes in western Central Asia and Afghanistan. Following the Turks came Mongols. In the thirteenth century the Mongol emperor Chinggis Khan invaded the west and set the stage for Mongol political domination in the appanages of his sons, Juchi in southern Russia and Jaghatai in western Central Asia. Although the leaders were Mongols, they drew into their successful armies many Turkic tribes. The result was a Turkicization of speech among the Mongols who remained in the west and the disappearance of Mongol speech in western Central Asia. There was a continued westward seepage of Mongols for two or three centuries after the invasion of Chinggis Khan, but the general process of Turkicization of language continued, and in the south the Iranicization of culture was such that by the early sixteenth century Babur, who was descended from Timur on the father's side and Chinggis Khan on the mother's side, looked on the Mongols in his army as foreigners with strange customs.[2]

The earliest known inhabitants of Central Asia, both sedentary and nomadic, were Caucasoid in physical type. Some tribal groups with Mongoloid characteristics began to appear during the first millennium A.D., as is attested by graves of that period,[3] but the Mongoloid type did not become pronounced in the population until the thirteenth century when the armies of Chinggis Khan stimulated the movement of other Mongols into western Central Asia. Mongoloid traits—straight hair, high cheekbones, "slant" eyes, and sparse beards—predominate in the north and northeast and gradually become attenuated as one moves to the south and southwest. They are absent in the Tajik population of the southeastern mountains.

The Mongol armies of Chinggis Khan and his successors constituted the last of the great tribal movements that had flowed westward through western Central Asia for over two millenniums. However, nomadic tribes continued to churn within Central Asia for several centuries. Timur (d. 1405), a Turko-Mongol descendant of Chinggis Khan, conquered an empire extending from China to the Mediterranean. In the fifteenth century the expansion of Muscovite power into southern Russia caused a reverse movement of Turko-Mongols from the appanage of Juchi, eldest son of Chinggis Khan. This appanage had become divided into the "Golden Horde," centered on the Volga River, and the "White Horde," extending eastward from the Caspian Sea and Ural Mountains into the steppes of what is now Kazakhstan and adjoining parts of southern Siberia. As Muscovite pressure on the Golden Horde increased and caused displacement as far as the White Horde, Abul Khaïr (1413–1469), chief of a branch of the White Horde founded by a fourteenth-century ancestor named Uzbek, tried to establish his rule over the northern steppes. Many of the nomads refused to accept his authority, but his grandson, Sheiban Khan, was able to conquer the oasis towns and cities of Turkistan. As a result of this conquest, the name Uzbek came to be applied to the Turkic-speaking peoples of the southern oases. The nomads in the northern steppes, retaining their independence, acquired the name Kazak or Qazaq, "free." [4] It was because of depredations by some of these southern Siberian tribes on Russian fur traders that the Cossack Ermak crossed the Urals in 1581 for the first step in the Russian conquest of Siberia.

A final, short-lived movement was that of the western Mongols (Oïrats) who, under the leadership of the Jungar tribe, in the seventeenth century established a state in that part of eastern Central Asia to which they bequeathed their name, Jungaria. In the early eighteenth century, pressed by wars with the Khalkha Mongols of the Mongolian Plateau and with China, one group of Oïrats forced its way across the grasslands of western Central Asia to the Volga River, where they became known as Kalmuks. This western movement caused a displacement of tribes along their path of march. Of greater import, the expansion of the Jungar state in the east reduced the grazing territory available to the nomads of western Central Asia at a time when Russian expansion was similarly restricting other boundaries. Early in the eighteenth century the slow but steady movement of Russian outposts onto the steppe from the north and west, began constricting the territory of the Kazaks and pushing them back on Karakalpaks, Turkomans, and Uzbeks. In 1718 a fortress was built at Semipalatinsk, completing a line of outposts ranging along the Irtysh River from Omsk on the Siberian border. In the

west, a Russian settlement was established in 1736 at Orenburg (later renamed Orsk) in the southern Urals, and in 1742
a new Orenburg (now known as Chkalov) was built on the
Samara River as anchor to a chain of forts leading to the
Caspian and Aral seas.

Of the Iranian, Turkic, and Mongol tribes who had
churned through western Central Asia over the centuries,
some remained in the area to be assimilated into the existing
population. Eventually all the tribal peoples became Turkic-
speaking, sorting themselves out into groups with ethnic
identities derived from adaptation to the geographic and cultural environment of the regions they inhabited, from the
particular mixture of ethnic strains that contributed to their
formation, and other historical circumstances. Throughout
this period of over two thousand years there had been a
steady filtration of tribal peoples into the oases. As they settled in the villages and towns, they gradually adopted the
culture of the oasis peoples. Thus, despite a turbulent movement of tribes and a confusing combination and recombina-
tion of tribal elements, the basic patterns of Central Asian
culture remained unchanged. Pastoral nomads occupied the
grasslands and deserts. In the south, town- and village-
dwellers raised crops in fields and gardens made fertile by
irrigation, and engaged in craft manufacture and in a trade
that linked the oases with the countries and cultures of southern and eastern Asia.

While tribal peoples were being drawn into the cultural
sphere of the oases, the oases were in turn subject to ideas and
techniques from neighbors with a long tradition of civilization. From prehistoric times, the strongest cultural influence
had been exerted by the nearest neighbor, Iran. In material
culture, economy, pattern of government, family life, the
arts, and religion, the oases belong to the Iranian culture
sphere. For example, Islam was introduced into the oases

7

within a century of its introduction into Iran, and although the Central Asians remained orthodox Sunni when the Persians adopted the Shi'a belief that the caliphate should have passed through Ali and his descendants, the Central Asians of the oases nevertheless gave cult attention to Ali as well as continuing to follow pre-Islamic Iranian rites. The oasis culture, influenced by tribal increments from the steppe and by trade relations with other regions, had a character all its own, but Persian elements were strong.

THE LAND

Central Asia, properly speaking, extends across the heart of the Eurasian continent from the Ural Mountains and Caspian Sea on the west to the Chinese borders of Mongolia. But a series of mountain chains, extending from the Pamirs in the south to the Altai in the north, set off western Central Asia from the eastern part of that area. These mountains, which have a generally east-west orientation and are broken in the north by valley corridors, did not prevent the free movement of peoples throughout history. They did, however, offer natural limits when expanding Russian and Chinese imperial interests collided and fixed a political boundary to mark their respective spheres of political and cultural activities. It is with western Central Asia that this study is concerned.

Western Central Asia is a land of grasslands, desert, arid plains, and mountains; Russia managed to bring a considerable part of the southeastern mountains within its power when political boundaries were being determined. In the west, the Ural Mountains and the Caspian Sea form a natural boundary, although there is a broad passageway between the southern foothills of the Urals and the northern arm of the Caspian which, both geographically and ethnically, leads so gradually into southern Russia that any line of demarcation must necessarily be arbitrary. In fact, the Soviet Republic of

Map 1. Soviet Central Asia. (Adapted from Central
Asian Research Centre map, 1958.)

Omsk

ALTAI MTS.

Irtysh R.

Semipalatinsk

LAKE ZAISAN

H — S — T — A — N

HUNGRY
STEPPE

LAKE BALKHASH

Kulja

Chu R.

Ili R.

zyl Orda

Alma Ata

ALA TAU

Sir Darya

Frunze

Turkestan

ISSYK KUL

TIEN SHAN

Chimkent

K I R G I Z I A

SINKIANG
(CHINA)

KUM

Sir Darya

Tashkent

Kokand

Fergana

ΤΑΝ

Samarkand

ALAI RANGE

ara

TAJIKISTAN

PAMIRS

Karshi

Dushanbe

Darya

AFGHANISTAN

HINDU KUSH

LEGEND

—··—··— Borders of the U.S.S.R.

——————— Limits of Union Republics

⊙ Capitals of Union Republics

▨ Sands

SCALE

0 50 100   200   300   400   500 KM

Kazakhstan extends north of the Caspian nearly to the Volga River. In the south, the Kopet Dagh, the mountains that mark the beginning of the Iranian Plateau, provide a natural base for the political boundary with Iran, while farther east the Amu Darya was fixed by agreement as part of the boundary with Afghanistan. In the north, the grasslands of the Central Asian steppe shade gradually in southern Siberia into the forest belt of taiga. This taiga marks the northernmost limits of the geographical and cultural entity of western Central Asia. Because the rich black earth belt just south of the taiga attracted Russian colonists from the time the first Russian settlers crossed the Urals into Siberia, the northern political boundaries of the Tsarist Governor-generalship of the Steppe and the Soviet Republic of Kazakhstan were fixed at a line through the black earth belt below which Russians had not been able to completely displace Kazaks.

Topographically, the area that came under Russian control differs from eastern Central Asia in that, within the circumscribing mountains, it is a lowland area. Some regions north and east of the Caspian Sea are below sea level. Considerable expanses in the southwest and north have an altitude of less than 500 feet and another broad area is under 1,000 feet. In contrast to these lowlands are the surrounding mountains. The Pamir Knot, an extension of the Himalayas straddling the borders of Russian and Chinese Central Asia, Afghanistan, and Kashmir, is one of the highest mountain masses in the world, with many peaks rising above 20,000 feet. The lower Kopet Dagh on the Iranian border has a high point of slightly less than 10,000 feet, while the Urals in the west average no more than 3,000 to 4,000 feet in their middle course.

As would be expected of the center of a large continental mass, the climate of western Central Asia is characterized by great fluctuations in temperature. In the north, the temperature swings from an average of about zero in January to 72° F. in July; in the south, the January average is well below freezing, while that of July is over 80° F. There is also considerable temperature range between day and night. In winter the foothills are less cold than the open steppe, which receives the full impact of the cold, dry, northerly winds that blow over Turkistan. On the steppe these sometimes reach gale force in the buran, which sweeps the ground free of snow. In the south, dry summer winds (*garmsil*) from the west shrivel everything they touch and often fill the air with clouds of fine dust.

Water resources are limited. In the north, westerly winds from the Atlantic retain some of their moisture after passing the Ural Mountains and drop a part of it in thunderstorms on the steppe, chiefly in the months of June, July, and August. Here the rainfall fluctuates from eight to sixteen inches a year. A much greater part reaches the Altai Mountains in the east, where the annual precipitation is over twenty inches. In the south, rains come chiefly in the spring, ranging from no more than three to six inches in the west to about fourteen inches in the hills where Samarkand and Tashkent are located to more in the higher mountains. The evaporation from the vegetation and canals of the oases also gives humidity to these islands of cultivation. The chief source of water, however, is the rivers that rise in the eastern mountains. The southern mountains, the Kopet Dagh, have no permanent snows, and only a few springs are to be found in their northern foothills. Farther east, two rivers rising in Afghanistan reach into the deserts of Turkmenia in their lower courses: the Tejend (called the Hari Rud in Afghanistan) and the Murghab. The two great rivers of Central Asia are the Amu Darya and the Sir Darya, the first fed by tributaries rising in the Hindu Kush, the Pamirs, and the southern flanks of the Alai Mountains; the second rising in the northern Alai and the Tien Shan. These two rivers flow across the southern plains to the Aral Sea. Farther north, the Ili River, rising on the northern flanks of the Tien Shan in China, finds its way westward to Lake Balkhash; and the Irtysh, which rises in the Altai Mountains, flows northwestward across the Kazak steppes to join the Ob River in Siberia. These four rivers notwithstanding, most Central Asian rivers are depleted by irrigation and evaporation until they disappear in the sands. Because they are fed by melting mountain snows and glaciers, they reach their peak of volume in summer, just when water is most needed for irrigating the thirsty fields and gardens.

The peoples of Central Asia distinguish between two kinds of water: *oqsu* or *aq su,* "white water," referring to the rivers fed by melting snow and glaciers; and *qara su* or *qorasu,* "black water," that is, underground water. White water—the rivers—are of particular importance to the settled peoples of the oases. Black water is essential to the pastoral peoples of the steppe and desert. No matter how luxuriant the grass and herbs after spring rains or melting of the snow, people and livestock require water, and the location of wells determines the usefulness of a grazing area. The Caspian Sea, the world's largest inland body of water, borders on Central Asia in the west. In the Middle Ages, when the Amu Darya flowed into the Caspian Sea, it formed a link in the thriving overland trade between Central Asia and the West, but after the Amu Darya shifted to find an outlet in the Aral Sea, the chief importance of the Caspian to Central Asia was in the evaporation that provided moisture for the parched area to the east. Only local groups residing on its shores exploited its resources for navigation or fishing and then only as a supplement to their normal economic activities. The smaller Aral Sea to the east of the Caspian also furnishes moisture through evaporation. The marshy delta of the Amu Darya forms a

11

geographical environment different in a number of respects from that found anywhere else in western Central Asia. In response to this the people occupying the delta area have evolved a distinctive way of life. In the east are Lake Balkhash and such smaller bodies of water as Issyk Kul and Lake Zaisan. Except for such moisture as they provide, they have been historically of little import to the peoples of Central Asia who, confirmed landsmen, prefer to keep their feet on solid earth and to eat food other than fish.

The vegetation of Central Asia reflects both the aridity of the climate and variations in the soil. In the far north is a belt of rich black earth which, moistened by the thawing of frozen subsoil in spring, bursts into a luxuriant growth of grass. Farther south in the true steppelands, where the soil is less fertile and precipitation uneven, the shallow-rooted "feather grass" grows in tufts, with the tufts becoming more widely spaced as aridity increases. The steppe is also brightened in spring with tulips and other bulbs and flowering plants, and dwarf thorny bushes are frequent. Between the Caspian and Aral seas the Ust Urt Plateau, rising to an altitude of from 500 to 600 feet, is devoid of streams. The only water is found in deep wells, often brackish, and in marshes and a few salt lakes that form in depressions in the clayey soil after the spring rains. After these rains there is a sudden growth of shrubs which disappear as quickly as they appear. South of the Aral Sea and the oases of Khiva (Khwarizm), the Kara Kum ("black sand desert") is largely a wasteland of shifting sand dunes and salt pans, with but a sparse growth of grass having underground creeper stems and of shrubs with long horizontal roots. Rising above these ground-hugging plants are forests of *saxaul,* a desert bush which grows in thickets up to twenty feet high and loses its branches in winter. These desert plants are capable of fixing the sands in place if the grass and shrubs are not destroyed by overgrazing and the *saxaul* cut down for its wood. The Kara Kum is southwest of the Amu Darya. Between the Amu Darya and the Sir Darya, to the northeast, is the Kyzyl Kum ("red sand desert"). More varied than the Kara Kum, its sand dunes are interspersed with lines of hills and with a region of clayey and sandy-clayey soils in which there is a rich springtime growth of plants. Altogether, these three desert areas, the Ust Urt Plateau, the Kara Kum, and the Kyzyl Kum, cover some 300,000 square miles, and there are many other areas, such as the Hungry Steppe west of Lake Balkhash, too arid to support more than a sparse population.

In the south and east, at the foot of the mountains, is a blend of fertile loess soil which needs only water to make it wonderfully productive. So rich is this loess that the oasis dwellers fertilize depleted soil with the remains of old mud walls and houses, but in the foothills of the Kopet Dagh, oasis plantings have been limited by the lack of water. The Russian geographer Woeikof, writing in 1914, noted only twenty-seven large springs along the three-hundred-mile route of the Transcaspian Railway between the Caspian Sea and the well-watered plains of the Tejend River. It is in the foothills of the eastern mountains that fertile loess soil is combined with mountain rivers to produce flourishing oases. Except for Khiva, on the lower Amu Darya south of the Aral Sea, all of the great oasis towns of history are in the eastern foothills. Bukhara, the traditional center of the trans-Asiatic caravan routes, is farthest out on the plain but draws water from two rivers. The others, Samarkand, Tashkent, and Kokand, are all in well-watered foothills. When the Russians sought a site from which to administer Semirechie Province, the territory of the eastern nomadic Kazaks, they chose a similar fertile, well-watered foothill spot which they named Vernyi, the present Alma Ata, capital of the Soviet Republic of Kazakhstan. Because even in these fertile zones of loess soil, effective fertility is dependent on the availability of water, vegetation flourishes only within the range of rivers and irrigation canals. At the end of the canal or river there is a sharp transition to arid tracts suited at best to dry farming of grains, more frequently only to seasonal grazing.

The unirrigated plains of loess have a rich growth of feather grass, wild barley, and similar plants which make excellent pasturage for livestock. Along the rivers grow poplars, willows, tamarisks, *jida* (*Eleagnus hortensis*), and a kind of reed (*Lasiagrostis splendens*) known locally as *chi*. In the irrigated areas, the vegetation is cultivated. Poplars are grown not only along irrigation canals but in little plantations, for poplar is the chief wood used for fuel, construction, and woodworking. Willows are frequent in oasis towns and villages, and a kind of elm is grown as an ornamental and shade tree. The winters are too cold for citrus fruits and olives, and only in certain sheltered spots in the foothills is it possible to raise oriental plane trees, figs, or pomegranates. The intense sunlight of summer gives a special sweetness to melons, grapes, and other fruits and vegetables and favors the growth of cotton. At higher altitudes in the eastern mountains, walnuts, pistachios, and apricots grow wild, and sometimes also almonds. At still higher altitudes, firs and junipers appear, widely spaced around grassy mountain valleys. Above the tree line, alpine meadows offer midsummer grazing.[5]

THE PEOPLE

In this arid land made habitable by life-giving waters from the mountains, the peoples who had been surging into Central Asia for over two millenniums eventually merged to form the ethnic groups known today. Almost all represent a mixture of elements which, largely through a common history, culture, and residence in contiguous territory, came to have enough feeling of ethnic identity to accept classification

I. Horses grazing in the foothills of the Alai Range, Kirgizia. (Sovfoto.)

II. Camel caravan and *saxaul* bushes in the Kara Kum, Turkmenia. (Sovfoto.)

as Uzbek, Kazak, or other name group. There was no sense of national solidarity; Turkoman tribes often showed as much hostility toward each other as they did toward non-Turkomans, and oasis people normally identified themselves as belonging to a certain valley or locality rather than as Uzbeks or Tajiks. Usually it was only in relationships with outsiders that they became conscious of being members of an ethnic group.

In the nineteenth century, the peoples of Central Asia had sorted themselves out into six major ethnic groups: Tajiks, Uzbeks, Turkomans, Kazaks, Kirghiz, and Karakalpaks. In addition, there were a number of small groups, such as Jews and Gypsies, who for centuries had managed to retain their own way of life and ethnic identity and avoided absorption into the more populous peoples around them. In the eighteenth and nineteenth centuries some new ethnic elements appeared, spilling over into Russian Central Asia from traditional homes in Chinese Central Asia or Iran. With Russian conquest, there began a flow of Slavic peoples into the area. Later, under the Soviet regime, still other peoples appeared, many of them non-Russian exiles from other parts of the Soviet Union. Although Central Asia had been ethnically heterogeneous since the beginning of history, culturally it had been fairly homogeneous with but two basic cultural traditions, those of the steppe and of the oases. Even those groups who were culturally the most divergent, the Jews and the Gypsies, fitted into the oasis-patterned mosaic of occupational specialization. The Slavic colonists, on the other hand, had an entirely different cultural tradition, as did some of the exiles who entered Central Asia under the Soviet regime. The present study is primarily concerned with discovering the effect of Russian rule—the imposition of Russian culture—on the traditional cultures of Central Asia, both pastoral and oasis. Since the number and variety of immigrants might be expected to have some impact on the traditional cultures of Central Asia, the stage will be set here by characterizing the whole population, including newcomers and small ethnic minorities of long standing as well as the major peoples.

Major Ethnic Groups

Tajiks. When history began for Central Asia, not long before the beginning of our era, the inhabitants of the oases spoke Iranian tongues and were what is known as Caucasoid or Europeoid in physical type. To judge from the present population as well as from skulls unearthed in ancient cemeteries, they were broad-headed, of a type known as "Pamir." Their culture was very similar to that of the Iranian Plateau, and as a result of continued trade and cultural contacts with Persians, their cultural development ran parallel with that of the Iranian Plateau; most of them eventually came to speak dialects of eastern Persian, closely akin to those spoken in the Persian province of Khorasan and in Afghanistan. In the high mountain valleys of the Pamirs, however, isolated villagers continued to speak eastern Iranian languages. Some speak Yagnobi, descended from a dialect of Sogdian. (The Sogdians ruled what is now Samarkand in the sixth century B.C. when the Persian emperor, Cyrus the Great, conquered that city.) Others, in a Pamir area extending into Afghanistan, speak Pamir dialects also belonging to the eastern branch of Iranian. Because of their isolation, each valley has its own dialect.[6] These Mountain Tajiks or Galchas, as they are known, missed much of the development of trades and crafts that occurred in the oases of the plains, and their cultivation was limited to tiny plots along mountain streams where they raised barley and such fruits, vegetables, and flowers as would grow at high altitudes. In their isolation, they retained not only their old speech, but also many elements of the Zoroastrian fire cult which had flourished in the plains before the introduction of Islam. They became Muslims, but, remote from oasis centers of Muslim learning, adopted the Muslim Ismaili faith led by the Aga Khan which was introduced into the mountains from India in the nineteenth century.

In the oases, the peoples of Iranian speech were subject to influence both from the Iranian Plateau and from the Turkic steppe nomads who settled in the oases over the centuries. As the number of Turks in the oases increased, many of the earlier inhabitants adopted Turkic speech although retaining their own oasis way of life. Because of this shift in language, the number of Tajiks has steadily declined through the centuries. In 1959 there remained only 1,397,000 Tajiks in the Soviet Union. Most of these (1,051,000) dwelt in the eastern mountain area that became the Soviet Republic of Tajikistan, but 311,000 in Uzbekistan still considered themselves Tajiks. Their culture is essentially like that of the oasis Uzbeks, many of whom are Tajik in origin, but the conservatism demonstrated by the Tajik retention of Persian speech is also reflected by a general resistance to changes in their way of life. The Tajiks are the most conservative of the native peoples of Central Asia.

Uzbeks. The Turks who settled in the oases adopted the oasis culture of the Tajiks but retained their Turkic speech and transmitted it to many of the Iranian-speaking inhabitants. By the early thirteenth century, for example, Khwarizm had become a Turkic-speaking city. In the early sixteenth century, the oasis cities were conquered by Turko-Mongol dynasties tracing descent from an ancestor named Uzbek. From this time the name Uzbek was applied to the dynasties and some of their tribal followers, but not to the Turkic town- and village-dwellers who had adopted the Tajik way of life. These came to be known as Sart, a word of Indian origin meaning "merchant" which the early Turks had applied to

17

the oasis people of Iranian speech as an alternative to Tajik. Under the Uzbek dynasties, Sart referred to a way of life and was applied by nomads to oasis dwellers in general, whether their speech was Persian or Turkic. Russians of the Tsarist regime followed the same practice, distinguishing between Sart, those of characteristic oasis culture—most of whom were Turkic-speaking—and Uzbek, those who retained some remnant of tribal culture. The Soviet regime, on the other hand, regarded Sart as pejorative and dropped it from the Russian vocabulary. In Soviet usage the name Uzbek was extended to include all the groups speaking related Turkic dialects: those formerly known as Sarts; settled peoples who retained some memory of tribal origins; and tribes who continued to lead a partly pastoral life on the fringes of the oases. Among these last were such separate tribal groups as the Kipchaks, who numbered 33,502 in 1926; the Kuramas (50,218); and the Turks (29,500).[7]

The name Uzbek thus now includes a fairly heterogeneous population, ranging in culture from fully sedentary merchants and craftsmen to seminomadic communities having a strong tribal orientation. In physical appearance there is similar variety. Many Uzbeks are Caucasoids of the Pamir type who differ in no way from their Tajik neighbors, but among some, even those known formerly as Sarts, a hint of Mongol ancestry is to be seen. Mongoloid traits are more noticeable among those of tribal memory or culture, but on the whole, Uzbeks are less Mongoloid than Kazaks and Kirghiz. Uzbeks are the most numerous of the native peoples of Central Asia; they comprise a majority of the inhabitants of the oases, which support a dense population. In 1959 the Uzbeks in the Soviet Union numbered 6,015,000, of whom 5,038,000 resided in the Uzbek SSR. Of the others, 454,000 lived in Tajikistan, a number which reflects a continuing shift among oasis dwellers from Tajik Persian to Uzbek Turkic speech. The

Map 2. Distribution of Ethnic Groups in Soviet Central Asia. (Adapted from *Ocherki Obshchei Etnografii: Aziatskaia Chast' SSSR,* Moscow, 1960, as reproduced by the Central Asian Research Centre, 1962.)

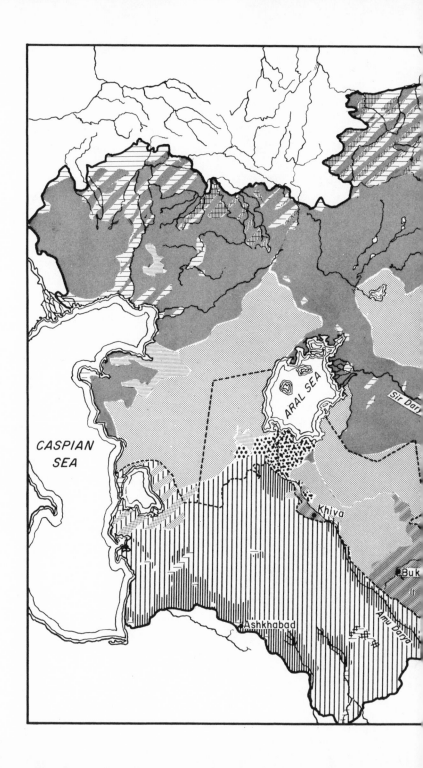

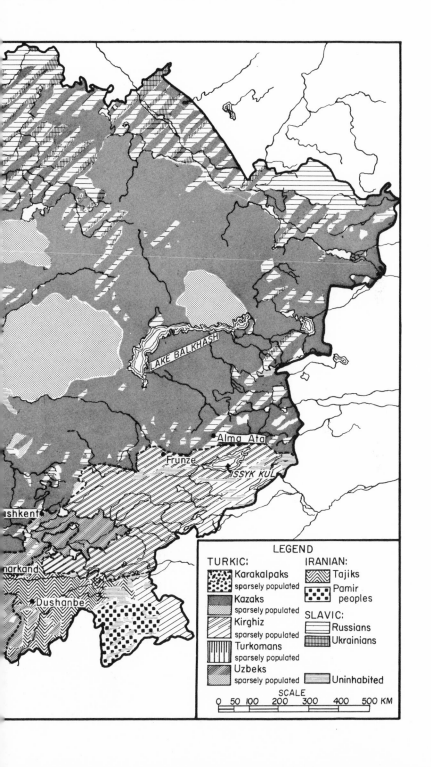

LEGEND

TURKIC:

Karakalpaks
sparsely populated

Kazaks
sparsely populated

Kirghiz
sparsely populated

Turkomans
sparsely populated

Uzbeks
sparsely populated

IRANIAN:

Tajiks

Pamir
peoples

SLAVIC:

Russians

Ukrainians

Uninhabited

SCALE

0 50 100 200 300 400 500 KM

LAKE BALKHASH

Alma Ata

Frunze

ISSYK KUL

shkent

narkand

Dushanbe

analysis of oasis culture made in this study is based essentially on traditional Sart culture. Where deviations in the direction of conservative Tajik or tribal Uzbek culture are mentioned, this will be specified.

Turkomans. The Turkomans occupy the arid southwestern part of Central Asia, a territory extending from the Amu Darya into northern Iran and northwestern Afghanistan. They are descended from Oghuz Turks who remained in Central Asia when most of their number moved on into southwest Asia in the eleventh century, but physically a majority are Caucasoid (Europeoid) of a long-headed Khorasan type which distinguishes them from both the Tajiks and most other Turks. Their language, unlike that of the Uzbeks, is most closely related to those of other descendants of the Oghuz, the Azerbaijani Turks of northwestern Iran and the Soviet Republic of Azerbaidzhan; the Qashqai of southern Iran, and the Osmanli Turks of Turkey. Dwelling in an area bordered by oasis people on the north and by village-dwellers of the Iranian Plateau on the south, they have been subject for many centuries to the cultural influences of these neighbors, and their culture reflects these influences. They have, however, clung to pastoral nomadism as far as possible although the aridity of their territory precludes a wholly pastoral nomadic way of life.

In 1959 there were 1,002,000 Turkomans in the Soviet Union, of which 924,000 lived in the Republic of Turkmenia. Most of the remainder (55,000) were found in neighboring Uzbekistan.

Kazaks. The Kazaks or Qazaqs, whom Tsarist Russians called Kirghiz or Kirghiz-Kazak, and whom Soviet Russians, since 1936, have called Kazakh, came into being in the fifteenth century. Contributing to their make-up were segments of the White Horde; tribes such as the Naiman who occupied much their present territory in the days of Chinggis Khan;

and other fragments of Turko-Mongol tribes in the grass-lands of northern Central Asia and southern Siberia who had rejected the attempt of the Uzbek Abul Khaïr to establish leadership over them. The Kazaks were classic Central Asian horse-breeding pastoral nomads. Removed at some distance from the political pressures that China exerted on the Mongols to the east and the Russians exerted on the Golden Horde to the west, and far from the cultural influences of the oases to the south, the Kazaks retained their nomadic way of life longer than most of the pastoral tribes of Central Asia. But when Russia began to expand beyond the Urals, the Kazaks were the first to feel the restrictions of encircling Cossack fortresses. Their fertile grasslands in the north and east attracted the bulk of Russian agricultural colonists during both the Tsarist and the Soviet regimes, and the development of mineral resources in some of the less fertile regions of their vast territory further impeded their nomadic movements. The Kazaks are Mongoloid in physical type, most strongly so in the north. They speak a Turkic language distinct from both Uzbek and Turkoman. Their territory is far more extensive than that of any other Central Asian ethnic group, but while they live much more widely dispersed than the sedentary Uzbeks, their population ranks second in size. In 1959 there were 3,622,000 Kazaks in the Soviet Union. Of these, 2,795,000 lived in the Soviet Republic of Kazakhstan, 335,000 in Uzbekistan, 70,000 in Turkmenia, and 20,000 in Kirgizia. Most of the remainder (382,000) lived in the RSFSR, outside Central Asia.

Kirghiz. The Kirghiz, known to Tsarist Russians as Kara Kirghiz, originally dwelt around the headwaters of the Yenisei River in southern Siberia. Some migrated southwestward to their present home in the western Tien Shan in the tenth century A.D. Those who remained in the north came under the rule of Chinggis Khan in the early thirteenth century and of the Jungars in the seventeenth. At the beginning of the eighteenth century this second group was forced south by the Jungars to join their kinsmen in the Tien Shan.[8] The Kirghiz resemble the Kazaks in their Mongoloid appearance and speak a closely related language. Cultural differences are chiefly a reflection of the difference in habitat; in the high mountains, for example, the yak has replaced the horse. In 1959 there were altogether 969,000 Kirghiz in the Soviet Union, of whom 837,000 resided in the republic taking their name. Of the remainder, 93,000 were found in Uzbekistan and 26,000 in Tajikistan.

Karakalpaks. The Karakalpaks ("Black Caps") are a people of mixed origin probably including in their ancestry ancient Massagetae, Oghuz and Kipchak Turks, and segments of the Golden Horde as well as of other Turko-Mongol tribal constellations who milled around the western desert steppes in the fifteenth century. In the sixteenth and seventeenth centuries most Karakalpaks occupied a territory along the lower and middle courses of the Sir Darya. In the eighteenth century, some united with Nogai and moved to the Ural-Emba region north of the Caspian Sea. A second group north of the Sir Darya became vassals of the Kazaks, while a third shifted southward toward Bukhara. Under pressure from Kazaks and the Emirate of Bukhara, most of the Karakalpaks of the second and third groups gradually moved westward to the delta of the Amu Darya, along the southern shores of the Aral Sea. In this new habitat of marsh and water, pastoral nomadism gave way to other forms of economy long established in the delta area. One group from Bukhara moved eastward into the valley of Fergana, where they came under the cultural influence of Uzbek village-dwellers.

The mixed heredity of the Karakalpaks is reflected in their physical appearance. Mongoloid traits are less pronounced than among the Kazaks, but more so than among the Uzbeks.

Their close association with Kazaks is evidenced by their language, which some linguists classify as a dialect of Kazak. In 1959 there were 168,000 Karakalpaks in Uzbekistan, which includes within its boundaries an autonomous Karakalpak republic.[9]

Minor Ethnic Groups

In addition to these major population groups, a number of small groups persisted for many centuries as ethnic islands in the oasis population.

Arabs. The Arabs were found scattered in small, compact enclaves in the eastern oases, many of them in the Zarafshan Valley from Samarkand to Charjui. Some believe themselves descended from the Arab armies who conquered Turkistan in the seventh and eighth centuries, while others have a tradition of coming to Turkistan in the fourteenth century during the reigns of Timur and his successors. In the 1926 census, 28,978 Arabs were enumerated, a majority of them in Uzbekistan. They spoke the Iraqi dialect of Arabic, although they were necessarily bilingual.[10]

Jews. The Jewish community in Central Asia is also of considerable antiquity. In the tenth century, according to the Russian Turkologist W. Barthold, Jews were more numerous than Christians in Turkistan, and there appears to have been a later Jewish immigration from Iran and Iraq. Known generally in the West as Bukharan Jews, Central Asian Jews were actually settled in a number of eastern oasis towns and cities such as Samarkand, Tashkent, Bukhara, Kokand, and Khatyrchi, as well as in rural villages. In 1926, 18,698 Jews native to Central Asia were counted. In addition to those who retained their Jewish faith, there was a community of Jewish origin known as Marranos or Chalas which had been forcibly converted to Islam in the nineteenth century by the government of Bukhara. Numbering only about a thousand, the Marranos retained an identity separate both from other Jews and from Muslims. For all the Central Asian Jews, a dialect of Tajik Persian was the language spoken in the home.[11]

Gypsies. Gypsies, known as Luli or Chugi, have long been a part of the ethnic scene in what are now Tajikistan and eastern Uzbekistan. Like gypsies everywhere, they lived a peripatetic life. Some provided music and singing at weddings and other family celebrations in small villages, even among the Mountain Tajiks, as well as in the bazaars of towns. Some made craft goods from materials available at points along their route. Bilingual in Tajik and Uzbek, they regarded Tajik as their native tongue but spoke an argot with a vocabulary derived largely from the argots of wandering dervishes and of guild entertainers and musicians. According to the census of 1926 there were about 5,000 Central Asian gypsies, but clearly many were not enumerated because of their wandering life. In 1959, 7,600 were counted in Tajikistan and Uzbekistan despite the fact that some of gypsy origin identified themselves as Tajik or Uzbek in the later census.[12]

Persians. Persians or Irani (Ironi) are of more recent introduction into the Central Asian population, at least those who form a group with a distinct ethnic identity. These trace their origin to the Persian inhabitants of Mary (Merv) who were led into captivity when the Emir of Bukhara captured that oasis in 1785. During the nineteenth century some Persians from Khorasan in Iran entered Central Asia of their own accord, possibly attracted by trade or by opportunities for employment as administrators in the khanates. Some prisoners brought across the border by Turkoman raiders and sold as slaves may also have risen in status to the point where they could join the Persian community, which maintained its identity through adherence to the "twelver" Shi'a faith.

23

Many Persians were absorbed into the Central Asian population; several of the emirs of Bukhara in the nineteenth century had Persian mothers. In the 1926 census 9,188 Persians were counted.[13]

Uighurs. Uighurs, who constitute the basic population of the oases of Chinese Turkistan, are closely akin to the Uzbeks in physical type, language, and customs, though in some ways, such as agricultural techniques, clothing, and food habits, they show Chinese influence. Uighurs began to enter western Central Asia in the second half of the eighteenth century, and there was a second movement in the 1880's, stimulated by political activities of the Manchu government of China. Those of the first migration originated in the Kulja region of Sinkiang and spoke a northern dialect of Uighur, Taranchi. They followed the Ili River westward into what was to become Russian Central Asia and settled along its banks, some of them working south toward Alma Ata. The second wave, emanating from Kashgar and speaking a southern dialect, settled in the Fergana Valley. In 1926, 108,570 Uighurs were enumerated.[14]

Dungans. Between 1877 and 1884, a number of Chinese Muslims, known as Dungans, sought refuge in Russian territory after an unsuccessful revolt against the Manchu government. A majority of them settled along the Chu River in Kirgizia and Kazakhstan, a few in the Fergana Valley in Uzbekistan. Skilled cultivators, they exerted a cultural influence beyond their numbers, which were 21,900 in 1959. The Dungans speak Kansu and Shensi dialects of Chinese." [15]

Kazan Tatars. When Catherine II of Russia published in 1785 a charter of tolerance of Islam and sought to educate the Kazaks, Tatar mullahs (men of Muslim learning) from Kazan were appointed as teachers, and thereafter Kazan Tatars not only dominated the schools established in Orenburg, Omsk, and elsewhere for the education of Kazaks, but traveled among the Kazaks as teachers and missionaries. Furthermore, Catherine gave Kazan Tatar merchants special privileges, so that before the Russian conquest of Central Asia, these merchants virtually dominated commerce between Russia and the oases and steppes. After conquest, Russian merchants replaced Tatars in the oases of Turkistan, but Tartars acquired considerable influence as interpreters between Russian and Central Asian officials and merchants. Kazan Tartars attained their position of eminence in Central Asia not only because of the strategic position of Kazan on the trade routes between Russia and Central Asia in the eighteenth century, but because of their origin. Descended from members of the Golden Horde who had remained in south Russia under Russian power, they were historically related to both the Kazaks and Uzbeks; linguistically they were particularly closely akin to the Kazaks. It is difficult to discover the number of Kazan Tatars in Central Asia, since in the Soviet census reports they are lumped with Crimean Tatars, many of whom were sent into exile in Central Asia when the Crimean ASSR was liquidated during World War II.[16]

Other Ethnic Groups. For many centuries, when Bukhara was a main transfer point for trade with India, there were small communities of Indian traders in the larger towns and cities of Central Asia. These Indians normally lived in caravansarais apart from the town and did not bring their wives with them. Information is not available on any present Indian population in Russian Central Asia. Oïrats (Western Mongols) are found in the easternmost region of Kazakhstan, and in the south, some Kurd and Baluchi tribesmen have moved across the border into Turkmenia in comparatively recent times. Under the Soviet regime, Korean "kulaks" were sent to Central Asia from the Maritime Province of the Far East. In 1959 there were 212,000 of these Koreans, 138,000 in Uzbekistan, the remainder in Kazakhstan. Also under the Soviet regime, Azerbaijani Turks and Armenians have been encouraged to settle in Central Asia to introduce new skills, but their number is inconsiderable.

During World War II, when several autonomous republics of southern Russia were liquidated, many of their inhabitants were exiled in Central Asia. The most numerous of these ethnic groups were the Volga Germans and the Crimean Tatars. Of the Germans, there were perhaps three quarters of a million in 1959, most of them in Kazakhstan.[17] Altogether, there were 780,000 Tatars in Central Asia in 1959, but the census does not distinguish between Kazan Tatars resident in Central Asia since the eighteenth or nineteenth centuries and Crimean Tatars, introduced during World War II.

Slavs

As a result of colonization under both the Tsarist and Soviet regimes, the largest ethnic group in Russian Central Asia was that of the Great Russians. In 1959 they numbered 6,215,000, over half of them in Kazakhstan. In addition, 1,035,000 Ukrainians were enumerated, over three-quarters of them in Kazakhstan. Almost all the White Russians in Central Asia, 107,000, resided in Kazakhstan. The grasslands of northern Kazakhstan attracted many Russian peasant colonists. Elsewhere the Slavic population has tended to concentrate in urban and industrial centers. The sheer numbers of Slavic immigrants has inevitably caused some population displacement in Central Asia. Even more, the proximity of millions of residents of European culture, combined with policy actions of a Russian-dominated government, might be expected to have had a profound effect on the culture of the

26

peoples of Central Asia. It is the intent of the present study to discover as far as possible the degree and extent of this cultural influence.

LANGUAGE

Before the Russian conquest of Central Asia and the introduction of new languages by colonists, the languages spoken in the area belonged to two language families: the Ural-Altaic family represented by Turkic; and the Iranian languages of the Indo-European family. Turkic speech in Central Asia is classifiable into three main branches: Southwestern Turkic, represented by Turkoman; Southeastern Turkic, the branch to which Uzbek and Uighur belong; and Northwestern, which includes Kazak, Kirghiz, Karakalpak, and Kazan Tatar.[18] Iranian is chiefly represented by Tajik, a language so closely akin to Persian that Tajiks claim it is Persian. Only a few thousand people in the high Pamirs speak eastern Iranian languages. Almost all Tajiks are bilingual. The Mountain Tajiks speak Tajik-Persian, while the oasis Tajiks also speak Uzbek Turkic. The differences among the several Turkic languages are not great, as evidenced by the fact that in the nineteenth century Kazan Tatars were able to act as interpreters between Russians and Central Asians in all parts of the area.

Kazak, Karakalpak, Kirghiz, and Kazan Tatar were so closely akin as to pose no serious impediment to communication, and within these languages dialectal differences were comparatively slight. Nomadic movements tended to retard divergence in speech. Among the settled people, however, each valley and region had its own dialect, and among the Turkomans, where tribal hostilities often prevented ready intercommunication, tribal dialectal differences were fairly marked. In normal circumstances, people were less conscious of speaking Uzbek, Tajik, or Turkoman than of speaking a

27

particular dialect. Most people thus identified themselves with their locality or tribe—the dialectal unit—rather than as members of the larger ethnic group to which they belonged.

Most Central Asians, whether Turkic- or Iranian-speaking, were illiterate. The oasis cities, however, had a long tradition of scholarship and had developed scripts for literary use among the small educated elite. Chaghataian was the language of a rich Turkic literature that had flourished in Central Asia from the fifteenth to the seventeenth centuries and persisted into the twentieth century. A separate Uzbek literary language, strongly influenced by Persian, began to come into use in the seventeenth century, and in the eighteenth century the Turkomans, who had had a literary language of their own in the fourteenth century, replaced Chaghatai with a literary language closer to Turkoman speech. The Tajiks, whose speech was very similar to Persian, used the Persian literary language in their writing; and Uzbeks also learned in their seminaries to read and enjoy Persian literature. The Arabic script was employed for all these literary languages of western Central Asia. The Kazaks, Kirghiz, and Karakalpaks had no literary language until they came under Russian and Kazan Tatar influence.[19]

II

Before Conquest:
The Pastoral Nomads

KAZAKS

THE Kazaks, who once dominated the grasslands of northern
Central Asia, had already come under Russian rule when
Tashkent was taken in 1865 and had long been subject to
Russian cultural influence. In order to understand the
changes that occurred under Tsarist as well as Soviet rule, we
will begin by describing the traditional Kazak culture.

Kazak pastoral nomadism was centered around the horse.
The small, shaggy horses of the steppe did not have the grace
and fire of Arab steeds, but they were fast and had great endurance; they gave mobility in the wars and blood feuds
(*barynta*) which frequently disrupted the peace of the
steppe; they were the object of cult attention; and possession
of large herds gave prestige unrelated to their economic
value. Children began to ride at an early age—there were special saddles for youngsters from two to four years of age—and
a Kazak disdained to walk even a hundred yards on foot; one
or two riding horses were always kept hobbled near the door
of the tent ready for mounting. Often Kazaks rode great distances for *tamasha* (entertainment) whether it was an exchange of news and gossip, the arrival of a notable visitor, or
a wedding or funeral. A family normally owned from fifteen

to thirty horses, while some wealthy families had over three thousand. But while the horse was the focus of cultural attention, sheep were of greater economic importance. Only rich chiefs had enough horses to permit the eating of horse flesh and the drinking of mare's milk in quantity, but every nomadic family had flocks of fat-tailed sheep to provide milk, meat, fat, wool, and hides. Some camels were kept—mostly two-humped Bactrians—to transport belongings from camp to camp, but they were not numerous and decreased in numbers from south to north. Even a rich family seldom kept more than fifty camels and a poor one no more than three or four. Cattle were rare until toward the end of the eighteenth century, but their numbers increased steadily during the nineteenth century along the edge of Russian settlements. Every camp was guarded by large, fierce watchdogs, and dogs were used in herding.[1]

Finding pasturage for the livestock entailed regular seasonal migrations by their owners. In winter the portable dwellings were set up in sheltered spots in the foothills, under the bluff of a river, or among bushy thickets of *saxaul* or growths of reeds. In spring the people moved out of their winter quarters, following the fresh growth of grass northward or, for eastern groups, upward into the mountains. Some groups who wintered in the southwest traveled as much as a thousand miles to summer pastures in Siberia, while those wintering at the base of the Ala Tau ranges often ascended no more than twenty-five miles to the high pastures of midsummer. The migration routes were never haphazard. Each tribal group had a traditional territory within which its member family groups migrated. Usually a group returned to the same location each year for winter quarters, where many clusters of tribally related families camped near each other. In spring this large group set out on its seasonal migration, with smaller groups fanning out into the summer residential unit, the *aul* or camp, which consisted of from three to as many as fifteen tents. Each family followed an established itinerary within the traditional territory of its tribal group.[2]

The Central Asian nomads traditionally stored no fodder. Through summer and fall, the animals grew fat grazing in their rich pastures, but the rigors of even a normal winter reduced them to scrawniness by spring. When snow lay on the ground, horses were first turned into a pasture to break through the snow with their sharp hooves (to *"teben"*) and eat the tops of the grass; then camels were sent in, and finally the sheep, who nibbled the remaining grass down to the soil. In a bad winter many animals died of cold and starvation, and if thawing snow froze into ice (*dzhut*) too hard to be broken by the horses' hooves, entire herds and flocks sometimes perished. During the nineteenth century, *dzhut* was reported to have occurred twenty times in one part or another of what is now Kazakhstan. If the winter had not been too severe, the beginning of the spring migration was a time of rejoicing, when people dressed in their finery and sang as they rode toward summer pastures. Summer and fall, when food was plentiful for man and beast, were the best times of the year for the Kazaks.[3]

In summer the Kazaks lived largely on milk products. For those who had many horses, the chief nourishment was kumiss, mares' milk fermented in a skin bag with frequent stirring. Those less fortunate made a similar fermented drink of sheep milk or added a little water to curds made of boiled milk. Buttermilk was drunk, and the cream (*qaïmaq*) from boiled milk was relished. Various cheeses were made, including a hard one, *kurt* or *kurut,* made by cooking down curds to a thick mass from which small cakes were shaped and sundried to a rocklike consistency. This was used for traveling or wintertime fare, when it was pounded and softened in milk

31

or water. Despite the wealth of animals, meat had a comparatively small place in the nomadic diet. At the beginning of winter, animals unlikely to survive its rigors were slaughtered. The flesh was smoke-dried; sausages were made, using horse entrails turned inside out as casing; and the tail fat of sheep was rendered and stored in leather bags for winter cooking. When the winters were severe, fallen animals were killed for food. At any time of year, hospitality required that a sheep be slaughtered on the arrival of guests, and animals were also killed especially for wedding and funeral feasts.[4]

By the nineteenth century, hunting played a minor role in Kazak economy, but foxes, antelopes, and other animals were hunted for their skins, to be used for clothing and to barter with neighboring peoples. Fishing was practiced by only a very few poor groups in the west. Most Kazaks scorned fish as a potential food.[5]

The Kazak dwelling, known to the Kazaks as *ui*, but to Russians as "kibitka" and to western Europeans as "yurt," was admirably adapted to both the nomadic life and the severe continental climate. Its walls were made of flexibly latticed wood sections which could be contracted for carrying and expanded when the yurt was to be set up. From five to nine of these sections (*qanat*) were set in a circle, with an opening for the doorway; curved rods were tied at intervals to the top of the *qanat* sections and the upper ends set in apertures in a circular wooden rim (*changaraq*) which crowned the dome-shaped dwelling. The doorway was framed by two wooden jambs, a threshold board below and a crossbeam above. Occasionally, wooden doors were attached by rope hinges to the jambs, but more frequently a strip of felt hung over the doorway. The wooden framework of the yurt was covered with several pieces of heavy felt, held firmly in place with ropes. At the top, over the circular *changaraq*, a felt piece was arranged in such a way that it could be flipped by a rope from one side of the smoke hole to the other, depending on the direction of the wind. A braided or woven band along the join between wall and roof strengthened the structure. In winter a felt lining was added for greater snugness, while in summer, particularly in warmer regions, the walls of the yurt were faced with openwork reed matting which, when the felt wall coverings were rolled up, gave privacy while permitting the free passage of breezes. When the nomads moved camp, the yurt was dismounted and the pieces loaded on camels or horses; at the new campsite, the yurt could be reassembled in an hour. For overnight stops, the wall sections alone were set up as a windbreak.[6]

In the interior of the yurt, the ground was covered with felt or *palas* (pileless woven rugs), and decorative felts often hung from the walls. Opposite the door, at the back of the yurt, were wooden chests usually covered with decorative felt cases. On the woman's side of the yurt, at the right of the door, were kept domestic utensils: skin sacks and bottles for storing liquid milk products and wooden bowls and ladles. In summer, just inside the entrance, the kumiss bag hung handy for stirring and quaffing. In the center of the yurt was the hearth, over which a large iron cauldron was suspended from a tripod. On the men's side of the yurt—the left—were kept saddles, harness, weapons, and other male appurtenances. The place of honor was at the back of the yurt, opposite the entrance. Occasionally, a wooden bed was seen in yurts of the wealthy, but normally, nomads slept on felt bedding laid on the floor.[7]

The felts used to cover and furnish the yurt, as well as those for clothing, were made by the women of the family, assisted by neighbors. Women also spun and dyed the yarn used for reed matting and, in the south, where weaving had been introduced from the oases, for pileless rugs and a camel's hair cloth. For weaving, a horizontal loom similar to that used by tribal peoples throughout Southwest Asia was employed. All women did embroidery and ornamental appliqué work on felt and made clothing, but only a few women were skilled in weaving. Both men and women worked leather. In ropemaking, horsehair was combined with sheep wool for greater strength. An effective soap was made of mutton fat and ash from a certain kind of plant. While Kazak families produced much of what they used, certain objects were made to order by itinerant craftsmen. Ironsmiths made cauldrons, knives, lance points, bridle bits, and other iron ware; silversmiths made jewelry, belt buckles, and saddle and harness ornaments, while infrequent coppersmiths made large copper pitchers as well as harness and saddle ornaments. Woodworkers produced saddles, the pieces forming the framework of the yurt, and chests, and, on a simple lathe, turned bowls and ladles from blocks of wood. Stoneworkers carved memorials to the dead.[8]

The Kazak costume, for both men and women, consisted basically of one or more *chapans*—a long, straight garment opening down the front and held in at the waist by a belt; trousers, very large at the top so that a rider, who might wear as many as six or seven *chapans* in winter, could tuck them inside; high-heeled boots; and a headdress which varied in form according to region and period. In the late eighteenth century, much of the clothing was made of skin—gazelle, colt, or squirrel—with an outer *chapan* of fox skin in winter; and of felt or home-woven camel-hair cloth. Even then, imported textiles were used when available, obtained either by barter or by robbing caravans. Throughout the nineteenth century, imported fabrics came increasingly into use, particularly for women's clothing, but even at the end of the nineteenth century high style for young men consisted of a *chapan* of horseskin, with the mane set into the shoulder seams for ornament. Both men and women frequently still wore leather trousers, and in summer men often wore an outer *chapan* of felt. Silver was the preferred metal for belt buckles, ornamental buttons, and women's jewelry—rings, bracelets, earrings, and hair ornaments. Often these were set with carnelians and other semiprecious stones.[9]

Kazak social life was organized around the family and more extended patrilineal kin. When an older son married, he received a yurt to be set up in his father's *aul*; only the youngest son remained in the paternal yurt after marriage to care for his parents in their old age and inherit the yurt on their death. The *aul* consisted of an extended family group of a man and his married sons and unmarried daughters, or of several brothers and their wives and offspring. The size of the *aul* was limited by the number of animals that could be pastured within range of one camp site. When the number of conjugal family units and animals became too large, one son might ask for his share of the family livestock and move off to form a new *aul*. A man rich in animals sometimes maintained two or three camps, with a wife and hired herdsmen in each. Ideally, the *aul* was made up of men related in the male line, together with their wives and children. In practice, it might include relatives of a wife. In the camps of wealthy families, there were often hired workers, orphans or men who had lost their livestock, who served until they had earned enough animals to set up on their own. These hired workers received food and clothing in addition to animals and were treated as members of the family.[10]

Although the camp was not always strictly a patrilineal family group in fact, the pattern of Kazak social organization was based on the assumption that it was. The Kazaks believed themselves all descended in the male line from one primogenitor. Tribal genealogies collected by nineteenth-century observers vary greatly in detail, even to the name of the primogenitor, but they all agree that he had three sons who, branching off to form separate *auls*, founded the three main branches of the Kazaks: the Great or Oldest Orda, the Middle Orda, and the Small or Youngest Orda. These three founders in turn had sons who, according to the tribal genealogy, split off to become the ancestors of lesser subdivisions in the ordas, and their sons in turn branched off to sire still smaller subdivisions, and so on down the line to the *aul*, where all the men and unmarried girls were usually descended from a common ancestor.

Thus the Kazak nation and all its subdivisions were regarded as ramifications of an extended family group. The tribal genealogies were highly idealized. Obviously, all a man's sons would not break off to found new camps, nor would new groups be formed consistently at every generation. Furthermore, the genealogies themselves often recognized the engrafting of unrelated groups by attributing one subdivision to an adopted son or by the name of the subdivision, such as Jetiru, "seven tribes." Followers of a strong leader often took his name for their group, and this name was in time incorporated into the tribal genealogy as that of an eponymous ancestor. Despite the often fictional nature of these tribal genealogies, they provided the framework for much of Kazak life. The larger subdivisions were territorial units. The Great Orda had a range in the eastern part of what is now Kazakhstan; the Middle Orda occupied the central and northern steppe; while the Small Orda extended from the Aral Sea westward to the Caspian Sea and Ural River. A fourth, the Inner or Bukeev (Bukey) Orda, between the Ural and Volga rivers, was formed at the beginning of the nineteenth century, when a part of the Small Orda flowed westward into an area vacated by Kalmuks. Within these general areas of the ordas, the larger subdivisions had their traditional territories, within which the smaller member subdivisions were free to migrate.[11]

Etiquette, marriage, and political organization were also tied to the tribal genealogy. When two strange Kazaks met, they at once established their genealogical relationship. Although hospitality to any visitor was obligatory, special assistance might be expected of close genealogical kin. In entertaining, honored positions in seating and the choice titbits of food were allocated according to the seniority of the line of the guests. In entertaining protocol, for example, a member of the Great Orda would take precedence over members of other ordas. In marriage, the Kazaks practiced genealogical exogamy. That is, it was forbidden to marry anyone related through descent in the male line from a common ancestor less than seven generations removed. During the nineteenth century, the number of generations was sometimes lowered to five, and because the average Kazak could not remember his genealogy for so many generations (chiefs who could afford a Tatar secretary kept written genealogies), there was an understanding that certain tribal subdivisions were too close and that others were far enough removed to allow intermarriage.[12]

Political organization, flexible as it often was, followed tribal genealogical lines. Pastoral nomads are notoriously resistant to the imposition of authority from above. Being nomads, they can move to a new territory if they feel imposed on by their chief. History makes some mention of paramount khans of all the Kazaks, notably the Khan Tauka (1680–1718) who, according to tradition, first codified Kazak customary law. However, little documentation is available on these khans, and it seems likely that they served either as temporary leaders against some common enemy or that their names appear in history because they were accepted by the Russian government as ruling over all the Kazaks. In the late eighteenth century, there were khans over two of the three ordas.

Despite their dislike of excessive authority, nomads do not live in a state of anarchy. They need leaders to settle disputes among themselves and to represent them in relations with the outside world. Below the orda level, therefore, the Kazaks had "big *biis* and little *biis*"—chiefs of larger and smaller subdivisions in the tribal genealogy. If families regrouped to follow a new *bii* and took his name for their group, the tribal genealogy was eventually modified to include this. At the base of this segmented political structure, the head of the family (*aqsaqal*, "white beard") made decisions for the *aul*. A group of related *auls* had a *bii* who in turn made decisions concerning the welfare of the group, with the advice of the *aqsaqals* of the member *auls*. Tribal subdivisions as far up the tribal genealogy as there was a need for leadership had similar chiefs, likewise counseled by lesser *biis*. In times of peace only the smaller subdivisions had effective chiefs. In times of stress, a number of subdivisions would rally to support and be protected by a strong leader. A chief's authority was based on the respect he inspired among his followers. The chief of the *aul* was head of the family, and in theory, chiefs of larger groups belonged to the genealogically senior family of that group. In practice, however, chiefship went to the ablest leader. If no member of the traditional chiefly family showed qualities of leadership, the tribesmen shifted their allegiance to someone else. The principal qualifications of such a leader were that he be wise and able, and that he have many relatives and the large herds and flocks needed to carry out his chiefly duties: the entertainment of followers and of visitors, and assistance to poor members of the group. Leadership at the various levels was essentially paternalistic and, except in time of war, fairly informal.[13]

There was a hereditary class principle at work among the Kazaks. An aristocratic class, called "white bones," traced descent from Abul Khaïr or some other illustrious ancestor and attempted to maintain their elite status by marrying only among themselves. Nevertheless, a white bone man could marry a woman of the "black bone," as commoners were called. The term "sultan," although it properly referred to those of white bone descent in both paternal and maternal lines, was in practice applied loosely both to those who claimed descent from the Prophet Muhammed and to any chief who had established himself as a strong leader.

Nowhere in the world had the heads of the nation and the aristocracy by birth so little meaning, so little real strength, as the Kirghiz [Kazak] Khans and Sultans. If any one of them attained to any influence, so as to be able to draw a crowd after him, he reached this not because of his "white bone," but on account of his personal worth, and personal qualities have gained exactly the same influence for simple Kirghiz of the "black bone." [14]

There were also slaves of sorts among the Kazaks: war captives; children who had been sold by their parents in time of famine; and a group known as Telengut who, according to tradition, were descended from slave retainers of early sultans, apparently on the pattern of the Turkic slaves who, in the Middle Ages, had gained control of the later Abbasid caliphate in Baghdad and of those who founded the Ghaznavid dynasty of Afghanistan. By the nineteenth century, the Telenguts had been freed, but some of them remained as privileged counselors of khans and sultans. Most of them, like other kinds of slaves, seem to have been assimilated into the Kazak group by intermarriage. The Kazaks were not very class conscious. [15]

Kazak marriages were arranged by families. Because of the exogamous taboo on marriage with anyone related within seven generations in the male line, the betrothed usually lived far apart before marriage, though aliens residing in an *aul* could marry into the camp in the first generation. Betrothals were often arranged between children. Among rich families, a boy was usually married between twelve and fifteen, and a girl often before puberty. Girls were usually married young because men preferred young brides; the girl's family was usually anxious to collect the bride price for use in obtaining a wife for a son; and early marriage assured the virginity of the girl and precluded the possibility of her elopement with a man of her own choice. Marriage established financial and social ties between families. The groom's family paid a bride price (*kalym* or *qalyng*), usually in livestock, to the bride's family. The *kalym* was so high that it was frequently paid in installments. Among poor families, men often had to postpone marriage until the age of thirty or over, or obtain a wife by "bride service"—working for the girl's father for a number of years in lieu of bride price. Sometimes two families avoided the expense of *kalym* by exchanging a son and a daughter in marriage. Once a substantial part of the bride price had been paid, the groom was allowed to visit the girl in her camp in a special tent set up for the purpose. The *kalym* was not payment for a chattel, as it was often interpreted by foreign observers. It was the "consideration" that made the contract valid; its size had a stabilizing effect on the marriage; the ability of the man's family to pay the *kalym* was regarded as an earnest of the family's ability to care for the woman and her children; and, finally, it gave social status to all concerned. The higher the bride price, the greater the prestige accruing to bride, groom, and both their families. Although most men were content with one wife, polygyny was permitted. A rich man might decide to take a young bride after his first wife had reached a certain age, and perhaps in time a third. Also, the levirate, under which, when a man died, his younger brother or other relative was expected to marry the widow and support her, often placed the responsibility of plural marriage on that member of the family most able to support two wives.[16]

Much has been written about the lowly status of Kazak women. Since marriage was arranged, the girl had little choice in a mate, but the same could be said for the young man. Only a wealthy older man had the opportunity to select a second or third wife. The Kazak woman was kept busy with her household tasks: cooking, caring for the children, milking the sheep, preparing milk products, sewing, making felt, weaving, setting up and dismantling the yurt, and sometimes saddling her husband's horse. She was ever busy, while her husband spent a good deal of his time sitting or riding off to visit friends. When visitors were entertained, the women prepared the meal and served it but did not eat until the men had finished. On the other hand, a woman was mistress of her yurt; indeed, she often owned it, for the dowry that a bride received from her family usually included a yurt as well as household equipment, clothing, and jewelry. Any livestock brought in the dowry was cared for by her husband but could be inherited only by her children, not those of another wife. A woman could divorce her husband or, on the death of her husband, marry a man outside his family. These required complicated financial arrangements, but the same was true if a man divorced his wife. Kazak women were not veiled, and girls associated freely with young men, in horse races, singing contests, and other diversions. As Wiener has pointed out, in the traditional heroic epics of the Kazaks the heroine was "usually endowed with qualities similar . . . to those of the *batyr*" (hero), and was "depicted as the equal of her husband or lover in moral worth and intelligence." [17]

Kazak religious beliefs and practices represented a mixture of ancient steppe spirit cult, of cult practices and beliefs emanating from Iran by way of the oasis peoples, and of those associated with Islam. Islam had had little foothold among the Kazaks until the Empress Catherine II (reigned 1762–1796), under the mistaken impression that the Kazaks were Muslims, ordered schools opened along the borders of the steppe under Kazan Tatar mullahs. Tatars also moved out among the Kazaks as merchants and missionaries and often attached themselves as secretaries to tribal chiefs, as did occasional mullahs from Khiva and Bukhara. In theory, the Kazaks were Sunni, but in practice few knew the difference between Sunni and Shi'a. Indeed, many of the mullahs were themselves little versed in the finer points of their religion. The so-called "five pillars" of Islam were little observed. 1. The name of Allah was more often heard in shamanistic incantations than in the profession of faith. 2. Prayer was performed on the occasion of a mullah's visit but never five times a day nor on Friday at a mosque; the nomads had no mosques. 3. There was no need for almsgiving; families took care of their own, and a poor man found a home with the family to which he hired out. There were some religious mendicants, but they seem to have made their way by fortunetelling and magical practices rather than as recipients of alms.[18] 4. There was no fasting. 5. Very few Kazaks made the pilgrimage to Mecca; those who did become *hajji* acquired so much prestige from this voyage that they were accorded the status of sultans.

Although the Kazaks ignored the obligatory duties of Muslims, they readily adopted some of the recommended practices. Circumcision was widely accepted and made the occasion for a celebration. The shaving of the head and the wearing of an embroidered skullcap seem also to have been readily adopted. For weddings, a mullah was called in, if one was available, but he was not essential. The bride went through the ceremony in the presence of the groom and was not hidden behind a screen or curtain as in the orthodox Muslim ceremony. For funerals, as for weddings, prayers were recited by a mullah if one were at hand, but the absence of a religious man was not regarded as a serious lack. Occasionally, a

42

niche was made in the side of the grave in Muslim fashion, and prayers were said at the grave on the fortieth and hundredth day after death. However, many of the death rituals were not Muslim. Sometimes a man's weapons and harness were buried with him, and his horse was killed. When the flesh had been cooked and eaten as part of the funeral feast, the bones were burned on the tomb. Among some tribal groups of the Great and Middle ordas, rich men who died in winter were wrapped in felt and hung from a tree until spring, when their bodies were taken for burial to the town of Turkestan, where there was a famous saint's tomb. Among the Kazaks a funeral, like a wedding, was an occasion for celebration, and on the day of the burial, the assembled guests built the tomb. For wealthy chiefs, whose funeral attracted several hundred celebrants, a great clay structure looking like a walled fortress, with turrets and sometimes a cupola, was erected. More humble graves were marked by piles of earth or, in mountain districts, of stones. A long pole with a black cloth attached was set up at the grave. After the monument had been built, there was a feast. One Muslim commemorative ceremony, readily adopted by those who could afford it, was that held on the first anniversary of the death. It was celebrated, however, in Kazak style. After the prayers had been recited, a white horse was sacrificed to the spirit of the dead, and its flesh was cooked and served with the rest of the feast already prepared. After the feast there was entertainment such as that enjoyed at weddings and funerals. This ceremony was expensive, but it was believed both that the spirit of the deceased would be annoyed and that the living members of the family would lose face if the celebration did not reflect the social and economic status of the deceased.[19]

The horse figured prominently in the ceremonial of Central Asian pastoral nomads. The birth of the first foal of spring was marked by ritual and feasting, as was the drinking of the first kumiss of the season. Among the Naiman Kazaks of the Altai Mountains, these events were celebrated in small family ceremonies as late as the 1920's. Shamanism, that psychological phenomenon characteristic of Central Asia, Siberia, and the Far East, also persisted into the early twentieth century. In this, the shaman (*baqshi*), believed to be possessed by a spirit control, went into a "trance state" to cure a patient, foretell the future, or find lost property. The shamanistic performance was essentially Central Asian in character, but changes in detail reflected influences from the south. During the nineteenth century, for example, the *dabyl* (a kind of tambourine), which was the traditional instrument by which a shaman worked himself into trance, was gradually replaced by the *kobyz*, a stringed instrument. The Arabic term *jinn* came to be applied to the spirits that caused sickness as well as those through which the shaman effected cures. Evil eye, not Central Asian in origin, came to be regarded as a cause of maladies. The incantations employed by the shaman in his ceremonies often invoked Allah and such Judeo-Muslim saints as Noah, Abraham, and David, as well as indigenous Central Asian spirits. These shamans were greatly venerated by the Kazaks. Wandering as they did from camp to camp, evoking ancient heroes in their chants, they kept alive the old legends and religious traditions of the people among the Kazak nomads. In addition to the shamans, there were diviners who foretold the future by burning the shoulder blade of a sheep or by throwing grease into a fire, and astrologers who studied the stars to determine auspicious and inauspicious days. The Kazaks also sought protection in amulets consisting of passages from the Koran written out by itinerant mullahs. By the late nineteenth century, it was not unusual to employ both a shaman and a mullah to treat a patient simultaneously.[20]

A cult of saints was found on the steppes and also a tree

cult. Sometimes a holy man after death acquired the status of saint. Often any grave might come to be regarded as that of a saint through some special circumstance. Because of the rarity of trees on the steppe, for example, the growth of a tree over a tomb was often enough to signal its sanctity. The most famous saint's tomb was that of the Khoji Akhmet at the town of Turkestan, but many districts had local saints at whose tombs people made votive offerings of pieces of cloth or the skull and horns of a wild sheep. Saints' tombs were also favorite places for burial, and cemeteries often grew up around them. Distinctive trees, even when not associated with a tomb, were often draped with votive offerings in the form of pieces of cloth, skin, or horse hair. Particularly in the southern steppes, some Kazaks marked their departure from winter quarters by rites similar to those performed in Iran at the time of Nau Ruz (New Year). Kazaks always welcomed the opportunity for a feast. Thus, many in the south observed the Muslim holidays of Qurban Bayram (commemorating Abraham's sacrifice) and Ramazan Hayit (feast at the end of Ramazan), though they did not fast during Ramazan.[21]

Important occasions for entertainment among the Kazaks were weddings, funerals, and anniversary mourning ceremonies for the dead. At the end of such a ceremony there was a great feast, for which relatives and friends contributed kumiss and animals to supplement provisions prepared by the host family. During and after the feast, various contests were held for the entertainment of the guests, with prizes offered for the winners. Long-distance races often taxed the endurance of even hardy Kazak mounts. Short races between young men and girls were tests of riding agility, with the girl trying to elude the young man who sought to cut across her path. Archery contests tested skill in shooting both from a standing position and while riding horseback at full speed. Wrestling was always popular, as were eating contests. Champion eaters, as well as skilled wrestlers and horsemen, were welcome at such celebrations and needed no invitation. Weddings were invariably held in late summer or early fall when food was plentiful and the animals fat. In winter, when the cold kept Kazaks indoors, young people played various games while sitting in a circle around the hearth in the yurt.[22]

Summer or winter, the chief entertainment was found in song. People sang to themselves. Women sang as they set out on the spring migration. There were ritual songs for weddings, funerals, and mourning ceremonies, for shamanistic performances and other religious rites. At any season of the year, the *aul* welcomed wandering bards (*aqyn* or *dzhyrshy*) who sang tales of legendary and historical events, sometimes of epic proportions. Young people gathered in the yurt on winter evenings to sing, and songs were sung between games at big festivities. A favorite form of entertainment was the singing contest, with first one side and then the other improvising verses. There was little variation in the music, but great improvisation, often witty, in the words. Sometimes the singing was accompanied by instruments—the stringed *kobyz* and *dombra* and the flutelike *chibyzga* were the favorites—but song was the great means of expression among the Kazaks. This rich literature, transmitted in the form of song, was oral. In the nineteenth century, few Kazaks could read or write, and even khans employed mullahs to handle necessary correspondence with the Russian government.[23]

Visual arts were limited to the decorative. Felt rugs were adorned by laying out a pattern of wet colored wool on a rug in process of manufacture and felting it into the rug. Another way of embellishing felt was the application of pieces of felt of contrasting color on the bag, chest cover, or rug to be decorated. Appliqué was also used for fur clothing, on which contrasting kinds of fur were inset. Embroidery was widely used—on clothing, horse caparisons, felt chest covers, and

III. The Sir Darya winding through the Fergana Valley, Uzbekistan. (Sovfoto.)

IV. Women making felt near yurts in a Kirghiz *aul*, Pamir Mountains. (Ullstein.)

bags. Colored wool yarns were employed in making the reed mats that covered yurt walls and in braiding or weaving the bands used to reinforce the yurt. Bone objects were carved, as were wooden chests, beds, door jambs, musical instruments, saddle pommels, and other objects. Gravestones were also carved in bas-relief. Silver jewelry, belt buckles, and harness mountings were incised with decorative motives and often embossed or set with carnelian and other semiprecious stones. In all this ornamentation, the motifs were highly stylized, often geometric, with straight lines, triangles, rectangles, diamonds, circles, and spirals around small embossed protuberances. Particularly favored in felt ornament were spiral motifs, often recalling the ram's horn motif of the ancient Central Asian animal style and in general reminiscent of Siberian art.[24]

OTHER PASTORAL PEOPLES

Kirghiz. The Kirghiz were very similar in culture to the Kazaks. Living in the eastern mountains, they used yaks as beasts of burden at high altitudes and had few cattle; Bactrian camels were more numerous than horses. Many Kirghiz were full pastoral nomads, but in some localities they wintered in clay or stone dwellings like those of the Mountain Tajiks and, in valleys below 8,000 feet, planted wheat and barley at winter quarters. Here some men remained to tend the crops in summer while women and boys took the livestock to high summer pastures. The Kirghiz normally moved in much larger groups than the Kazaks, with a hundred or more yurts in an *aul.*

Like the Kazaks, the Kirghiz had a tribal genealogical social organization, with *bii*s or *manap*s leading tribal segments of varying levels ranging from the *aul* up to the tribe. Soviet literature presents these *manap*s as comprising a wealthy hereditary aristocracy that exploited the Kirghiz masses, but nineteenth century reports corroborate the statement of the Russian Turkic scholar, W. Barthold, that "the Kara Kirghiz had neither princes nor nobles; the elders . . . were not chosen by any kind of election, but owed their position entirely to their personal influence." [25] The Kirghiz were even less ready than the Kazaks to accept an authoritarian leader and often fought among themselves, as well as against attempts to subdue them by the khans of Kokand and Kashgaria and the Chinese governments. Again like the Kazaks, the Kirghiz were only nominal Muslims.[26]

Karakalpaks. The Karakalpaks were formerly pastoral nomads of the steppe, but during their residence along the Sir Darya in the sixteenth and seventeenth centuries, they became acquainted with agriculture. When they were pushed into the area of marsh and desert along the delta of the Amu Darya, their way of life changed in adaptation both to the new natural environment and to the cultural influence of the khanate of Khiva.[27] The Karakalpaks continued to dwell the year round in yurts, but became semisedentary, moving only a short distance from the reedy protection of winter quarters to summer quarters where they planted grains and melons in crudely irrigated fields, as well as herded sheep and goats. Horses gave way to cattle, which were useful in agriculture for drawing plows and *arba,* two-wheeled carts, and which did not require the broad pasturage needed for horses. Poor Karakalpaks along the shores of the Aral Sea fished, trading fish for grain with the cultivators. Their diet, as described in an old Karakalpak saying, consisted of "three months of milk, three months of melons, three months of pumpkins, three months of fish—any way to live." [28] These foods were supplemented by bread flaps and other grain dishes. Karakalpak craft work showed oasis influence. Blacksmiths made a variety of objects used by cultivators and fishermen. Jewelry, the work of a few craftsmen, was transitional in style between that of the nomads and of the oases. Some carpenters specialized in yurt frames, others in saddles, while Uzbek carpenters scattered among the Karakalpaks made the great *arba*s employed for transportation, as well as the boats used by fishermen. Housewives wove woolen textiles, such as bands to reinforce the yurt and chest covers, on simple horizontal looms like those of the Kazaks. In addition, on an Uzbek-Tajik type of loom, they wove cotton material for clothing.[29]

Despite changes in their economy, the Karakalpaks retained their tribal genealogical social and political structure, with each tribal segment enjoying rights to a section of territory within which it planted crops and pastured its animals. Under the influence of Khiva, some leaders seem to have made the transition to the status of feudal landowners,[30] and some lands had come under *waqf* (religious) tenure. A few Karakalpaks had become prosperous by engaging in trade. The Karakalpaks, who took Islam more seriously than the Kazaks and Kirghiz, had a number of small mosques. Their interest in music and song was apparently comparable to that of the Kazaks, but their decorative arts show some differences. A. N. Kharuzin, who had an opportunity to compare Karakalpak yurts with those of Kazaks in the 1880's, noted that the Karakalpaks made little use of decorative felts and instead hung embroidered cloths on the walls. Storage chests were often painted in the Uzbek manner; where chest covers were used, the embroidered or woven designs were frequently more reminiscent of Turkoman motifs than of Kazak. In clothing, cotton fabrics of plain colors, stripes, or the fluid pattern obtained by tie-dyeing the yarn before weaving, reflected oasis influence as contrasted with the Kazak preference for prints in purchased fabrics. The men wore head coverings of black lamb fur, which gave the Karakalpaks (Black Caps) their name.[31]

Turkomans. Although the Turkomans had long been in

contact with the settled peoples of the oases and the Iranian Plateau, they had not readily renounced their tribal pastoral heritage. They remained pastoral as far as possible, but the desert region they inhabited was too arid to support life by stockbreeding alone. Some of them, like the Tekke at Merv, had occupied oases formerly tilled by sedentary cultivators. All had a mixed economy. The Turkomans of the nineteenth century were categorized as *charva* ("nomad") and *chomur* ("settled"), but there was no clear division between the two. Very few tribal groups were completely sedentary, and just as few were fully nomadic. The Turkomans combined, in varying proportions, stockbreeding, agriculture, crafts, trade, war, and, on the shores of the Caspian, fishing. Ideally, from the Turkoman point of view, some members of the family herded the camels and sheep while others cultivated the fields or supervised their cultivation by slaves. Turkoman girls spent much of their time in embroidery and weaving. A girl thought first of her dowry, but having woven a few fine rugs and embroidered a suitable number of garments for this purpose, she and her sisters wove additional rugs and saddlebags for sale to merchants—the fine rugs known in Europe and America as "Bukhara" or "Merv." [32]

The Turkomans were notorious for their warlike proclivities. When not violently resisting the attempts of the rulers of Khiva, Bukhara, and Persia to subdue them, they hired out as mercenaries to these states in their wars against each other. More important in their economy, Turkomans raided the villages of "unbelievers," chiefly Persian Shi'a Muslims, although they were not averse to attacking Russian Christians when the opportunity presented itself. In these raids they took horses, goods, and people. Captives were ransomed if their families had the money to pay. If not, they were either retained as domestic slaves or sold in the slave markets of Khiva or Bukhara. Ransom was regarded as the more profitable. Horses, although not numerous in comparison with the great herds of the Kazaks, were of great importance in Turkoman raiding activities. These horses, unlike the short, sturdy mounts of the Kazaks, were graceful, mettlesome steeds with a considerable infusion of Arab stock and, like the horses of the Bedouin Arabs, were brought up in camp and carefully tended. Only mares, which were seldom ridden except for short distances, were sent out to pasture with the other animals. The arid desert, which occupied much of the Turkoman territory, was more suitable for camels than for horses. As in all pastoral Central Asia, sheep and goats were the chief livestock. Grazing was limited by the location of wells or the availability of rain water. In the south, along the foothills of the Kopet Dagh, some springs and streams permitted patches of irrigated agriculture, and along the Tejend and Murghab rivers in the east there were more extended oases. Here the crops were of the type generally cultivated in the oases of Turkistan: barley, wheat, millet, and, occasionally, rice; and melons and fruit.[33]

The diet reflected the economy. Few Turkomans had enough horses to provide milk for kumiss, but the prosperous served a similarly fermented drink of camel's milk. Curds (*gatthuk*) made of sheep and camel milk were much eaten, as well as a soft cheese made from this. Bread flaps, either baked in an oven or cooked in fat, formed the dietary staple, often served with green tea brought by merchants from China. Even when hospitality required the killing of a sheep, often a portion of the flesh was served chopped and cooked in broth and the remainder sold, a practice not found among the Kazaks. The great Turkoman delicacy was the rendered fat of the tail of the fat-tailed sheep in which chopped meat was cooked. In the oasis regions, melons and fruits were much eaten in the warm months, and melon slices were dried for year-round use. Pilau, the standard oasis dish, was often made of barley rather than rice and cooked only with fat and per-haps wild carrot; pieces of meat and dried prunes were added only on special occasions. Except for those living along the Caspian, the Turkomans avoided fish. The Turkomans had acquired the use of narcotics and stimulants from their seden-tary neighbors. They were so addicted to the use of the water pipe (*kaliun*) that they had developed a traveling substitute, a hole in the ground in which tobacco was placed on live coals and the fumes inhaled. They also had a kind of snuff, called *gugenas,* made of powdered tobacco mixed with lime ash, which was placed under the tongue for its astringent effect. Some opiüm was smoked among oasis Turkomans, but this practice was not widespread.[34]

Despite the fact that most Turkomans depended to some extent on agriculture, they clung to the portable yurt of their nomadic past. Even the fishing village of Gömüshtepe on the Caspian Sea was made up entirely of yurts when Arminius Vambery visited it in 1867. In the Merv Oasis, where Ed-mund O'Donovan spent some months in 1881, people owned mud houses of the oasis type, but these were used chiefly for storage or for entertaining visitors. The people preferred to live in yurts, often set up beside the house. The Turkoman yurt differed from that of the Kazaks only in interior furnish-ings. Over the felt floor covering were spread woven pile rugs, and the walls were adorned with woven saddle bags in-stead of felt chest covers. On the woman's side, most of the containers were of wood, metal, or gourd, rather than leather, and there was a horizontal hand mill for grinding grain. Outside the yurt was an oven, a crude variation of that used by the oasis peoples. Clothing was similar to that of the Kazaks in the basic form of shirt, coat, and trousers, but the men favored coats of the black and yellow striped material made in Bukhara and wore high sheepskin hats. On the feet, they wore sandals of moccasinlike leather footwear instead of high-heeled boots. The only other skin garment was the sheepskin cloak with very long sleeves similar to the *pustin* of Iran and Afghanistan, worn with the skin side out in good weather and the fur side out in rain and snow. Women favored purples and reds in their clothing, which was often richly embroidered. For state occasions, a sleeved cloak, with the sleeves crossed in back, was draped over the headdress, in the fashion of sedentary oasis village women who used such a cloak to cover their faces when they went out. The Turkoman women, however, did not cover their faces. Their silver jewelry, which was more elaborate than that of either Kazak or oasis women, featured necklaces with pendant cylinders containing amulets.[35]

Turkoman tribes were much more distinct than those of the Kazaks. There were several independent tribes, often hostile to each other. The major tribes were: the Yomud, with a territory extending eastward from the Caspian Sea; the Goklan, along the Atrek River on the Persian border; the Salor, east of the Goklan, also on the Persian border; the Saryk, whose territory extended along the Murghab River into Afghanistan; the Tekke, who occupied the Merv (Mary) oasis in the mid-nineteenth century; and the Ersari, just north of Merv, who had established a *modus vivendi* with the Tekke by the time both these tribes came under Russian rule. These Turkoman tribes retained the tribal genealogical social structure characteristic of the tribal peoples of Central Asia, with each tribal group having its own traditional territory. There was little class distinction. As among the Kazaks, khans had to be rich to afford the entertaining required of the position, but their authority depended on personal qualities of leadership. The title of "khan" was also given to the descendents of khans, that of *sardar* to those who had distinguished themselves as leaders of raids, and brave fighters were honored with the title of *bahadur* or *batur*, but these were courtesy titles. Slaves on capture were treated with inhumanity, but of those who survived, women were often married by their masters.[36]

The Turkomans had acquired the Muslim preference for cousin marriage and regularly married within their own tribal group. Girls were often married at the age of twelve and boys at fifteen, but because of the high bride price and, in the oases, the cost of purchasing land or water rights, poor men often had to wait some years before they could afford to marry. The status of Turkoman women appears to have been similar to that of the Kazaks. Women did all the house work and set up and dismantled the yurt, whereas "once a man passes the age of forty, he delegates all his work to the younger members of his family, and never dreams of doing anything himself." [37] The woman was mistress of her house, however, and went unveiled. In the 1880's the widow of a khan at Merv exerted considerable political influence in the tribe.[38]

The Turkomans were more strongly Muslim than the Kazaks. Although the mosque was frequently only an earth platform or a large yurt, most larger communities had a place for praying, and some Turkomans said their daily prayers or at least said grace after eating. Arminius Vambery, traveling among the Turkomans in 1863 in the disguise of a holy man from Istanbul, concluded from experience that mullahs and religious judges (*qazi*) exerted more influence over the people than their *aqsaqals*. *Qazi*s regularly attended the courts of tribal and subtribal chiefs to pass on such cases as concerned religious law. Any one who could afford it made the pilgrimage to Mecca. The Turkoman attachment to Islam, like other aspects of Turkoman culture, appears to have been transitional between that of the Kazaks and that of the settled oasis peoples. The feast of Qurban Bayram was celebrated by some, but not the fast of Ramazan.[39] A wedding or a death was the occasion for a feast, but the diversions of Kazak festivals were absent from funerals; at weddings, there were races and various games on horseback, including *baïga,* a mounted contest for the carcass of a goat. Otherwise, the chief entertainment seems to have been chess and a game played with sheep's knucklebones. Music at the time of Russian conquest appears to have been provided principally by professional bards.[40] The chief decorative arts were those of woven pile rugs and saddlebags, and embroidery done by girls and women; and women's jewelry made by professional silversmiths. The embroidery often showed Persian influence in its stylized floral motifs, while that on skull caps was often more reminiscent of Kazak felt ornamentation. The designs of woven pile rugs and saddlebags were strictly geometric, devoid of the curves of either the highly stylized ram's horn motif of Kazak felts or the floral design of Persian rugs. In the geometrical angularity of design they show an affinity with Seljuk rugs of the thirteenth century and Anatolian rugs of the fourteenth and fifteenth centuries. Each Turkoman tribe had its own characteristic style.[41]

III

Traditional Oasis Culture

OASIS culture includes that of the cities and market towns and of isolated rural villages both in the plains and the high mountains in the east. Everywhere in the oasis area the people were sedentary, dwelling in permanent houses huddled together in population clusters along life-giving streams and irrigation canals. Where the water ended, the desert began. The settlements were indeed oases, islands of watered fertility set amidst the desert. In the east, Tajiks tended to cling more tenaciously to ancient ways than did many of the Uzbeks; in the Khiva Oasis, far to the west of the central cluster of trading cities, the Uzbeks retained some elements of their former tribal culture. Beyond this, there were smaller regional variations in culture, with each region set off a little from others by idiosyncrasies in speech, clothing, technology, and social and religious practices. Although these regional differences were sufficiently marked to be of concern to later Soviet administrators, the way of life throughout the oasis area, from the Pamirs to Khiva, was essentially the same. It is thus valid to describe an "oasis culture" in contrast with the pastoral nomadic culture of the steppe and desert.

The oasis economy was based on agriculture, craft manufactures, and trade. In the arid climate of Central Asia, irrigation was essential to the raising of crops except for some cereals. Grain was grown by dry farming in mountain patches and along the edges of the oases, but although the quality was high, the yield was low and uncertain. To support the dense population concentrated in the oases, a great deal of time and attention had to be given to the irrigation systems. Even small upland valleys had small channels leading water from mountain streams into the fields on either side. Along the large rivers there were intricate networks of canals which had to be kept free from silting and regulated to insure an equable flow of water among the fields served. Water rights were more important than land rights. Among the grains grown, wheat was the preferred cereal for humans; barley, fed to horses by those who could afford to eat wheat, was eaten by poorer people. Millet, which required little water, was widely grown by seminomads in unirrigated lands and eaten in both bread and porridge. Durra or sorghum (*jukhori* or *jughara*), which gave a high yield, was an important crop for rural farmers; the seed provided food for man as well as for horses and poultry, and the stalk was used for fodder, fuel, and for matmaking. In smaller amounts, farmers raised some beans and various oil seeds, particularly sesame. In the lowlands where water was plentiful, rice, favored for feast-day dishes, was grown, as well as alfalfa, cotton, the opium poppy, flax, hemp, and tobacco. The oases were long famous for their melons, both muskmelons and watermelons. In addition, several types of gourds were cultivated, some for eating, others dried and made into containers.

Most fruits and vegetables were grown in gardens surrounded by high walls which often also encompassed the farmhouse and its outbuilding. Prosperous town-dwellers often maintained summer dwellings and gardens outside the town, where they spent the warm months of the year living on the produce of their gardens. Wherever space allowed, grape arbors provided shade in the courtyards of dwellings, and in the orchards were apricots, peaches, quinces, figs, pomegranates, apples, almonds, and other fruits and nuts. There was usually also a vegetable garden within the walled compound, with carrots, onions, turnips, peas, radishes, cucumbers, and red pepper. Mulberry trees grew widely in the oases; their fruit was dried and pounded into a meal used for sweetening food, and the leaves were fed to silkworms. The people were very fond of flowers, and even in the high mountain valleys the Tajiks managed to raise marigolds and poppies in their tiny gardens. Poplars planted along streams and canals served as windbreaks and as a source of timber for woodwork and construction; willows and elms provided both shade and ornament in the towns and villages. Travelers approaching a town often saw only trees rising above the walls.[1]

Stockbreeding played a comparatively unimportant role in the oasis economy. All men who could afford it rode horses, and although some of these were bred in the oases, many were purchased from nomads and seminomads. The poor man's beast of burden was the ass. Both horses and oxen were employed to draw plows and *arba*s, the high, two-wheeled carts that were the normal conveyance for women, family parties, and farm produce. Camels for the caravan trade were obtained from nomads. In country districts villagers often kept some sheep and goats, sending the village flock out to graze under a shepherd. Much of the mutton and wool used in the towns and cities came from seminomads and nomads on the fringes of the oases.[2]

The oasis diet was varied. Basic to any meal was bread, baked in thin flaps. Sometimes it was unleavened, more often leavened with sour dough held from the previous day's baking. Usually it was eaten hot, fresh from the oven. Chinese green tea, introduced in the nineteenth century, was quickly adopted by all but the poorest families and most isolated villages. It was served on many occasions: for breakfast, seasoned with salt and the cream of boiled milk, eaten with bread; for the entertainment of guests; and as an accompaniment of relaxed conversation in the bazaars. Tea and bread also constituted the basic midday meal. Melons and fruits were eaten in quantity as between-meal snacks during the summer; they were also dried for winter use. The chief meal of the day normally came in the evening. The great favorite was pilau —rice cooked with fat and seasoned with carrots and dried fruit and, when it was available, with mutton. Even the wealthy did not have pilau every day; the well-to-do served it on Friday evening, at the end of the Muslim sabbath; the poor could afford it only on special feast days; in mountain villages it was made with barley instead of rice. Everyone knew how to cook pilau. Women prepared it in the home, but for family and community feasts men did the cooking out of doors and took pride in their skill.[3]

Most oasis-dwellers could not afford to eat meat very often. Such meat as was available—mutton, sometimes chicken or goat, and occasionally sausages or other dishes made of horse flesh—was extended to go as far as possible. Broth was the basis of a number of dishes containing pieces of mutton and whatever meal, grain, or beans were at hand, sometimes with sour milk added. Pasties filled with meat chopped with onions, pumpkin, herbs, or red pepper, were cooked in broth or baked. Milk products were much less used than among the nomads, although the oasis diet included curds, the cream from boiled milk, and dried and salted cheese. Clarified butter was used in cooking when available; the fat of the fat-tailed sheep was also greatly relished as a cooking fat, but most families made do with sesame and other seed oils. Whereas the nomads subsisted happily on fermented milk during the summer, the oasis people gorged on melons and fruits; and where the nomads killed a sheep for the entertainment of guests, the oasis people served *dastarkhan*—tea with as many varieties of sweets, nuts, and fruits as could be assembled. The oasis people had little more use for fish than the nomads, but some fried fish was sold in town bazaars. They were very fond of sweets and had a considerable variety, but these were never made at home. Confected by professional sweetmakers, they were, like pilau, a luxury which poor families could afford only on feast days. Sweets had a special place in ritual. At weddings, for example, the family of the groom gave *halva* to the bride and her friends, and during Ramazan a confection of sugar and egg was eaten.[4]

In an area where wood was precious and stone nonexistent except in mountain regions, the most plentiful building material was mud—the loess soil which gives the oasis region its fertility. The dwelling and its outbuildings and courtyards were surrounded by a thick wall built up of lumps of loess mud. Against the inner side of one or more of these outer walls stood the house, which had thinner walls of tamped earth or sun-dried brick reinforced by a frame of upright poles. The uprights supported horizontal roof beams, across which were laid straw, reeds, or mats. Over this was spread a coating of mud. Even in two-storied city dwellings, the floor of the second story was of this construction. Houses had no foundations. The walls were built directly on the ground except in prosperous city dwellings, where a floor of fired brick was laid. A house had no windows facing the street, only a closed wooden door, strongly barred at night. To anyone walking along the blank-walled street, only the door gave a clue to the economic status of the residents. Upper-class dwellings were distinguished by double doors, richly carved. If the street door opened onto the only courtyard of the dwelling, where women worked, a short clay wall facing the door on the inside effectively blocked the view of passersby when the door was open. Upper-class dwellings had two courtyards, the first used only by men, the inner one reserved for women. The house itself was oriented toward the court-yard; on that side, the house walls were punctuated by open-work plaster grills or wooden doors which were usually kept open in summer for ventilation and light. Also facing the courtyard was a roofed veranda which protected the rooms from the direct rays of the summer sun. Extending beyond the veranda was a packed clay terrace, the *aivan*. In the court-yard, a bread oven stood near the kitchen; in a corner where two walls met was a toilet; and along one or more walls there were stalls for animals. Within the courtyard, grape arbors gave shade from the intense summer sunlight. Uzbek families who had not forgotten their nomadic tradition often set up a yurt in the courtyard for living quarters, using the house for storage and the entertainment of guests. In the suburbs and in the country, the walls of the courtyards were extended to embrace a vegetable garden and fruit orchards.

Oasis dwellings were constructed of the building materials most readily available—the basic loess soil was ready to the hand of the landowner and cost only the effort of making it into walls. Furthermore, these dwellings were admirably adapted to the climate. Mud walls keep out summer heat and hold in interior winter heat better than do kiln-fired bricks. In city homes where the courtyards were small, summer rooms faced the north, while winter rooms faced the south to catch the sun's rays for warmth. Where courtyards and gardens were more spacious, the family spent most of its time during the long summer months in the courtyard. Rugs were laid out on the *aivan,* and there people cooked and ate their meals and spent their leisure time. Women napped on the *aivan* in the heat of the day, and at night families slept there. In win-ter, women often went onto the flat roof of the house to catch the warmth of the midday sun. Fuel—dung, wood, or charcoal —was scarce. In the short but cold winters, families huddled in the kitchen before the hearth or snuggled around the *sandal,* a low wooden table placed over a charcoal brazier set in a hole in the floor, with covering quilts channeling the heat to the legs of people sitting around it. People ate at the *sandal* during the coldest months, and slept near it.[5]

The arrangement of the dwellings was also adapted to the oasis custom of secluding women. Muslim law forbade that a woman's face be seen by any man other than her husband and close relatives. Wealthy homes had two courtyards, a first where men entertained, a second where the family lived and women were free to go unveiled. In more modest homes, a man received guests in the *mehmankhane,* a front room with a separate entrance from the street. In the homes of craftsmen, hired workers often lived in the front or men's quarters (*tashkar*), leaving the *ishkar*—women's quarters—for family use. In houses too small for such a division, women either covered their faces or took refuge with a neighbor when men called on the head of the house.[6]

Household furnishings were simple. Reed mats were laid on the mud floors, and over these were spread felt or pileless woven rugs. In the homes of the rich, the floors were laid with Bukharan pile rugs or, most highly prized, Turkoman rugs. Niches in the mud walls held teapots and other household articles ornamentally arranged. Opposite the entrance to the family living room was a large niche to accommodate a chest containing cherished clothing and jewelry. On and beside this chest, colorful quilts and cushions were neatly piled with an eye to aesthetic considerations. Across one corner of the room stretched a cord or pole from which hung clothing in everyday use. Other than the *sandal* and chest, there was little furniture. People sat on rugs and cushions on the floor. In nineteenth-century Bukhara and Tashkent, there was a fashion of serving food on low tables, but in most households a cloth was spread on the floor for meals. In some areas, the kitchen had a fire hole over which a cauldron was suspended on a tripod, with a chimney to carry out the smoke. Elsewhere, a kind of kitchen range was made of clay, with fire pits fed from openings in the side and cooking utensils placed over holes in the top. Cooking was also often done on a charcoal brazier. In addition to the ubiquitous iron cauldrons, the kitchen was stocked with knives, ladles, bowls and platters of various sizes made of pottery, wood, or tinned copper, and jugs of pottery or brass. Grains and other dry foods were stored in large clay jars or in pits, while cheeses and melons were hung from the rafters. In summer much of the cooking was done in the courtyard.[7]

The clothing of the oasis people was similar in form to that of the nomads, but the materials differed and there were many regional variations in details. For both men and women there was a shirt or tunic, opening down the front. The men's shirt was tucked into full, baggy trousers; the women's tunic, worn over the trousers, extended to mid-calf or ankle. Townswomen in the privacy of the home and farm women at work wore just the tunic and trousers, adding a long, loose cloak (*khalat*) like a dressing gown only for entertaining or, in winter, for warmth. Men usually wore one or more *khalat*s, the number depending partly on the temperature, partly on the social status of the wearer. A man of some standing normally wore two at home, but added several more when going out or receiving visitors of distinction. The basic garments of shirt and trousers were made of cotton cloth, usually white for men. The *khalat* was made variously of cotton, quilted cotton, a silk-and-cotton fabric peculiar to the oases, silk, or velvet. In the Pamirs and among some seminomads, wool cloaks were more frequently worn. In winter, men often wore great cloaks of sheepskin, with the skin side out in fair weather, the wool side out in rain or snow. The rich lined silk *khalat*s with fur. The *khalat* was held in place with a girdle; among the upper classes, the richness of the buckle gave a clue to the rank of the wearer. The men, following Islamic custom, shaved their heads and covered them with an embroidered skull cap, which usually formed a base for the turban. In Khiva, men wore high sheepskin hats, and elsewhere high conical headdresses of fur or fur-trimmed velvet were often worn in winter. Women also wore a cap, topped by a kind of turban. The shape and embroidered designs on the cap and the arrangement of the turban varied according to locality. When townswomen ventured out of the home, they covered the head with a black horsehair veil reaching to the waist, and over this wore a *paranja* (cloak) of a dull gray or dark color extending to the ankles. The sleeves, very long, were fastened in back, and there were slits in the sides of the *paranja* through which the hands could be thrust. In country districts, the *paranja* was not worn except at funerals or other formal occasions, but not every woman owned one. Country women simply turned away if they saw a strange man or put a child-size *khalat* over the head when going into the village street.[8]

In Khiva and some other regions there were separate farmsteads, but in most places cultivators lived in villages. In the old cities, the central part of the city was crowded, like the cities of medieval Europe, within the old city walls. There was little space for large courtyards in the dwellings, and buildings were pushed up to two stories. Around the dense central core, however, courtyard walls enclosed orchards and gardens, and there were craftsmen's suburbs where men worked out of doors. Whether in city, town, or *qishlaq* (village), the narrow and often winding streets were lined with blank walls, broken only by the closed doors or gates of dwellings. Trees rose over the tops of the walls but houses and gardens were invisible. By the mosques were open spaces, often with trees and sometimes a pond, and before the Friday or congregation mosque, found only in cities and large towns, there was a great open space where men gathered for the Friday prayer. Family life and women were hidden behind walls.

The life of the towns and cities was in the bazaars. These consisted of little shops opening onto narrow streets or side lanes. In some bazaars there were arcades along the street; in others, a roofing of reed mats gave shelter from the summer sun and the snow and rain of winter. Following the Iranian pattern, silk merchants were clustered in one section of the bazaar, jewelers in a second, grain merchants in a third, for example, with the sellers of each commodity grouped together. Many craftsmen, such as jewelers, coppersmiths, and woodworkers, practiced their craft in the bazaar, selling such finished objects as they had in stock or making things on order. Cook shops sold prepared food to customers who brought their own bowls, and there were confectioners and venders of pilau and other special delicacies. In Khiva and Bukhara there were also slave markets where the captives of Turkoman raiders were sold.

Buying and selling was a leisurely procedure, involving a good deal of conversation interspersed with shrewd bargaining. The Sarts had a cultural vocation for the market place, enjoying the ceremony of buying and selling as much as the profits derived from the transaction. The bazaars of the towns and cities were always crowded, except in the early afternoon heat when shops were closed. The *chaikhanes*, teashops, were social centers where men could enjoy conversation and, if they wished, send a boy to buy fruit, confections, or other food in nearby shops. In addition to the main bazaars of the towns and cities, there were shops where butchers, bakers, and other purveyors catered to the daily needs of households in the neighborhoods. Some craftsmen, such as leather tanners, potters, and certain kinds of carpenters, plied their crafts in special suburbs. Merchants engaged in foreign trade often had offices in the caravansarais. Some of the large villages held weekly bazaars, where men from neighboring villages brought their produce and traders from the nearest town or city came to buy and sell. At seasonal markets along the edge of the oases, nomads sold livestock. There was often a special relationship, "trade friend," for the exchange of goods between a nomad and a village-dweller on the edge of the steppe.[9]

This trade which linked village with town and city, and the steppe with the oases, was a concomitant of specialization of occupation. Ideally, the steppe nomad family was economically self-sufficient, though the nomads used trade goods when these were available. The oasis family was not self-sufficient. In rural communities, housewives spun woolen yarn and wove it into cloth for family clothing. Also for family use, they wove pileless rugs and saddle bags, made felt rugs, and did embroidery. Although the chief purpose of their activities was to satisfy family needs, they produced a surplus for sale whenever possible. Similarly, men tried to raise a surplus of grain and other products to exchange for meat and other goods. In many country villages some men were part-time specialists, weaving cotton cloth or making pottery, shoes, or other objects when not busy in their fields and gardens. In the towns and cities there were many full-time craft specialists, organized into craft guilds. Among these urban specialists, some metal workers made agricultural tools, for example; others made knives, guns, or cast-iron cauldrons; locks and keys; basins, trays, and pitchers of copper or brass; and bells or lamps. Jewelers worked in silver, occasionally in gold. Some specialized in filigree work, others in niello, still others in damascene inlay. Often the wives of such craftsmen helped their husbands, working on certain processes in the home.

In textiles, the ginning of cotton and the spinning of cotton yarn were the work of women, as was the raising of silkworms. But unwinding the silk from cocoons was the work of master craftsmen, as was the dying of yarns and fabrics and the weaving of cotton, silk-and-cotton, and silk taffetas, satins, and velvets. Leather workers were also specialized, some tanning one of the several types of leather used, others cutting shoe soles or uppers, still others making sheepskin harnesses. Specialists in closely related crafts usually worked in adjoining sections of the bazaar, so that a customer who had purchased an ax head could have a wooden handle hafted on at a nearby shop. Jewelers frequently sent objects to a second jeweler for the addition of ornament. In the production of ceramics, objects made in one town or village were often sent to another for ornament and glazing. Towns and villages specialized in certain crafts, such as a particular type of woven fabric or style of pottery.

In the towns and cities, families produced little of what they consumed. Householders bought meat, milk, grain or meal, fats and oils for cooking and illumination, fuel, confectionary, and often fruits and vegetables. They hired craftsmen to build their houses and their ovens; bought the fabrics for their clothing; and had their shoes and jewelry made to order. They also purchased tools and utensils and most of the furnishings of their homes. Craftsmen bought the materials they processed for sale and often employed assistants to help with the work. Trade itself was a specialized occupation. Some traders went to country markets where they bought grain and local craft goods or livestock for resale in the towns and cities. Others financed caravans to bring goods from Iran, Afghanistan, India, Kashmir, and Kashgar, as well as from Russian trade fairs held on the edge of Central Asia. In the bazaars, money changers served those engaged in foreign trade. Thus, because of the complex economy, urban centers drew into their orbits rural villages within the oasis area and pastoral nomads on the periphery. In addition, they acted as focal points for dissemination within the area of goods and ideas from neighboring countries.[10]

In social organization, the oasis people, like the pastoral nomads, held the extended joint family as the ideal. Such a family household typically comprised a man and his wife, married sons and their wives and children, and unmarried daughters. The family owned jointly the dwelling and culti-vated land, as well as domestic animals, agricultural tools and equipment, and food stores. On the death of the father, or, more often, when the first grandson was married, the sons usually set up separate households. The size of the family depended on the amount and fertility of the land or, in the cities, on the prosperity of the family business. The house-hold of a well-to-do family was often extensive. As late as the 1930's, Tajik households of fifty or more members were counted. In a poor family, one or more sons might have to go off to seek his fortune in another district.[11]

Marriage, as among the nomads, was a transaction between families, although the bride price and reciprocal dowry were not as substantial. When a girl was considered ready for mar-riage—usually between the ages of eleven and fifteen—the women of the family took her visiting, so that the women of other families could see her. A boy usually married at fifteen or sixteen, though a man sometimes attained the age of thirty before his family was able to scrape together the bride price. When he was ready for marriage, the women of his family passed on the likely candidates suggested by some older woman, usually a friend, who acted as matchmaker and knew what girls were available. It was regarded as important that the families of the boy and girl be of the same social and economic status; for example, the son of a *hajji* (one who had made the pilgrimage to Mecca) was expected to marry the daughter of a *hajji*. As among other Muslim peoples, there was a preference for cousin marriage, although cousins brought up in the same extended family household would never marry. Once the families had agreed on the suitability of a match, the boy sometimes persuaded the matchmaker to arrange for him to catch a secret glimpse of the face of his prospective fiancée by hiding him in a room the girl was to enter. The girl was not consulted at all in the choice of her mate.

Bargaining over the bride price was often spirited, and sometimes neighbors were called in to mediate between the two families. In addition to the bride price (*kalym* or *qalyn*) the groom's family provided the food for the wedding feast. The dowry, which included clothing as well as rugs, bedding, ornamental covers that the bride had embroidered, and utensils the bride would use in her new home, was often equivalent in value to the bride price. The *kalym* was often paid in installments; when half had been paid, the contract was fully binding, and if the girl died, her family was expected to provide another bride in her place. Among Uzbeks in country villages, the groom was allowed to visit his fiancée; he was led to her secretly by the wife of her brother, because the groom was not supposed to be seen by her family until the wedding. When the *kalym* had been paid and provisions for the marriage feast delivered, the wedding was held. A mullah witnessed the contract enumerating bride price and dowry and performed the Muslim marriage ceremony, at which the absent bride and groom were represented by their fathers or other male relatives. In addition, particularly in country districts, there were pre-Islamic rites, such as the bride's circling around or jumping over a bonfire. The wedding feast held at the bride's home was as elaborate as the families could afford, attended by the friends, relatives, and neighbors of both families. As at all important family feasts, uninvited guests were welcome. The bride remained in seclusion throughout the feast, while the wedding guests were entertained—men and women in separate courts—with dancing, singing, and other diversions. After the feast at the bride's home, the bride was conducted to her husband's home, where she was ritually introduced—"showed her face" —to the members of her husband's family. Just as her brother's wife had arranged meetings with her fiancé before the wedding, so in the new home the wife of her husband's brother helped her to adjust to the new household.[12]

Woman's life was a secluded one. A small girl was allowed to play freely with boys, even go into the street, but at the age of eight or nine she was expected to adopt woman's decorum, learn household skills, and begin to embroider the coverlets that would be part of her dowry. In order to obtain the money to buy silk yarns for this, she frequently embroidered objects for sale. Town girls often had the same interest in finance as their fathers and earned money by hatching the eggs of silkworms, then investing the profits in more eggs or in silk yarns for embroidery. Meakin wrote of one fourteen-year-old wife and mother in Kokand who earned a respectable income embroidering caps and copying books for sale. Women were forbidden to show their faces to any man other than members of the family. They had the freedom of the inner courtyard and of the roof tops, where they could enjoy the winter sun and gossip with women on neighboring roofs. It was forbidden for a man to go on a roof or tower without first giving a warning call, which sent women scurrying to shelter. Although a woman could not go to the bazaar and thus had to ask a brother or other male relative to make purchases for her, she could visit other women; shoes placed at the entrance of the women's quarters were a sign to the men of the family that they should not enter because of visitors. When a townswoman went out, enveloped in a *paranja,* she

shrank into a side street or turned her face to the wall on encountering a man. In country villages there were often no
separate woman's quarters in the dwelling. Women did weed-
ing, gleaning, and other tasks in the field, and their spinning
and weaving were frequently done in a courtyard on which
several houses faced. To wear veils while engaged in such
outdoor activities would have been inconvenient, but these
country women kept their distance from men and turned
away when they met one on their path.[13]

Neither love nor compatibility was considered in arrang-
ing a marriage. Men worked apart from their wives. In the
towns and cities men spent most of their free time in the
bazaar talking with friends at a *chaikhane.* In country towns
and villages, during the winter months, groups of men met in
the evening in the *mehmankhane* of each member in turn for
an evening of convivial conversation. Husband and wife usually had little occasion for conversation; one man was reported as saying that he talked to his wife perhaps three or
four times a year. Although a wife could get her way by guile
or nagging, her life was narrow. According to Muslim law, a
man may have four wives. The high bride price, however,
limited plural marriage in Central Asia to the prosperous.
Among poor families—that is, among most of the population
—monogamy was the rule. Occasionally, a man took a second
wife under the levirate, the customary law requiring that a
man marry the widow of his elder brother or other relative.
Among the well-to-do, women dreaded the prospect of being
one of several wives and, it would appear, men had occasion
to regret the discord of a household with plural wives. Men
with extensive landholdings often had a wife heading the
household of each estate, and a trader sometimes had a wife in
each town he visited regularly. Where there were several
wives in one household, each usually had her own room. Few,
other than the khans, maintained harems with concubines in

addition to the full Muslim complement of four wives. Under Muslim law, a man could divorce his wife at will, but the value of bride price and dowry made divorce an expensive luxury which few could afford. A woman could divorce her husband for certain causes, or by mutual consent, but there were occasions on record when a woman chose poison as a simpler way of ridding herself of an unwanted husband. It is unlikely that divorce was much practiced except among prosperous families in the towns and cities. Among craftsmen and rural cultivators, where women made a substantial contribution in labor to the family economy, divorce would have been prohibitively expensive.[14]

Among Sarts, that is, Tajiks and Uzbeks with a long oasis tradition, kinship ties and obligations faded out beyond the extended family. Among Uzbeks who retained some tradition of tribalism, traces of the old tribal genealogical kin structure persisted. Those who had been settled for several generations still remembered their tribal genealogies and felt some sense of kinship with and obligation toward others of the same tribal group, even when geographically separated. Often tribal kin groups had settled in the same locality, so that in the villages and, sometimes, in cities, extended kin groups retained some sense of solidarity long after settlement, because they remained neighbors.

The strongest social unit in cities, towns, and large villages, however, was the ward. A ward consisted of a street or segment of street, with the lanes and cul-de-sacs branching from it—an area including roughly from thirty to sixty houses together with the mosque that served the residents. Formerly, in the days when wars and raids were frequent, each city ward had been separated from its neighbors by a gate which was locked at night; some of these gates were still in use in the Emirate of Bukhara in the second half of the nineteenth century. Although many city wards were ethnically heterogeneous, others were populated by a single ethnic group. Tajiks lived in some wards, Uzbeks in others, and the small Jewish communities had their own wards. Indians, who left their families behind in India when they came to Central Asia to trade, lived in special caravansarais in Bukhara, Tashkent, and Andizhan. The ward was a close-knit community, governed by a council of elders. An outsider could not buy a house in the ward without the permission of the community. The mosque was for the use of all male residents, as well as the rooms where men warmed water in winter for ablutions preceding early morning prayer. Large kettles were also kept in these rooms for cooking pilau for family or community festivals. All the residents contributed to the maintenance of these rooms and of the water channel that ran through the ward providing water for the residents. The men of the ward embellished the mosque by planting trees near it and sometimes by digging a pond. In addition, they sometimes employed a sweeper to keep the street clean and to water down the dust of summer. Families of the ward helped each other with their family celebrations—circumcisions, weddings, funerals—and joined in celebrating religious festivals. In Khiva and certain other regions where each extended family lived in a separate farmstead, neighboring farmsteads shared a mosque. Small country villages had a similar organization, under the direction of a council of elders, and enjoyed mutual cooperation.[15]

For cultivators dependent on irrigation for their livelihood, the most important community project was maintenance of the irrigation canals and regulation of the flow of water. Water rights to a plot of land were of greater value than the land itself. All the families using the water were expected to contribute labor in keeping the canal clear. To supervise this work and to see that each landholder received the flow of water for the number of days to which he was entitled, there was a special community official, the *mirob* or *mirab*. In small valleys, a *mirob* chosen by the village or several neighboring villages could act by himself, for everyone knew his own rights and those of his neighbors. In the complex network of canals of the large oases, a head *mirob* was needed to oversee the work of the local *mirob*s. In the khanates, one of the chief officials of government was a *mirob* who stood at the head of a hierarchy reaching down to that at the local level. The *mirob* was in many respects the most important official of government, and at the higher levels, these officials were not averse to accepting remuneration for favors granted in the allocation of water.[16]

The governments of the khanates did not grow out of the local community organizations; rather, the khanates were imposed on these from above. The hereditary khans were Uzbeks, but the pattern of government was Iranian, adopted by the Uzbek rulers when they conquered Turkistan. (In the nineteenth century, several of the khans had Persian mothers who, one might suppose, would have reinforced this pattern.) The ruler was a despot, responsible to no one. Living in pomp and luxury, with harems of dancing boys as well as of wives and concubines, often spicing his feasts with the wines forbidden to his subjects, he appointed his favorites to high posts and made them generous grants of land. These men, while they remained in favor, filled their chests with the gifts and bribes of those they administered, but if they roused their ruler's ire, their property was confiscated and they were sometimes executed. Intrigue and peculation were the order of the day, from the chief ministers to their lowliest officials and servants. Provincial lords were mulcted by the ruler and his officials and in turn mulcted those under them. Some of the most fertile lands and most lavish water rights went to military leaders and the relatives of officials in favor. In addition, many rich estates were *waqf*, owned by seminaries and other religious institutions. The amount of *waqf* land was constantly increased through gifts of the devout, who by their act of piety stored up grace in the afterlife and often assured themselves a tax-free income for their lifetime. The people at the bottom of the pyramid paid many kinds of taxes; Soviet scholars studying old documents found twenty-five kinds of tax recorded for the Khanate of Khiva, and no less than fifty-five kinds in the Emirate of Bukhara. In addition, the farmers contributed labor for the upkeep of the irrigation channels as well as for the building of dams and bridges and, further, owed a certain number of days' labor a year on the khan's land. In the nineteenth century the governments of the khanates were decadent. Taxes were onerous; more and more cultivators were becoming tenant farmers on the expanding feudal estates of the khans, their favorites, and the church. However, the governments of the khanates, while demanding much, offered little security. Turkoman raids stocked the slave markets of Khiva and Bukhara and provided slaves to serve the wealthy, but they also drove cultivators from exposed lands in the south of the khanates. Khiva was often dependent on the support of Turkoman warriors to maintain itself.[17]

In the khanates there was a pronounced class structure, based on family, property, status in relation to the government (including that of military leaders), and religious position. Although, in the upper echelons, rank and its visible symbols were rather narrowly fixed—a man knew just how far he could go in the design of his belt buckle and in the number and richness of his *khalat*s—there appears to have been a certain amount of social mobility among the classes. A man could be granted or deprived of land and other benefits as he rose or fell in the favor of the khan. Dancing boys sometimes rose to high position, and Persian slaves, though usually mistreated, on occasion achieved high rank. Education gave status, and a man might advance his social position by making the pilgrimage to Mecca or hiring someone to make the pilgrimage for him. Class distinctions were strongest in the cities, towns, and large estates. In country villages there appear to have been few.[18]

Craftsmen and entertainers had a special kind of social organization, the guild. In the cities, towns, and any population center where there were a number of master craftsmen of any special craft, there was a guild, through membership in which the craftsmen of suburban communities were linked with those of the nearest town. Apprentices served with a master until they were initiated, in a special ceremony, into the guild corporation. Each craft guild had a patron saint— Noah was the patron saint of carpenters, for example, David that of metal workers. Each guild had a written record, the *risola,* which contained the origin legend of the guild and a code of rules concerning its cult and technology. The affairs of each guild were managed by a council of elders and certain administrative assistants. Among the weavers, for example, one assistant spent his time in the bazaar, regulating the selling price of goods, while another was in charge of the guild cult and supervised sacrificial rites to the patron saint. The council of elders also acted as an employment agency, and guild members often frequented a special teashop that served as their social and business center. The guild corporation was a close-knit social as well as economic group; its members played a role similar to that of relatives and neighbors on the occasion of family festivals.[19]

The Islamic religion was dominant in the nineteenth-century khanates of Turkistan. Bukhara was regarded as one of the great Islamic centers, "the true support of Islam," and all the khanate governments enforced Islamic practices in the towns and cities. There it was obligatory for men to perform the first prayer of the day at the ward mosque, though the other four daily prayers could be said anywhere, and to attend the weekly service held at the Friday or congregation mosque. A special official, the *reïs,* described as "a sort of church- and school-inspector," had power to impose fines or corporal punishment for religious lapses and even stopped men in the bazaar to catechize them on important points of dogma. Ranking high in the khanate governments were the *qazi*s, who judged cases coming under religious law, Shariat. Since *qazi*s were appointed for life and had no fixed administrative district, an individual could take his complaint to any *qazi* he chose. A *mufti* (secretary or scribe) recorded evidence and judgment and could interpret the law. *Ulema*s, men learned in the Koran and its interpretations, were consulted by a *qazi* in difficult cases and also by the khans. Religious men were everywhere. The title "mullah" was applied to anyone who could read, and since all education was religious, mullahs presided over mosques and shrines and were called on to officiate at circumcision, marriage, funeral, and other cere- monies. *Imam*s were mullahs who presided at the Friday or congregation mosques. At the head of the many dervish orders that flourished in Turkistan—some sixty were repre- sented in Bukhara alone—were *ishan*s. Under these were *sheikh*s, holy men who had been accepted into the order by virtue of having passed rigorous tests, such as repeating a prayer many times without drawing breath, and having fa- vorable dreams. *Sheikh*s usually lived in hostels or supervised *mazar*s (shrines) for the benefit of the order. These dervish orders, which included the Qalandar, singing dervishes; the order of Naqishbandi, who danced; and a hermit order whose members had no hostels but slept under the stars; lived on the gifts of the pious. Vambery, who traveled through Turk- istan in 1863 disguised as a holy man from Istanbul, learned at first hand the reverence accorded holy men by the people. He and his traveling companions, Central Asian *hajji*s returning from a pilgrimage to Mecca, received food and shelter wherever they went. Everywhere, as a learned man from the then capital of the Islamic world, he was besieged by people who thought to receive grace from his touch or breath, by entertaining him, or having him write a verse of the Koran as a charm. *Saids* (*sayyid*), who received deference as descendants of the Prophet Muhammed, were comparatively rare in Turkistan. Holy men ranged from scholars to *devannah*s (imbeciles or insane ones whose souls were believed to be with God). Many took opium, and by the nineteenth century, scholarship had reached a low point, even among the most learned. The people revered these holy men chiefly for their magical powers against ills and misfortunes attributed to spirits, evil eye, and other malignant supernatural forces.[20]

Although the khanate governments insisted on adherence to Islamic form in certain religious practices, even formal practice had its own Central Asian character. For example, *zakat,* the tithe Muslims are expected to give to the poor, was in Turkistan converted into a tax collected by the khanate governments. Among the people, some "recommended" practices were much more strongly entrenched than *fars*— obligatory acts. In much of the popular religion there was only a thin veneer of Islam over a body of non-Islamic beliefs and practices that were often accepted by the clergy as a part of Islam. Few could afford to make the long and dangerous pilgrimage to Mecca; those who did, or who hired someone to make the trip for them, acquired great prestige. Nevertheless, there were many places of pilgrimage in Turkistan, usually the tombs of saints. The people flocked to these, encouraged by *ishan*s who, financially interested in the success of the shrines, propounded the dogma that visiting several large *mazar*s was the equivalent of a pilgrimage to Mecca and Medina. Most famous of these shrines was the tomb of Baha-

V. The old and new in Kazak transportation. (Sovfoto.)

VI. A Karakalpak in traditional headdress plays the *qobyz*. (Sovfoto.)

ed-din Naqishbandi, founder of the order of dancing dervishes, near Bukhara, which attracted pilgrims from as far
away as China. There were *mazar*s scattered all the way from
the Caspian to the high Pamirs, some the object of local cults,
some drawing pilgrims from afar either because they were the
tombs of patron saints or of great heroes, or because they
were reputed to cure some particular malady. New *mazar*s
were often built at the grave of some famous *ishan*. *Mazar*s
were usually signaled by a horse tail (or, in the Pamirs, by a
yak tail) on a pole and by the horns of a wild ram. Frequently, votive offerings in the form of bits of cloth fluttered
from the pole. Whenever a shrine became popular, it was
taken over by some dervish order and a *sheikh* posted to receive the gifts of the pilgrims. At the shrines of patron saints
of towns, annual celebrations were held.

In addition to cult ritual attached to shrines, there were a
number of other cults. The oasis people who, as Sunni Muslims, regarded Shi'as as worse than unbelievers, nevertheless
had some cults that were essentially Shi'a in origin. One was
the cult of Ali, son-in-law and, in Shi'a belief, the true suc-
cessor of Muhammed in the caliphate. Ali, "king of man-
kind," was the patron saint of dangerous professions, such as
those of warrior and digger of *qariz* (underground water
channels). The martyrdom of Hussein, son of Ali and, according to Shi'a belief, rightful caliph succeeding Ali, was
celebrated each year in the days leading up to the tenth day
of Muharram, the anniversary of his martyrdom, by sacrifices,
ritual lamentations, and the reading of poetic stories about
the battle of Kerbela. Fatima, daughter of Muhammed and
wife of Ali, was the object of a woman's cult as protector of
brides and women who had borne children, and also was the
patron saint of spinners. Other patron saints of women were
Bibi Seshambeh (Lady Tuesday) and "Lady Solver of Problems," in whose honor ritual feasts were offered with the

reading of appropriate stories. All the guilds gave cult attention, with food offerings and other ritual, to their patron saints. Cultivators and shepherds also had patron saints, and the agricultural cycle was marked by ritual.[21]

The passage of an individual through life was marked by a series of rituals, some small domestic affairs, some as elaborate as the family could afford. The ceremony for first-born sons was not Islamic. After the birth of the child, a candle was kept burning to ward off evil eye until the ninth day, when the grandmother, accompanied by other women of the village or ward, brought a cradle and clothing for the infant. Then a feast was held. No men attended this celebration. One of the most important family ceremonies was that of circumcision, a practice recommended by Islam but not obligatory. Although a mullah performed the operation, the elaborate ritual, feast, and ensuing entertainment were characteristic of the Central Asian oases rather than of Islam. At marriage, a second major family ceremony, a mullah witnessed the marriage contract and read the marriage agreement, but the bride price and dowry followed the Central Asian and not the Koranic Arabic pattern. A propitious day for the wedding was determined by divination (astrology, scapulimancy, and the Koran were variously employed in divination) and the ceremony often included such non-Islamic rituals as having the bride jump over or run around a bonfire. Death ceremonies deviated somewhat from the Islamic pattern. After funeral prayers at the ward mosque, the procession to the cemetery was interrupted by a stop at every mosque on the way, and the mullah was called out to recite a prayer. The deceased was cleansed of his sins by a symbolic sale to the mullah or grave digger, and a lamp, coin, or other object was often deposited on the grave. A feast—an important part of any Central Asian ceremony—was given on the day of the funeral; there was a memorial service, with reading of prayers and food, on the seventh, fortieth, and hundredth day (or, according to some sources, on the third, ninth, and fortieth day), and on the anniversary.[22]

The oasis people fasted during Ramazan, feasting at night. Among people of modest means, families in a ward or village often took turns feasting their neighbors at night, while among affluent town-dwellers, entertainers were sometimes hired for the night-time feast. In the cities there were night bazaars during Ramazan. At the end of Ramazan came the Kichik Bayram or Ramazan Hayit (*'id al-fitr*), the breaking of the fast, with feasts.

The second great Muslim festival was Qurban Bayram (*'id al-adhu*), commemorating Abraham's willingness to sacrifice Isaac. Families who could afford to sacrificed a sheep; other families pooled their resources for a joint sacrifice. Even the poorest tried to make such a sacrifice at least once in a lifetime. The sacrificial meat was distributed among neighbors and kin, and the most honored piece, as well as the skin, was given to the mullah. After the sacrifice and prayers, there was a general celebration in some open space in or near the town; merchants offered special holiday goods, particularly children's toys; and entertainment was provided by stiltwalkers, puppet shows, clowns, and others. On the first day of such festivals, women visited the cemetery, and those in whose family a death had occurred during the year performed a ritual of mourning. After the mourning ceremony, the women in some cities went to special closed teahouses near the place of the men's celebration, where they could enjoy a good gossip and sometimes buy bazaar goods and watch entertainers. All of this was in the towns. Tajiks in the high Pamirs did not observe either the fasting or feasting of Ramazan, nor did the Uzbek seminomads.

A third annual festival was the anniversary of Mavlud, the birth of Muhammed. This was not celebrated everywhere. In

Tashkent both men and women observed it; in Samarkand, it was celebrated only by women. In some places Mavlud was associated with Nau Ruz, the Iranian New Year, which the oasis people also observed. Unlike the Muslim festivals, which were based on the lunar calendar, the date of Nau Ruz was fixed by the Persian solar calendar and so was regularly held in the spring, the Western month of March. In some places in Turkistan, Nau Ruz was preceded by the Persian popular practices of breaking clay pots and tossing them over the wall of the household compound and by jumping over a bonfire, both symbolizing a discarding of the ills and misfortunes of the old year and a ritual cleansing in preparation for the new. Houses were freshly plastered with clay, and everyone who could possibly afford it had new clothes. Special food was prepared, often also symbolic. The celebration of Nau Ruz, like that of all other major festivals, was accompanied by feasts and entertainment.[23]

Education was traditionally associated with religion in Turkistan. In each town ward there was usually at least one *mekteb* (elementary school), but in remote country villages, instruction was limited to that given by itinerant mullahs. In towns and cities every boy was expected to enter school by the age of seven at the latest, and often they began at five or six. The teacher was paid by the parents, who gave him a small sum of money for the term and, in addition, gifts in kind every Thursday and on the occasion of the great religious festivals. When a boy completed his course of study, the teacher was given a robe. Throughout the year, school was held from after sunrise until time for the late afternoon prayer. There were weekend holidays on Thursday afternoon and Friday, the Muslim sabbath, and a week's vacation for each of the two great Muslim festivals, Kichik Bayram and Qurban Bayram. Poor boys often dropped out of school at the age of ten or eleven to work for their fathers; those of more prosperous families continued up to the age of thirteen. Despite this long course of study, students in most *mekteb*s learned very little. They were taught the Arabic alphabet and memorized verses of the Koran and of several other books, including the Farz'ayn (Book of Precepts) and Chahar Kitab (four books of the Koran). Few students learned to read or write or to understand the books they had memorized. Thus, despite this schooling in the *mekteb*, enforced by the *reïs* in the towns and cities of the khanates, most men were illiterate.[24]

After completing the seven-year course of the *mekteb*, some boys went on to study at the *medresseh*, seminary. Most peasant and artisan families could not aspire to an advanced education for their sons, but for those with ambitions there was ample incentive for continuing study in the *medresseh*. This was essential to appointment in the administrative hierarchy of the khanate governments as well as in the church. Doctors needed this training in order to study the medical works of the past; no medical or other scientific research was being done in nineteenth-century Turkistan. To be able to read and write was extremely useful to merchants whose trade went beyond that of a shop in the bazaar. In addition, education enhanced a man's social status. Bukhara was the center of learning in Central Asia. There were some two hundred *medresseh*s in that city in the 1860's. There were also a number in Tashkent, Khiva, and Samarkand, though many of the famous old seminaries of the latter city had fallen into ruins by the nineteenth century. There were a few *medresseh*s in other cities, including a special *medresseh* for Turkoman students at Karshi, on the border between the Emirate of Bukhara and Herat.[25]

The *medresseh*s were usually founded by some wealthy family, in the hope of thereby obtaining grace in the afterlife. The establishment, which was often near and sometimes associated with a mosque, characteristically consisted of cell-like rooms built around an open courtyard. Classes were held in the ground floor rooms. The students occupied cells on the second story. The school was supported by *waqf*, productive estates owned by the *medresseh*. Wealthy students often lived at home and attended classes during the day; others, once admitted, received not only a cell in which to live but a small fixed annual income from the *waqf*. During the long vacation, poorer students had an opportunity to earn supplementary income needed for food and other living expenses.

Students were free to attend classes at other *medresseh*s, and very ambitious ones went on to study in Istanbul and Mecca. The chief subject of study was theology, which included Koranic law. The instruction also included history, logic, rhetoric, mathematics, astronomy, and poetry. The students studied Arabic and the Persian or Uzbek Turkic language. Although Sunni Muslims, they had a predilection for Persian poetry and were great admirers of Hafiz and Sa'di. In the *medresseh* they learned to read and, if they carried on their studies rigorously, to write. The usual method of instruction was by disputation. The professor would read a passage; the students and any visitors who happened to be present discussed its meaning, after which the professor gave the correct interpretation. This method was time-consuming, and some students spent their entire lives in the *medresseh*. Many withdrew after seven or eight years, before completing the 137 books of the standard curriculum. Those who did finish the course were qualified to act as professors in their turn or to become *qazi*s or *ulema*s. The level of scholarship in most cases was comparable to that of Europe in the late Middle Ages, limited to hairsplitting interpretations of old texts. The work of the fifteenth-century Ulugh Beg was studied in the *medresseh*s; indeed, the *medresseh*s he had founded in Samarkand and Bukhara were still operating in the late nineteenth century, though by that time stimulus for further scientific investigation had disappeared.[26]

Despite the fact that most boys attended *mekteb* for several years and some went on to study at the *medresseh,* the general rate of literacy among men was very low. Most people did not even understand the Arabic prayers they repeated five times a day. In the usual village, only one or two men might be able to write, and none in isolated rural hamlets. Even in the cities, so few men could sign their names that most "respectable" men wore seal rings of lapis lazuli with which they stamped their seal on documents in lieu of signature. For most women, schooling was nonexistent. They did not need to know by heart the five daily prayers, since no *reïs* would penetrate their seclusion to catechize them. In only a few upper class families were educated women to be found. There were a few girls' schools in large cities such as Tashkent and Bukhara. These were usually taught by the wife of the *qazi,* and she in turn trained a daughter or, if she had none, some promising student, to succeed her. These women could read; one woman, the wife of the leading *qazi* of Samarkand, was said to have read over two thousand books. Often these educated women could also write. Untrammeled by the disputatious requirements of religious scholasticism, they read legendary history and travel stories. The number of educated women was small, but many of those who had attended school kept up their studies after marriage, as if in this way to reach beyond the confines of their secluded homes.[27]

Recreation for the oasis people was largely of the spectator variety. The steppe nomads amused themselves with singing, races, and other diversions in which they actively participated; their only professional entertainers were the troubadors who wandered from camp to camp. The oasis people, on the other hand, were more inclined to sit and watch the entertainment provided by others. Psychologically sedentary, they responded eagerly to *tamasha,* the all-encompassing term for any diversion, from that of watching the behavior of a foreign traveler or a dogfight to an elaborate program of dancers and other professional entertainers. Characteristic of the Sart attitude was a story recounted of a minister of the Emir of Bukhara who was taken to a ball in St. Petersburg in the late nineteenth century. He greatly enjoyed the spectacle of watching the dancers, but when his Russian host wished to join the dancing, the Bukharan minister was horrified. "I am quite satisfied with the amusement that your dancers have afforded me. Do not . . . exert your own person for my benefit." [28] Few men hunted for sport, even in areas where game was plentiful. Uzbeks who still retained traditions of a tent life engaged in the Turkoman sport of *baïga,* in which horsemen contended for the carcass of a dead goat. In this, following the steppe pattern, uninvited quests were welcome to join in the game and compete for the prize. For the most part, however, people sat. In communities large enough to boast *chaikhanes*, men spent much of their free time at these establishments, drinking tea, talking, and often playing chess or gambling at such games as tossing coins or dice. In the larger towns, public readers took their stand outside a mosque or *medresseh* and recited religious poems, Persian poems, legends about Timur or some saint, or parts of the history of Bukhara, Samarkand, or other cities. In winter, particularly in the villages, men provided their own entertainment in the home. Groups of men of the same age met in the *mehmankhane* of each member in turn, with the host providing the refreshments. Younger men, less affluent, chipped in to pay for food and drink. Elders or youths, they provided their own entertainment. Perhaps the most popular sport in the oases, at least in the towns and cities, was a fight between animals—rams, cocks, and quails—in which the spectators bet on the outcome. Henri Moser, who visited Khiva shortly after the Russian conquest of the city, accounted ram fights the national pastime of the Uzbeks of that city. Every rich man kept fighting rams for entertainment. In Bukhara, cock or quail fights were held at festivals, and in spring, young men organized such fights at the city wall. Quail fights, on which the audience often bet heavily, were frequently held at teahouses near the bazaar.[29]

For special entertainment there were professional performers. When rich people entertained guests; on bazaar days in market towns and cities; in large open parks for the great Muslim festivals or those honoring the patron saint of the city; and for family festivals of circumcision and marriage, these professionals were called in. Most of the entertainers— musicians, dancers, comics, puppeteers, acrobats, jugglers, stiltwalkers, and animal acts—were members of guilds and usually worked in troops of varied performers. On bazaar days and for public religious festivals, comics who played the clown or acted out satirical skits, as well as puppeteers, acrobats, jugglers, and animal acts, could be counted on to attract a crowd. For circumcision parties, clowns, acrobats, and jugglers were most in demand. Musicians accompanied most troops. Musicians and dancers seem to have been most popular for weddings, where comics and puppeteers were also enjoyed. Particularly in the eastern part of Turkistan, there were migrant troops of gypsies "from Afghanistan" (in Afghanistan they are said to be "from India") who provided entertainment for isolated villages.

Except for the gypsies, whose women would sing for anyone who paid them, almost all the professional entertainers were men. The only women professionals were the dancers and musicians who entertained women at wedding parties and other domestic festivals while the men enjoyed their own diversions apart. Although educated women sometimes played the *dutar,* a stringed instrument, or danced to the accompaniment of tambourines, this was in the privacy of the home, for their own entertainment or that of their husbands. Professional women dancers were *déclassée* in most parts of the Muslim world, but Central Asians particularly frowned on their performing before men, who in any event much preferred *bacha*s (dancing boys). The dancing of *bacha*s was the favorite entertainment of prosperous Sarts in the towns and cities. Khans and wealthy begs kept their own harems of *bacha*s, and even comparatively small oasis towns on the trade routes could muster a troop of *bacha*s to entertain visiting dignitaries. European travelers who attended such performances were unanimous in noting the enthusiasm with which hosts and local guests greeted this entertainment. Although prostitution was forbidden in the khanates, there were women prostitutes in the cities for the accommodation of such unattached men as traveling merchants and unmarried craftsmen.[30]

Despite Muslim proscriptions against the use of stimulants and narcotics, almost everyone—men and women alike— smoked the water pipe. Men also used tobacco in the form of *nos (nas)* a compound of powdered green tobacco, charcoal or lime ash, and flavoring, a pinch of which was placed under the tongue for its astringent affect. Much less widely used were opium, usually drunk in an infusion but sometimes smoked, and *bang,* an infusion of hemp. Although the use of alcoholic beverages was strictly forbidden in the khanates on pain of death, secret drinking occurred where wine was available. The khans themselves frequently indulged, as did great begs, and drinking parties were not unknown among students in the *medresseh*s. Meyendorff, who visited Bukhara in 1820, noted that quite a few older men drank to the point of inebriation. The conviviality of the winter evening parties held by village men in their homes, as reported by Soviet ethnographers, may have been due to alcoholic stimulant. Grapes were grown in every garden, and there was an ancient tradition of wine making and wine drinking in Turkistan. There is more than a suggestion that the Muslim taboo on alcohol had simply driven wine drinking indoors, not eradicated this time-honored habit. Uzbek seminomads who did not raise grapes made a beer (*buza*) of millet.[31]

In the arts, the oasis people had a more varied and sophisticated development than the nomadic steppe dwellers. Because they were technologically more advanced and had much greater specialization of occupation, some men could devote their careers to the acquisition and practice of special artistic skills. Although the work was distinctive of Turkistan and of the regions within it, the decorative arts owed much in both technology and spirit to influences carried along the caravan and pilgrim routes from Turkey, Persia, India, and Kashgar. By far the strongest artistic influence emanated from Persia. Persian inspiration was particularly marked in the decoration of prosperous homes. The wood carving of doors and pillars and the *ganch* [32] ornamentation of interior walls often showed highly stylized and graceful motifs inspired by flowers, leaves, and trees. In copper work also, the flowing tracery of the engraving often followed the curves of leaves on a stem, sometimes framing an angular star or other motif. Flower medallions were popular motifs both for Bukharan (Beshir) rugs and for the coverlets that girls embroidered for their dowry, with spaces between often filled in with palmettos and leaves. Stylized flower motifs were also found in block-printed cloth. Embroidered caps, as well as pottery styles, varied considerably from district to district. Cloth was often striped or had the fluid design obtained by tie-dyeing the yarn before weaving. Where plain colored cloth was used for clothing, women embroidered designs along the borders, on the sleeves, and sometimes in back.

In general, Sarts did not like blank spaces in their ornament. In wood carving, *ganch,* copper and other metal work, as well as in many of the textiles, the ornamental design covered almost all the space. There was also a good deal of color. Within upper class houses, trees with large flowers were painted on some of the walls, and the woodwork was often brightly painted. The silks and velvets worn by both men and women who could afford them were usually of rich hues, and the striped cottons worn by poorer women at home were also often colorful. Silver jewelry was brightened with insets of semiprecious stones of which the most popular were carnelian, turquoise, and lapis lazuli. Copper utensils, some golden, some red, gave color to a room. The better pottery, such as was placed in niches in the living rooms, seems also to have been colorful. The glazed ware of one village, for example, was distinguished by a bright blue-green color; of another, by a dark brown background; while in Tashkent the ware had bright varicolored designs on a cream background. All this ornamentation and color was not, however, overpowering even to Western eyes. Outside the home, the blind walls of the houses were of the same dull yellowish gray as the surrounding soil from which they were built, and only the green of trees growing around the mosque or peeping over garden walls relieved the drabness of the landscape. Indoors, the basic tone of the walls was the same. Only certain walls were ornamented with painted *ganch,* and the painted or carved woodwork occupied little space. There was no furniture except for the *sandal* and chest. Thus, all the aesthetic enjoyment derived from decorative arts was concentrated in a few places—the rugs on the floors, piles of cushions and of quilts for bedding, painted or carved woodwork, *ganch* or painted murals on an occasional wall, and in the clothing. In the homes of the poor, who could not afford such luxuries as carved woodwork, pile rugs, or rich-hued silks and velvets, the chief color was provided by quilted bedding, the subdued tones of felt and pileless woven rugs, and a few utensils of copper or pottery.[33]

IV

Culture Change
under Tsarist Rule

TRIBAL PEOPLES: KAZAKS

LONG before the Russian conquest of Tashkent in 1865, the Kazaks had been subject to strong Russian influence. It was the expansion of Muscovite power into southern Russia that had caused the dislocation of tribes in the Golden and White hordes and contributed to the formation of the Kazaks as a people. Furthermore, the Russian conquest of Siberia began in the late sixteenth century with a Cossack incursion across the Urals to protect fur traders from the depredations of nomads in the process of achieving identity as Kazaks. From these beginnings, Russian expansion continued along the western and northern fringes of Kazak territory. By 1725, when Peter the Great died, a line of Cossack fortresses extended along the Irtysh River in the north from Omsk to Semipalatinsk and in the west through Kazak territory to the Caspian Sea. During the following century the encroachment continued, with Cossack outposts creeping into the steppe and encircling it on the east. By 1865, when Tashkent was captured, most Kazaks had long since been brought under Russian administrative control.

This steady Russian movement around and into the steppes reduced the area of pasturage available to the nomads, and this constriction was accentuated in the eighteenth century by the rise of Jungar (Oïrot) power in the east and the push of one Oïrot group, the Kalmuks, westward across the Kazak domain to the Volga River. In the first half of the nineteenth century, there was also pressure in the south when Kazaks were driven out of their traditional winter pastures near the Amu Darya by the expanding power of Khiva. At the same time, while the economic independence of the nomads was impaired by loss of pasturage, a new breach on Kazak economy was made by the appearance of trading posts and seasonal fairs along the borders of the nomadic territory; these, by offering manufactured novelties in exchange for animals and furs, created new needs. Moreover, the effects of Russian encroachment were not limited to the economy. The Tsarist government was anxious that peace be maintained in the steppes bordering Russian settlements. To achieve this, it recognized and supported tribal chiefs believed to be powerful enough to control the tribesmen under them. Frequently, in the early years, they were disappointed in this hope; tribal segments declined to respect chiefly authority and often the chiefs called for Russian help against external enemies such as Khiva. However, as Kazak pasture lands became scarcer, families and tribal sections could not as readily express their disapproval of a chief by moving off and attaching themselves to another chief. Furthermore, in the scramble for pastures among themselves and the encroachment of aliens on all sides, Kazak nomads needed strong leadership. As a consequence, Russian policy, combined with unsettled conditions on the steppe, tended to favor wealthy chiefs who were sometimes more concerned with augmenting their own power and prosperity than with assuming the paternalistic responsibilities normally expected of their leaders by pastoral nomads.

These tendencies—a reduction of pasturelands, an increasing dependence on trade goods, and a weakening of paternalistic leadership—were intensified when Russia established control over the whole of Central Asia. Russian conquest of the Kazak steppes was piecemeal. In a series of sorties from the line of forts established during the reign of Peter the Great, military posts were gradually planted throughout the steppe. The area between the Ural and Emba rivers had come under Russian control by 1824; Akmolinsk in the north was founded in 1830, Vernyi (Alma Ata) in 1854. By 1867 the Tsarist government was sufficiently in control to set up a new administrative organization which included the whole territory of the Kazaks, dividing it among three governor-generalships: Orenburg, West Siberia, and Turkistan. Up to this time, the Russian outposts had been settled chiefly by Cossacks who were given land and subsidies in return for their military services. Few Russians other than exiled criminals settled in the steppes before the 1870's, when Russian colonists began to appear in numbers. Then, although government plans for Russian colonization along the main post roads were not always successful, there was a considerable unauthorized movement of Russian peasants into the most fertile parts of the northern steppe. Fields of grain began to appear at winter campsites or to block the migration routes between summer and winter pastures. This influx of Russian colonists into the most fertile parts of northern and eastern Kazakhstan—the Steppe *oblast*s (provinces) and Semirechie—continued until the outbreak of World War I. By 1914 almost half the total population of these regions was Russian. In Semirechie also there was an influx in the 1870's and 1880's of Uighur and Dungan refugees from Sinkiang who established agricultural colonies along the Chu, Ili, and other rivers. In addition, Russian pacification of the Kazak steppes encouraged land-hungry Uzbek peasants to extend their cultivated fields along the southern edge of the steppe.[1]

Under the influence of settled neighbors, Kazaks began to

change their way of life. Some nomads cut hay for winter fodder and built winter shelters for a portion of their animals. Some began to spend their winters in dwellings of wood, sod, or mud, depending on the house styles of their nearest neighbors, or to put up a clay wall around their encampment of yurts. Deprived of their richest pastures, many Kazaks were forced to give up pastoralism partially or completely. Some who lived near lakes or rivers took up fishing which, as Meyendorff observed during a journey made in 1820, was a sure sign of poverty.[2] Many were driven by need to engage in agriculture. Of these, some planted a little millet or other grain at winter quarters, leaving a poor family or two to care for the fields while the rest of the group went on its summer migration. Some settled at the edge of Russian colonies and eventually became a part of the settled community. Others hired out as mine workers or as agricultural laborers at harvest time. Much of this employment appears to have been temporary or seasonal. Of the 29,392 passports issued in 1881 in the Semipalatinsk region to Kazaks seeking employment, 17,151 were for one month only, 1,635 for a year, and only 4 for two years. At the Spassky mines, many of the Kazak employees were young men who worked only long enough to earn a bride price, then returned to the *aul*. For some years Kazaks had a lucrative business supplying the caravans used for transporting furniture and other goods required by Russian colonists and administrators in Turkistan as well as local produce destined for Russia, but this camel traffic was curtailed with the opening of the Orenburg-Tashkent Railroad in 1906.[3]

In addition to the Russian trading towns and seasonal markets at the edge of the steppe which tempted the Kazaks, there were Sart merchants from Turkistan as well as Kazan Tatar merchants who carried goods to temporary markets within the steppe. Most Kazaks, unfamiliar with the ways of commerce, paid high in produce for the cheap trade goods they received, but a few became commercial entrepreneurs. One traveler through Central Asia in the mid-nineteenth century reported that "every sultan and chief has his merchant, as well as his mulla, or priest, and both are very important personages in the tribe." [4] Some Kazaks turned moneylenders, exacting as much as 100 per cent interest on their loans. Of the trade goods made available to the Kazaks, many were fripperies whose chief attraction was novelty. Some goods, however, became a part of Kazak culture: green tea and tea bowls from China, for example, and the Russian samovar for heating tea water.

Textiles from both Turkistan and Russia were received with enthusiasm, particularly for women's clothing, and a sleeveless velvet or velours redingote jacket (*kemsal*), fashionable among Russian ladies in the nineteenth century, became standard attire for many Kazak women, worn over a *chapan* cut on traditional lines but made of brightly printed cotton or silk. Kazak women also began to wear a headdress of white cotton cloth, possibly inspired by the traditional turbans of oasis women. Cloths embroidered in cross-stitch, possibly of Ukrainian influence, became popular for decorating the interior walls of yurts.

The purchase in markets of metal objects of all kinds, as well as of saddles, appeared to spell the doom of Kazak craft work, but in the late nineteenth century, when lack of grazing land drove many Kazaks to seek alternative means of earning a living, there seems to have been a resurgence of professional craft work. Often adopting the techniques of neighboring peoples, including Russians and Ukrainians, Kazak blacksmiths, silversmiths, woodworkers, and stone and bone carvers traveled from *aul* to *aul* producing goods on order, living as a guest in the home of the customer, and being paid in livestock. The hope of these itinerant craftsmen seems always to have been to acquire enough animals in payment to be able to return to a pastoral way of life.

In the early twentieth century, some craftsmen began to work in craft centers. In southeastern Kazakhstan, for example, carpenters making the framework of yurts set up shop in localities where wood was plentiful, and nomads came to them to obtain new yurt frames. In making felt, which was saleable in Russian markets, men often assisted the women of the family in this traditionally woman's work. Cattle became increasingly important in the economy, particularly among those Kazaks living near settled communities; horses decreased sharply in numbers.[5]

Many Tsarist officials had difficulty in understanding the flexible nature of Kazak political organization. Seeking responsible leaders to maintain order on the steppe, they had khans elected for the ordas and invested them ceremonially in office, only to discover that these khans had little control over most of the tribesmen. Indeed, they often expected Russian protection against their enemies, including China and the Khanate of Khiva. In the Russian administrative system that was eventually set up dividing the area into governor-generalship, provinces (*oblasts*), counties (*uezds*), and districts (*volosts*), the larger divisions were administered by Russian army officers, while the *volosts* were under native elective officials: an *upravitel;* chief, and *biis*, judges. The *upravitels* received a fixed salary, while the *biis*, in accordance with Kazak custom, were dependent on gifts from the litigants. Under Russian rule, nomads were taxed a specified number of rubles per yurt, the amount increasing through the years. In the western steppe, some tribes reacted so violently to this system that it was modified to permit appointment of judges and payment of the yurt tax in kind. In the east, where many of the nomads were accustomed to being taxed by the Khanate of Kokand or the West Siberian Government, the imposition of Russian administration provoked no strong resistance.[6]

The Russian system of administration was disruptive of Kazak culture in several ways. First, the money tax pushed the Kazaks farther from family self-sufficiency and barter toward dependence on alien markets where money could be obtained by selling goods or services. Also, taxing the tent rather than livestock weighed most heavily on the poor nomad family for, poor or prosperous, a family normally needed only one yurt. Second, nomads registered as residents of one *volost* frequently migrated in other *volost*s during a part of the year. Given the cumbersome bureaucracy of the Russian administration, this created many complications. Third, Kazaks were not accustomed to the type of election administered by the Russians. Traditionally, the head of the family was head (*aqsaqal*) of the *aul* in which his family lived. The chief of the next higher group in the tribal genealogical structure was usually head of the senior family of the lineage. If there was any question about the succession, the *aqsaqal*s met and argued until they had reached a consensus. The Russian election, itself an unfamiliar method of selecting a leader, introduced a type of competition among *aqsaqal*s as foreign to the Kazaks as was the idea of a fixed salary. These people were also unaccustomed to the notion of electing permanent judges. Traditionally, Kazaks called on anyone whom they respected to judge the merits of their disputes, and since they entered the case with confidence in the judge, they usually accepted his decision. Forced under the Russian administration to go to a judge not of their own choosing, they were less inclined to accept his judgment. The Russian administration provided a court of appeals, a regional council made up of all the *bii*s in one or several *volost*s which met at intervals, but this was inconvenient both for the litigants and for the *bii*s, who often did not attend.[7]

Kazak dislocation was exacerbated by the corruption of many Russian officials, whose standard of living bore little relation to their salaries. Furthermore, since these officials seldom learned to speak the native language, they were dependent on interpreters—usually Kazan Tatars—for the supervision of elections and other dealings with the Kazaks. The Kazak *upravitel*s and *bii*s in turn, who were seldom literate, were also dependent on clerks—again usually Kazan Tatars—to keep their records. This gave the interpreters and clerks enormous power, for they could interpret and record matters to suit their own mercenary interests. It is thus small wonder that Grodekov, only a few years after the system was established, noted a weakening of the tribal structure as evidenced by lawsuits among near tribal kin and the frequent nonpayment of penalties.[8] This weakening of the tribal kin structure was also reflected in a widening gap between rich and poor. In the old way of life, an individual who had lost relatives or livestock through misfortune could work as shepherd or herdsman for a prosperous stockbreeder, living with the family of his employer until he had earned enough animals to set up for himself. Under Russian rule, there were ever fewer prosperous tribesmen able to employ young men, and of those who retained or acquired wealth, some had done so by adopting Russian values and forgetting kin responsibilities. Thus, many poor Kazaks were forced out of the pastoral way of life and into settlements.

There was also a change in the concept of land tenure. Traditionally, land was not owned. Each tribe or major tribal subdivision occupied an established territory, within which its member *aul*s had the right to migrate. In times of peace, families normally returned each winter to the same protected camp site and during other months of the year followed an itinerary fixed by custom. Thus, families enjoyed rights of usufruct within the territory of their tribal group, but no one owned land. Under the influence of Russians on three sides and sedentary Uzbeks and Tajiks on the fourth, Kazaks began to recognize private ownership of land. First, associated with the construction of permanent winter dwellings, there came family ownership of winter quarters. These were normally inherited within the family, following the pattern of inheritance of a yurt, but winter quarters could be sold. Next, with the cutting of hay for winter fodder, meadow lands came to be held as family property, to be inherited by a son, but capable of sale. In the northern steppes, Kazaks rented land to Russian colonists who, when they had become firmly established, persuaded provincial officials to recognize their ownership of the land. In some areas, rich Kazaks became the landlords of former tribal lands, reducing their less prosperous fellow tribesmen to the status of tenant farmers. This transition to private ownership of real estate seems to have occurred chiefly around the fringes of the steppe.[9]

Although the Tsarist government had at one time encouraged the spread of Islam, the over-all influence on Kazak religious beliefs and practices was comparatively slight. In the field of education, however, changes were more marked. When the Kazak Bukeev or Inner Orda moved west into the area between the Urals and the Caspian, its khans became interested in the education of their people. Zhangir, who became khan in 1823, issued a decree that mosques and schools be built and a *mekteb* course instituted, with classes held during summer in yurts. From these schools, particularly bright students were sent to Russian gymnasia until a Kazak gymnasium was opened in 1841 under the direction of a Kazan Tatar. The Tsarist government also began to provide a Russian education for Kazak students. Kazak classes were opened in the Russian military school at Omsk in 1813 and at Orenburg in 1825, and in the late 1850's N. A. Il'minskii, a Russian orientalist with lively theories concerning the education of non-Russian peoples, exerted considerable influence as member of the Orenburg Border Commission. One of his students, Ibray Altynsarin (1841–1899), carried his ideas and methods into the steppe as inspector of education in Turgai *oblast* from 1879 until 1889. In addition to a number of elementary schools, he founded four Russian-Kazak secondary schools with dormitories for Kazak students, a Kazak teachers' training school, and, in 1887, a dormitory for Kazak girls in a Russian girls' school. But even in Turgai province, efforts to develop education were impeded by a shortage of funds and interminable bickering among administrators over educational policy. In other provinces progress was much slower. In 1913, in all of what is now Kazakhstan, there were only 267 *aul* schools in the Russian system and 157 Russian-Kazak schools. Few Kazaks attended Russian gymnasia or other schools of advanced training.[10] Education for Kazaks in the Russian schools was designed chiefly to train clerks and interpreters for the Russian administration. Most Kazaks remained illiterate, concerned with the affairs of pastoral life or the struggle to survive on the fringes of settled life.

Yet, limited as educational facilities were, a small intellectual élite did emerge. Some sons of khans educated at the cadet school at Omsk became army officers and grew to be more Russian than Kazak. However, a number of educated Kazaks established a bridge between the Russian and Kazak worlds, translating the Western ideas that came to them through the medium of Russian literature and Russian teachers into Kazak and Central Asian terms of reference. Most famous of these was Choqan Valikhanov (*ca.* 1837–1865) who became a friend of the most illustrious Russian Central Asian scholars of his day and was made a member of the Imperial Russian Geographical Society for his research on Kazak and Kirghiz culture and folklore. Another was Ibray Altynsaryn who, in addition to developing a school system in

Turgai Province, devised a Kazak alphabet based on the Cyrillic, translated Russian literature into Kazak, and introduced a new literary form into Central Asia—secular prose— which he employed in a series of short stories, many of them based on Kazak folk tales. A third great Kazak intellectual of the nineteenth century was Abay Qunanbay (1845–1904), who was educated in a Muslim *medresseh* in Semipalatinsk before beginning Russian studies. A scholar familiar with Arabic and Persian literature as well as Russian and Western European literature read in Russian translation, he translated into Kazak such Oriental classics as the *Arabian Nights* and the *Shah-nama* in addition to works of Lermontov, Pushkin, and even Goethe and Byron. His own prose and poetical writings reflected the humanistic influence of his reading in Greek classical literature and such Western scholars as Darwin, Spencer, and Spinoza. They also showed a preoccupation with Kazak themes and were couched in a simple, direct style devoid of the ornate verbal garlands of the Persian literature known in Central Asia. A reformer like Altynsaryn, he presented many of his ideas in the form of verse set to music which was widely disseminated by Kazak *aqyn*s (bards). These three intellectual leaders did not forget their cultural heritage. Rather, they used their Russian-acquired learning to illuminate their own culture and the cultural needs of their people. Choqan Valikhanov, who dressed like a Russian dandy in St. Petersburg and wrote in Russian, used Western scientific methods to study the culture of Kazaks and Kirghiz and present his findings to Russian scholars. When stricken with tuberculosis, he returned to the steppe to die in a yurt among his kin. Ibray Altynsaryn struggled to bring education to his people. Abay Qunanbay applied the insights gained through his Russian education to the problems of a changing Kazak world. So penetrating were these insights that he incurred the distrust of both Kazak mullahs and tribal chiefs and of Russian administrators, and he died a lonely old man on the steppe. Nevertheless, his works, published both in Kazak and in Russian translation, continue to inspire his Kazak people.[11]

Until the abortive Russian Revolution of 1905, the Russian government had forbidden the publication of periodicals in the Kazak language. After 1905, several newspapers and other periodicals appeared, and there was some publication of books in the Kazak language, including collections of poems by Abay Qunanbay. In the early twentieth century, Kazak writers showed the influence of the Western political and social thought of the times. Some introduced the theme of class struggle, others were concerned with preserving Kazak culture from Russian engulfment. All employed the Arabic script in writing Kazak, although one, Ahmad Baitursun, introduced changes compatible with Kazak phonemics and strove to develop a literature peculiarly Kazak. Most employed poetry, the traditional form of Kazak oral literature, but in 1908 the first Kazak novel, by Ispandiar Köbey, was published. The Kazak intelligentsia, though small, was caught up in the political and social ferment which preceded the Bolshevik Revolution of 1917.[12]

OTHER TRIBAL PEOPLES

The Kazaks, by their location, acted as a buffer between the encroaching Russians and the other nomadic peoples of Central Asia. When Tashkent was taken, the high eastern mountain territories of the Kirghiz were still the object of exploration, and the introduction of the Tsarist administrative system failed to break the influence of tribal leaders. Although many Kirghiz continued their traditional nomadic way of life into Soviet times, however, there was a considerable increase in agriculture during the Tsarist period as well as a development of trade and mining. Of these changes in the economy, the Kirghiz bard Moldo Klych sang: "When money made its appearance, the well-being of the people went away." [13]

The Karakalpaks at the time of annexation had only recently become established on the lower Amu Darya and southern shores of the Aral Sea. There they were struggling for subsistance on a transitional economy based on stock-breeding, grain and melon culture, fishing, and subordinate trade with neighboring Kazaks. Karakalpaks on the left bank remained under the Khanate of Khiva until the Revolution of 1917. When those on the right bank came under Russian rule in 1873, they resisted taxation of any kind. They were successful in their efforts to avoid taxation as settled farmers and were all classed as nomads. This ruling had the immediate advantage of lower taxes but in the long run hindered the economic growth of the area. For under the Tsarist administrative classification of nomad, they could not sell land or use it as security on loans for the development of cotton culture. Furthermore, because most of the tribal chiefs had forcibly opposed even the kibitka tax imposed on nomads, these men were barred from election as *volost* administrators. As a consequence, no tribal chiefs rose to wealth by supporting and being favored by the Russian administration, as occurred among the nomadic Kazaks; nor did there emerge a class of bourgeois landowners and entrepreneurs grown rich on cotton as happened in the oases. Although some individuals achieved prosperity on the fringes of the Russian cotton and money economy, Karakalpakia in general remained an economic backwater, notable chiefly for its proliferation of small mosques and dervish orders.[14]

The Turkomans were the last of the Central Asian peoples to come under Russian domination, resisting in a series of bloody battles which ended only in 1885. Once Russian forces had subdued these impassioned fighters, the government moved to abolish slavery and the raids for slaves which had been an integral part of Turkoman life. This deprived the tribesmen of an important source of income. In the oases occupied by Turkomans, it placed a new burden on the women, whose labor replaced that of slaves in cultivating the fields. The cessation of slave raids resulted in the impoverishment of the Turkomans. It also deprived many men of their chief interest in life. Henri Moser, who traveled among the Turkomans in 1881, not long after the second battle of Geok Tepe, commented on the number of men who were turning to alcohol and opium. Some Turkomans were drawn into the Russian cotton complex and, after 1905, into Russian or Jadid (reform Muslim) schools. A majority, however, continued their tribal way of life as best they could.[15]

THE OASES

Russian conquest of the oases of Turkistan came later than that of the Kazak steppe and was effected much more rapidly. An abortive campaign against the Khanate of Khiva in the winter of 1839–1840 was defeated by the weather. In 1847 a fortress was planted on the Sir Darya near the Aral Sea and in 1853 troops moved up the river and captured Ak Mechet. In 1864 Chimkent fell and the next year, Tashkent. The Emirate of Bukhara submitted to Russian might in 1868, and the Khanate of Khiva five years later. The Khanate of Kokand was finally reduced to submission in 1876, and the warlike Tekke Turkomans were brought to terms in 1881. A limit was set to Russian expansion in the area when the boundary with Afghanistan was established in 1885. In less than forty years, Russia had extended its domain, by military conquest, over the vast and populous land of Turkistan. Bukhara and Khiva were allowed to continue as autonomous states, but at Russian pleasure; the Emir of Bukhara was de-scribed as "a sort of gilded marionette in the hands of his Russian adviser." [16]

On the steppes, gradual Russian military encroachment had been followed by large-scale Russian peasant settlement, but in Turkistan until 1910 a clause in the statute of govern-ment barred Russian peasants from settling on lands other than those newly brought under irrigation. As a conse-quence, in 1911 there were only 202,290 Russians in the *oblast*s of Sir Darya, Fergana, Samarkand, and Transcaspia, out of a total population of 5,291,152.[17] These consisted largely of government administrators, the military, traders and entrepreneurs, and, with the coming of the railroad, of employes in railroad and industry. Almost all were settled in the towns and cities; in most such urban centers, Russians had their own communities, built apart from the old native towns. In the khanates of Khiva and Bukhara, Russian resi-dents were rare. In the oases of Turkistan, the Tsarist gov-ernment was anxious to reap the economic rewards of con-quest, obtaining raw materials for its own industry and finding markets for its manufactured products, but Russian communities had their own social life, little touched by the people in whose land they lived. Although its ultimate goal was Russianization, the administration was mindful of the rapidity with which Russian armies had conquered Turkis-tan and of the exiguous size of its army in comparison with the large native population. It therefore moved cautiously in instituting changes affecting the local culture, fearful of en-gendering active resentment.

The early impact of Russian rule was thus primarily eco-nomic, though changes associated with the Russian occupa-tion often had far-reaching cultural effects in some regions. For the most part, however, Russian culture filtered out from Russian centers to that small part of the native population able to observe and emulate Russian manners. The spear-heads of Russian economic colonialism were raw cotton from Turkistan in exchange for Russian manufactured goods. At the beginning of the nineteenth century, raw cotton and cotton textiles had been Turkistan's chief export to Russia, but the local cotton was a short-staple variety, laborious to process and suitable only for inferior yarns and textiles. Russia's own textile industry was expanding, and when the outbreak of the American Civil War cut off Russia's usual supply of American cotton, prices shot up. In response, an American variety of cotton was introduced into Turkistan, and in 1884 the first small shipment was made to Moscow. The acreage planted to cotton increased rapidly, as did shipments of cotton fiber to Russia. Before the introduction of the American variety, cotton had been grown by Uzbek and Tajik peasants on small holdings, as a cash or barter crop supplementing grain and other food crops. Russia, with its increasing demand for cotton, sought to convert the region to a one-crop economy, turning all suitable land to cotton culture and shipping in grain from Russia.[18]

This policy had far-reaching effects. Under the government of Turkistan, the *mulk* estates of the great landlords had been broken up and given to the peasant families cultivating them; taxation of the *waqf* lands of religious foundations had also resulted in a reversion of some land to the actual cultivators. Thus, families whose ancestors had been sharecroppers for generations were faced with the responsibility of managing their own land—of finding oxen and tools to cultivate their land, obtaining seed, and providing food for their families between crops. This was difficult enough in itself, as has been demonstrated more recently in Middle Eastern countries where there has been a redistribution of land. At the same time, these former sharecroppers, as well as other peasants who already owned their own land, had to adjust to

107

a new crop more expensive and time-consuming to raise than grain, and to a money economy in which they sold their whole crop and bought much of their food instead of bartering or selling a part of the crop for locally produced goods. In response to this situation, there arose entrepreneurs who advanced seed and other necessities against future crops and, on those occasions when the peasant was unable to repay these advances out of income, obtained title to the land. In 1914, 25 per cent of all the farms in Fergana *oblast* were worked by people who did not own the land.[19] The peasants thus did not necessarily benefit from Russian rule. Some received land only to lose it again, exchanging a traditional landlord with whose ways they were familiar for a strange entrepreneur landlord or employer. They found Russian taxes more onerous than those of the khans, both because the taxes had to be paid in money and because the methods of extortion of the new tax gatherers were unfamiliar and so less easily evaded than those of the old. Their dealings over water distribution with a *mirob* elected by Russian procedures also confused them. When pressed for money, they turned to seasonal work in the industries that were springing up or on the railroad. Some left the village and agriculture entirely and became urban workers. Those who remained cultivators were often faced with the conflicting pressures of planting all their acreage to cotton, as they were strongly encouraged to do, or of planting some grain to provide food lest grain shipments from Russia fail to arrive.

While the peasants in areas suitable for cotton cultivation often felt themselves worse off than before, the merchants, traditionally sensitive to a good business deal, profited by the economic changes. Many became entrepreneurs who financed the peasant and sold his cotton to the agents of Russian textile manufacturers. Since cotton could not be shipped to Russia in the form of bolls picked from the plant, there arose industries to clean the cotton, process the fiber, and press its seeds into oil. Vodka distilleries and wineries were set up to cater to the thirsty local Russian population, and other processing plants attracted local enterprise. Thus, there arose in the oasis cities a new and prosperous middle class, in a position to observe Russian cultural behavior and financially able to imitate such parts of it as seemed desirable.[20]

The stimulus of increased trade with Russia had a multiple influence on oasis crafts. First, the influx of Russian trade goods in competition with local craft wares weakened and sometimes destroyed local craft. Second, the demand in Moscow for art work from Turkistan often had a deleterious effect on art styles and craftsmanship, since craftsmen did not take the same pains with work destined for an alien and distant market as for the face-to-face customers examining wares in the shops of the bazaar. Metal workers were particularly hard hit by the influx of Russian goods. Iron casting had been a highly developed craft in the mid-nineteenth century, when cauldrons, jugs, lamps, and braziers were often elegantly adorned. Under Russian competition, iron casters were reduced to making the tips of plows and the hubs of wagon wheels. Fergana Valley had been famous for its guns, but by the beginning of the twentieth century this craft was almost extinct. In the teashops of the towns the Russian samovar replaced a similar local device for boiling tea water. Locksmiths gave up their craft in the face of imported Russian locks, but they acquired a new and profitable craft making objects of tin imported from Russia. Some of the jewelers catered to the Russian trade, like the one who adorned European studs and scarfpins with a turquoise mosaic. Others sought a popular local market, making ornaments of thin sheets of silver stamped and laid over a filling of putty to give substance. Of the copper and brass work, Miss Meakin, an Englishwoman who visited Turkistan in 1896 and 1902, complained that few good pieces were to be found in the bazaar because the best work was being sent to Moscow. Weavers and potters also suffered in competition with Russian manufactured goods, as did leather workers. Woodworkers lost trade when metal-bound trunks were shipped from Moscow by the thousands to replace the carved and painted chests that traditionally constituted the chief piece of furniture in the oasis home.[21]

There was also a deterioration in home crafts. Meakin reported that Uzbek and Tajik girls embroidering for the Moscow market were less careful than when working on pieces for home use and that among Turkoman rugs in the bazaar at Merv, "cheap work and cheap designs abounded, but the Turkoman carpet of world-wide renown was not there." [22] She was able to pinpoint the time of change in Bukhara:

As for the Bokhara of seven years ago, the Bokhara of Vambéry, Schuyler, and Curzon, it was gone forever. . . . In the bazaars that once had not their equal, there is hardly a booth that has not procured its wares direct from Moscow. I spent hours in searching for curios that I could take to friends in England, but there was literally nothing Bokharan left except a few knives.[23]

This was Bukhara, the former great trade and craft center of Central Asia, still governed by the Emir of Bukhara, who would not let the railroad approach too closely to his city because his subjects regarded it as the "*arba* of the devil." Some Bukharan upper-class homes boasted European chairs, tables, beds, and lamps. Even Russian stoves were built into the wall for show although the Uzbeks did not use them, complaining that the heat gave them headaches.[24]

The building crafts, however, received impetus from the new prosperity of entrepreneurs and traders. The Russian new towns were laid out on broad, tree-lined avenues with rivulets running along the curbs and neat frame or brick dwellings and impressive brick administrative buildings.

VII. A Turkoman head shepherdess on a karakul sheep-breeding farm in Turkmenia, wearing traditional costume. (Sovfoto.)

VIII. Turkoman sitting on a tribal rug and playing the *nai*. (Max Klimburg.)

Rich Sarts began to build dwellings in the Russian style. Sometimes the part of the house reserved to the men was built and furnished in the European manner, while the women's quarters followed the older fashion. Elsewhere, men built impressive houses in the European fashion for entertaining, but kept their families in traditional homes. The chief prestige symbols, in addition to European furniture and *objets d'art,* appear to have been glazed windows and kiln-fired brick walls. Trading firms and banks also advertised their prosperity by constructing brick buildings, not only in the Russian-administered cities of Turkistan but also in the capitals of the khanates. Nevertheless, while making this bow to modernity in dwellings and places of business, the rich also acknowledged their success by having new mosques constructed in the wards. These were elaborately adorned in the native style, with *ganch* carving, murals, and columns.[25]

Russian influence on oasis social culture was for the most part limited and superficial. Farm women spent more time in the fields picking cotton than they had in the days of mixed farming, but their status in the family and in society seems in no way to have changed. In Tashkent and other Russian towns, there was an increase in prostitution among women who preferred this life to unfortunate marriages. The number of such prostitutes was small, but the fact that they went unveiled hardened general resistance to the unveiling of respectable women.[26]

The Tsarist government interfered little with the religious practices of the people, but on occasion lack of interference had its affect. The khanate governments had exercised some control over *waqf* property, for example; under Russian inattention, mosques and *medressehs* often fell into disrepair while mullahs pocketed the *waqf* revenue. The Russian administration recognized Shariat law but arranged the election of *qazis* and assigned each to a specific district. This caused dislocations in several directions. Whereas the khans had usually appointed religious scholars of the highest reputation to the post of *qazi,* lesser men frequently won in the unfamiliar elective process. Furthermore, persons seeking judgment under the Shariat were required to go to the *qazi* of their district instead of seeking a judge of their own choice. All this led to a loss of prestige by *qazi*s and other mullahs. This loss of prestige also had its affect on the *medresseh*s where scholars were trained, for students who had formerly been attracted to the honored *medresseh*s of Samarkand now often went to Bukhara or even to Istanbul or Cairo for their education. The position of *reïs,* guardian of prescribed Muslim practice in the towns, was abolished by the Russian administration, and as a consequence, attendance at the mosques dropped off sharply in Tashkent and other cities under direct Russian rule. Many town-dwellers became lax in performing their daily ablutions and prayers. There was also a marked increase in public intoxication among town- and city-dwellers. On the other hand, there was a great increase in pilgrims to Mecca. As a result of the new prosperity and the great ease of travel provided by the new railroad, many thousand pilgrims went to Mecca each year by way of Batum and Istanbul. Also, prints of Mecca produced in Istanbul, Bombay, Kazan, and even St. Petersburg began to appear in oasis homes, as well as religious literature published in Kazan and Orenburg.

As by-products of Russian rule, therefore, there was an increase in interest in international Islam at the same time that local Turkistani religious leaders were losing status and authority and some of the population was falling away from traditional Muslim practices. Many mullahs resented this loss of prestige and used their still considerable influence over the people to stimulate anti-Russian feeling. Some of the dervish orders were particularly active in stirring up popular feeling against the Russians; a number of revolts in Fergana were inspired by dervish leaders. This led the Russian administration to forbid the dervish order of Qalandars to hold services in public because of the seditious nature of some of their sermons. The tombs of saints were also affected. The Shah Sindeh, a shrine dedicated to a medieval saint martyred by infidels, which had been one of the most popular places of pilgrimage in Central Asia, lost such prestige by the Russian conquest that it was practically deserted in 1884. Another victim was a tomb of Daniel near Samarkand. Daniel, like certain other Central Asian saints, was believed to grow in his grave, so that the tomb had to be lengthened from time to time. After the Russian conquest, the belief took hold that as long as Daniel continued to grow, no foreigner would gain complete possession of the country. It was therefore a great blow to the people when the Russian administration built a wall around the tomb to stop further growth.[27]

A significant change in oasis culture during the period of Tsarist rule was in the field of education. As had happened earlier among the Kazaks, some upper-class oasis families found it desirable to work in harmony with their Russian overlords and, in due course, sent their sons to Russian schools where they became acquainted with the ideas stirring in nineteenth-century Europe. Before Russian conquest, in the eighteenth and early nineteenth centuries, the Tatar city of Kazan on the Volga River had been the center through which much of Russia's trade with Turkistan was channeled. During this period Kazan was subject to strong cultural influence from Bukhara, then the center of Muslim learning in Central Asia, and Bukharan teachers were welcomed in the *medresseh*s and *mekteb*s of the Tatar city. After the Russian conquest of Turkistan, however, Kazan not only lost its virtual monopoly as intermediary in Russian-Turkistan trade relations, but found itself in danger of engulfment by Russian Christian proselytism. Thus pressed, young middle-class Tatars, fearing lest the Tatars lose their ethnic and religious identity completely, were moved to reform Islamic education and practices in order to bring them more in tune with the modern European world. Therefore, following the Russian conquest of Turkistan, the direction of cultural influence was reversed. No longer did Kazan look to Bukhara as the center of learning. Instead, the small group of intelligentsia in Turkistan, to whom a new world had been belatedly opened by their contacts with Russians, looked for leadership to the Tatars who had already begun to adapt European concepts to Muslim needs. An increasing number of Tatars came to teach in the *medresseh*s and *mekteb*s of Turkistan, where they introduced a synthesis of Russian and, after 1905, of Western European ideas distilled in other Muslim countries, particularly Turkey, Persia, and India. Both the Kazan Tatars and the middle-class intelligentsia of Turkistan were especially attracted to the program of the Crimean Tatar, Ismail Bey Gaspirali (1851–1914), known to the Russians as Gasprinski, who advocated such changes as school reform on European lines, a common Turkic literary language to be used by newspapers throughout Muslim Russia, and even the emancipation of women. Gaspirali's newspaper *Terjiman* ("The Translator") had readers in Central Asia. One of these, the Imam Munevver Qari (1880–1933), founded the first *usul-i jadid* ("new method") school in Tashkent in 1901, and in the following year published a text that was to become a standard in the Jadid schools.

Already, with the rise of a new middle class, attendance at the traditional *medresseh*s had been increasing steadily. Faced with competition from both the Jadid schools and those operated by the Russian government, inadequate as these latter often were, and further faced with meeting the needs of students who would have to follow careers in a

Russian-dominated society, even the traditional schools were jolted out of their medieval stagnation. By 1908, nearly 10,000 students attended the *otin-bibi,* girls' schools. In 1911 the Tsarist government became so disturbed by the mounting sense of pan-Turkic, pan-Islamic, and nationalist solidarity being fostered by the Jadid and other native schools that new regulations were introduced governing the operation of Muslim schools in Turkistan. These regulations were so burdensome as to slow down the growth of the reform schools, but the requirement—aimed specifically at the Tatars who had been propagating the new method in Central Asia —that *mekteb* teachers (other than Russians) be of the same nationality group as their students was less burdensome than anticipated. By 1911 there was a new intelligentsia of Sarts able to carry on the new method adapted to the needs of Turkistan. On the eve of the revolution in 1917, there were 166 Jadid schools in the Russian-governed area of Turkistan as well as 18 in the Kazak province of Semirechie. The number of people affected by this educational movement was small; in 1917 only 2 per cent of the Uzbeks were literate. The movement had, however, produced an educated nucleus which looked not inward to traditional Bukhara, but outward to the new world that existed beyond the confines of the Russian empire.[28]

V

The Pastoral Tribes
after 1917

JUST before the outbreak of World War I, the Kazaks seemed to be making some adjustment to changed conditions. On the borders of Siberia, at least, where Kazaks had been longest subject to Russian rule and colonization, statistics showed a marked decrease in the number of households without animals and a population increase greater than that of Russia. The first effect of World War I on Kazak nomads was a sharp decline in the number of Russian colonists swarming in to settle on the best pasture lands; but then came higher prices for the commodities to which the nomads had become accustomed, increased taxes, and the requisitioning of goods and services. In 1916 a decree was announced with little explanation that non-Russians were to be drafted for war work. In an alarm turning to panic, Kazaks and Kirghiz rose against the *volost* heads charged with making up the conscription lists and against Russian settlers. Some tribesmen fled to China, often with loss of life or of livestock. Russian colonists, in turn, panicked and took reprisals on any natives they encountered or seized the occasion to appropriate nomad land and animals. How many were killed in the bloody fighting or died of starvation through loss of animals has not been determined. It has been estimated that some three hundred thousand fled to China.[1]

Scarcely had an uneasy peace settled on the steppe when the Menshevik revolution brought to Central Asians a hope of freedom from Russian rule. Kazak engineers, doctors, and other professionals serving in the war had used the opportunity to spread among other Kazak conscripts their Western ideas of nationhood. They now organized an Alash Orda provisional republican government which, after the Bolshevik revolution, rallied the forces of Kazak resistance to this new threat of Russian domination. When Bolshevik forces cut their communications by capturing a part of the Orenburg-Tashkent railroad, Kazaks in the west joined Bashkirs and Ural Cossacks while those in the east joined the White army of Admiral Kolchak in Siberia. A hint of the losses suffered in this struggle is found in statistics for Semirechie Province, where between 1917 and 1920 the number of livestock decreased by 51.67 per cent. After nearly three years of bitter fighting, the Soviets set up a government for the Kazaks but prudently placed the capital at Orenburg, a Cossack settlement at the edge of Kazak territory. In 1924 the capital of the Autonomous Socialist Soviet Republic of Kazakstan was moved onto the steppe—at Ak Mechet (Qzyl Orda)—but only in 1928 was it considered safe to move on to the Russian town of Vernyi, renamed Alma Ata, the present capital. The Kazaks and their neighbors the Kirghiz were the last of the Central Asian peoples to be accorded full status as socialist soviet republics, in 1936.[2]

The Tsarist government had been generally cautious about introducing changes in the culture of the newly conquered Central Asian peoples, but Soviet leaders showed no such hesitation. Once they were in control, they pressed for rapid change, and like the governments of other countries having a minority population of pastoral nomads. Soviet leaders began with the firm belief that agriculture was a higher and more desirable way of life than pastoralism. They were also aware that nomads are not easy to control. Thus, the first goals of Soviet policy in the area were to settle the nomads as quickly as possible and to destroy the tribal genealogical kin ties which were fundamental to tribal social and political life.

In 1921–1922 came the land-water reforms, under which government land to the extent of 1,161,370 acres (470,000 hectares) was distributed among poor Kazaks in Semirechie and Sir Darya provinces. In 1926–1927 there began an intensive program of taking arable and meadow lands from the tribal leaders usually referred to in Soviet literature as "*bay*s and wealthy families" and redistributing them among poor families. Altogether, 3,360,560 acres (1,360,000 hectares) of meadow and 2,888,750 acres (1,250,000 hectares) of arable land were redistributed at this stage. In 1928, the Soviets made a further attack on viable nomadism by confiscating 145,000 animals from 696 "big *bay*s" and distributing the stock among 25,000 poor and middle-class families. The earlier redistribution of land had been made to families in the hope of encouraging agriculture. The 1928 redistribution of animals, in contrast, marked the beginning of a collectivization program which, under the direction of enthusiastic Russian officials, was rushed through at breakneck speed, far ahead of plan and much more rapidly than in Russia itself. In the first year, 50,000 households were "settled" in collectives, and by the beginning of the Second Five-Year Plan, the settlement of the Kazak nomads was regarded as basically complete.

Thousands of nomadic families were forced into collective encampments where their animals often starved to death for lack of adequate grazing. Those who resisted were labeled "reactionary *bay*s" and either liquidated or expelled, their animals confiscated. Many Kazaks fled to the Chinese side of the border, some sought refuge in Afghanistan. Those who could not escape often killed their animals. Altogether, the Kazak population decreased by nearly 900,000 between 1926 and 1939. Although, despite the losses of the civil war years, the number of livestock in 1929 had increased by 35.9 per cent over the 1913 figure, between 1929 and 1934 the number of sheep and goats decreased from 27,200,000 to 2,261,000 and of horses from 4,200,000 to 221,000.[3]

The collectivization program, which emphasized settlement of the nomads and development of agriculture, was accompanied by the impoverishment, exile, or liquidation of tribal leaders. At the same time, mining and industry were developed in regions that had been the pasture lands or winter quarters of the nomads; in the south, cotton culture was extended into former grazing areas. Before and during World War II, many thousands of dissident Koreans, Ukrainians, Volga Germans, Crimean Tatars, and other nationality groups were transplanted to Kazakhstan, and throughout the Soviet period there was an influx of Russians in the guise of administrators, agitators, technicians, and "fraternal helpers." Finally came the "virgin lands" program inaugurated in 1953 to convert the remaining grasslands of northern Kazakhstan into a Russian breadbasket.

Given all these forces militating against nomadism, it seemed unlikely that the pastoral nomadic way of life could survive. Yet survive it has, in modified form, and has even been accepted as the most efficient way of exploiting grassland and desert. Terms have changed: Russians now describe nomads as *otgonnyi* ("roving") instead of *kochevoi* ("nomadic"); herders are "specialists" skilled in the care of livestock; and the nomadic family is a "brigade," with each member holding an official title. They are, nevertheless, pastoral nomads moving in family groups according to season to find grazing for their animals. It is difficult to ascertain just how many Kazaks remain pastoralists. The report of the 1959 census findings published in 1961 analyzes occupational categories only for the U.S.S.R. as a whole and not according to republic. In the Soviet Union as a whole, the census enumerated 753,600 shepherds and herders, an increase of 29 per cent over the 1939 total of 583,300. It might be inferred that a large majority of these were found in the Central Asian republics of Kazakhstan, Kirgizia, and Turkmenistan, which are the traditional herding areas. In another occupational category, farm managers are lumped with leaders of livestock brigades, and there is no way of discovering how many of the 217,600 total belong to livestock brigades. It might perhaps be safely inferred that only full-time shepherds and herders are included in that occupational category and that those pastoralists who do some dry farming in addition to herding animals are included in the comprehensive category of those engaged in agriculture without special designation. Similarly, Kazaks engaged in dairying would be included in that occupational classification, one that is not peculiar to Central Asia. The occupational census thus seems to set a minimum figure of three quarters of a million people, most of them presumably Central Asians, who are devoted to pastoralism. Statistics on the livestock in each republic are available. In Kazakhstan the number of sheep and goats rose from a low of 2,610,000 in 1935 to 30,404,000 in 1962, nearly double the 1916 figure of 18,364,000. Since census figures on privately owned livestock were obtained by a spot check of one farm in ten, it is possible that the sheep and goat population is higher than enumerated. (Given the Central Asian propensity for avoiding any enumeration that might have the affect of raising taxes, it is unlikely that the livestock population might be lower than that indicated by the spot check.) In any event, the number of sheep and goats has been growing steadily for three decades.[4] Sheep, because of their grazing habits, must be shifted from pasture to pasture at intervals. Thus, a possible inference from these statistics is that pastoral nomadism may be increasing rather than declining.

By a process of elimination, it is possible to obtain a rough idea of how most Kazaks live. In 1959 there were 2,794,500 Kazaks living in Kazakhstan. Some hundred thousand of these were employed as workers in industry and construction. In 1960, 34,800 Kazaks had received a higher education and might be expected to have nonpastoral occupations, such as the 2,064 who were engaged in research. In the same year, there were 31,351 Kazaks in VUZ (institutions of higher education). Allowing for other categories for which statistics are not at hand, it would appear that a large proportion of Kazaks in Kazakhstan, perhaps two and a half million in all, were attached to kolkhozes (collective farms) and sovkhozes (state farms). Some of these may have been employed as mechanics or drivers, but it has been reported that on the sovkhozes of Kazakhstan only 26 per cent of the mechanics and other skilled workers are Kazaks. Some Kazaks may be engaged in intensive agriculture, but since Soviet anthropologists accept it as fact that Kazaks have no particular skill for intensive agriculture, the numbers engaged in this occupation are presumably small. One might hazard a guess that perhaps half a million Kazaks migrate from pasture to pasture throughout the year, while perhaps as many as two million raise some livestock but also plant some grain or engage in dairying and live in yurts during only a part of the year.[5]

The number of sheep and goats has, as we have seen, increased steadily over the years. The horse, that animal traditionally most esteemed by Kazaks, has not increased so consistently. From a low point of 241,000 in 1935 the number increased to 1,801,000 in 1953, but after that fell gradually to 1,110,000 in 1962, only a quarter of the 1916 horse population of 4,340,000. Yet, all Kazak kolkhozes described in recent anthropological literature had herds of horses. The usefulness of sheep to the Soviet economy is obvious; they provide wool, flesh, and hides for all, as well as milk for the shepherds. The usefulness of horses in an industrial society, however, is less evident. The stockbreeders themselves ride horses, and horses are used as draft animals on kolkhozes when mechanized equipment breaks down. In general, the literature is silent on the use of horses except that Kazaks continue to make kumiss from mare's milk. It appears likely that the continued vitality of horse breeding among the Kazaks is a reflection not of the economic importance of the horse, but of the cultural predilection of Kazaks for that animal. Kumiss for every Kazak may be the Soviet cultural equivalent of the "chicken in every pot" of the American 1930's.

Cattle, latecomers among Kazak livestock and less resistant to the extremes of steppe climate than Kazak sheep and horses, multiplied rapidly with Russian colonization. They numbered 5,062,000 in 1916, rose 7,400,000 in 1929, fell to 1,591,000 in 1934—a much smaller decrease than among sheep and horses—and numbered 6,139,000 in 1962. Whereas the 1962 sheep population had surpassed that of 1929, the cattle population was still well under the 1929 figure. In the past, cattle were usually associated with settled cultivators, both Russians and oasis peoples, and were usually taken up by Kazaks near Russian settlements. Although statistics are not available on the present distribution of cattle between Kazak and non-Kazak kolkhozes and sovkhozes in Kazakhstan, Kazaks appear to be raising them in considerable numbers, and cow's milk has become established in the Kazak diet. While sheep, horses, and cattle have flourished, camels never recovered from the loss suffered during the period of rapid collectivization. In 1962, Khrushchev pointed out that the number of camels in Kazakhstan had dropped from 1,100,000 in 1927–1928 to 137,500 in 1962. In earlier years, Soviet administrators had scorned the camel as a symbol of all that was archaic, but Khrushchev in his speech called for a revival of camel breeding, pointing out that camels should survive in deserts unsuitable for other livestock and that camels' milk, meat, hair, and even their use as transport were not to be ignored. The first reaction to Khrushchev's call came in Turkmenistan, where in 1963 prizes for successful camel breeders were ceremoniously awarded at the Ashkhabad opera house.[6]

The general increase in livestock has been helped by the introduction of veterinary practices which have reduced the incidence of the diseases that formerly took periodic toll of the nomadic herds. The cutting and storing of fodder for emergency winter use had reduced the loss of animals in times of heavy snow and ice—*dzhut*—which decimated flocks and herds several times during the nineteenth century. Every kolkhoz has a considerable acreage of natural hay lands where grass is cut for winter use. Furthermore, the development of water resources in Central Asia has included a program for drilling wells to bring new lands into use for pasturage. In desert regions of western Kazakhstan where stockbreeders have been cut off from their traditional summer pastures, areas of fodder are planted in which animals can be turned out to graze. Elsewhere, wells make it possible for nomads and their flocks to rove in grazing lands formerly empty because of lack of water.[7]

By the 1960's the great drive of the late 1920's and 1930's to turn the pastoral nomads into settled cultivators had passed. The Soviet economy needed the meat, hides, wool, karakul fur, and dairy products traditionally produced in the steppes and deserts of Central Asia. It was recognized that many parts of Central Asia are best suited to stockbreeding and that caring for livestock—particularly sheep—requires a nomadic or "roving" way of life. There has thus been an official acceptance of pastoral nomadism and an appreciation of the value to the Soviet economy of the traditional stockbreeding skills of Kazaks, Kirghiz, and Turkomans. Although a theory has been advanced concerning the inherited fitness of these peoples for living and working in harsh natural conditions, there is solicitude for the welfare of the nomads. In 1961, Khrushchev called for the mass production of synthetic materials for yurts, more durable than the traditional felt and wooden frames. Shepherds "fulfil a very important function in the national economy," he stated, and "as long as there are shepherds, yurts are indispensable." [8] Yurts were, according to an ethnographic policy article, eminently practical for local conditions, and were discouraged only by leftist-minded people. However, suggested *Pravda* in 1962, since mass production of synthetic yurts had not yet been organized, some sort of mobile dwelling on wheels might be provided, and the harsh living conditions of the shepherds might be alleviated by the mass production of such articles as portable gas stoves and warm sleeping bags.[9] This solicitude does not seem to have been motivated by a need to keep Kazaks and other pastoral peoples at their traditional occupation of livestock breeding. By all accounts, the Kazak preference for yurts is such that even settled people tend to spend their summers in a yurt beside their stationary clay house. The high-level Soviet interest in mass-produced alternatives may perhaps represent an attempt to gain a firmer control on the traditionally independent stockbreeders.

Central Asians, like Russians, have been allowed to keep a few animals for family use. Among Kazaks and other Central Asian peoples of stockbreeding tradition, private ownership of animals was accepted with such enthusiasm that in one extreme case a kolkhoz was reported as owning 560 sheep and goats while its members owned 10,470 privately. This was undoubtedly unusual, but newspaper complaints were numerous of kolkhozniks who were too busy caring for their own animals to work on the kolkhoz; of "townsmen" grazing their stock on kolkhoz pastures; of the death of kolkhoz animals in hard winters because the emergency fodder was fed to private livestock. In 1961, Kazakhstan, Kirgizia, and Turkmenistan enacted decrees limiting the number of privately owned livestock. In Kirgizia, for example, workers on kolkhozes and sovkhozes who were regularly engaged in livestock breeding in remote pastures were limited to one cow, one milk mare, and five sheep and their lambs for each family. Even Uzbekistan, which, although most of its population is concentrated in the oases, has many nomads and semi-nomads outside the irrigated area, felt the need in 1963 to impose a tax on livestock owned by kolkhozniks who had not worked a minimum number of days on the kolkhoz and on other able-bodied citizens who were not engaged in "socially useful work." The need to limit private ownership of livestock was apparently felt to be so great that the Kirghiz law forbade the ownership of any livestock by kolkhoznik households other than those of herders, though in the early 1950's such ownership was so taken for granted in Kazakhstan that there was a normal procedure for herding animals owned by families who lived in the kolkhoz center. They were often cared for by retired workers who were paid in money or meat for their services. After Khrushchev's retirement, there was a change in Soviet policy to encourage the private production of food throughout the Soviet Union. One might expect the Kazaks and other Central Asian pastoralists to take full advantage of this new policy.[10]

A number of Kazak kolkhozes have been described for the period between 1949 and 1953. One was a kolkhoz of the Bukeev Orda in the far west; the others were in southeastern

Kazakhstan between Lake Balkhash and the border of Kirgizia. All had been formed by the consolidation of very small artels or kolkhozes. For example, in the Chu River Valley of southeastern Kazakhstan, thirty-one artels had been combined to form thirteen kolkhozes in one district, while in another, twenty artels had been merged to form eight kolkhozes. The number of families in a Kazak kolkhoz ranged from 116 to 266 and the number of kolkhoz workers from 120 to 400.[11] In the histories of the kolkhozes described, there had been a progressive increase in the number of livestock. At the time studied, the number of sheep and goats ranged from 5,385 (1949) to 22,000; of horses from 373 to 1,839; of cattle from 468 to 1,775. One eastern kolkhoz had 64 camels, that in the Bukeev Orda, 237. There were chicken farms on some kolkhozes, and on one (obviously with European members), hogs and bees. One kolkhoz devoted entirely to livestock breeding had 32,000 sheep and goats, 1,500 horses, 7,400 cattle, and 200 camels. Usually each kolkhoz had a center, but in some cases several small kolkhozes shared a center. Such headquarters typically had a miller, a blacksmith, and a carpenter, as well as a cultural "club" and an elementary school. These kolkhoz centers had few, and sometimes no, year-round residents except for multinationality kolkhozes with some intensive agriculture. Most services were provided by regional centers where there was usually a store, clinic, hospital, school, library, and post office; on occasion, there was also a radio station, a hotel for visiting kolkhozniks, and a public bath and a hairdresser. These regional centers served as links with the outside world.

The lands belonging to a kolkhoz were divided into pasture land (the largest area); meadow land (fairly extensive), from which fodder was cut for winter use; and cultivated land, most of which was devoted to dry farming (*bogarnyi*) of grain. For some of the kolkhozes described, there is mention of alfalfa, which requires irrigation, and maize raised for fodder. Patches of potatoes or melons are also mentioned and occasionally fruit orchards. None of the descriptions give data on the ethnic groups other than Kazak represented on the kolkhoz. Where irrigated agriculture is practiced extensively on a kolkhoz, it is reasonably safe to infer the presence of Uzbeks, Uighurs, Russians, or other *narodnost* (nationality). On the other hand, where comparatively small areas are planted to atypical crops, it is not clear to what extent these indicate non-Kazak residents or to what extent they reflect a Kazak adoption of oasis patterns. The *bogarnyi* lands were often scattered at some distance from the center, and kolkhozniks assigned to their cultivation lived in yurts spring and fall during the planting and harvesting, as did the tractor brigades assigned to plowing and reaping. Cattle were kept in stalls at the center during the winter and pastured within a radius of ten or twenty miles of the center during the summer, when the herders lived in yurts. Herds of sheep, horses, and camels migrated throughout the year, following seasonal itineraries similar to those of prerevolutionary times and ignoring kolkhoz or republic boundaries as casually as nomads had ignored national boundaries in Tsarist times. In the Chu Valley, for example, brigades moved out onto the steppe in spring, up into alpine meadows (sometimes in Kirgizia) in summer, back onto the steppe in fall, and to sheltered spots in the foothills or near Lake Balkhash in winter. Their stops along the nomadic itinerary are reported as following an official schedule but appear to have differed in no way from the stations, determined by the availability of water, characteristic of the precollective period.[12]

Some nomads seldom go to the kolkhoz center; in recognition of this, Red Yurts—mobile centers for adult education—are sent out to visit the nomads. However, many maintain permanent dwellings at the center where older members of the family and school children reside during the winter months. Members of the cattle brigades also spend the winter in permanent dwellings at the center, as do those assigned to cultivating *bogarnyi* fields. In summer, school children and elders join their families at summer pastures, and often the center is completely deserted in summer.

The kolkhozniks are formed into brigades, with each assigned to tending either a flock of sheep or a herd of horses, of camels, or of cattle; or to care for cultivated fields or to cut hay from the meadows. This would seem contrary to the old practice in which the extended family of the *aul* had a variety of animals, though these were herded separately according to kind. In practice, however, the "brigade" does not seem very different from the traditional *aul*. It consists of a family group, and in addition to whatever type of animal it is charged with herding, there are riding horses and pack camels. The family would have some sheep for its own use. Since the Kirgizia enactment of 1961 was very strict in other respects, one might interpret its limit of five sheep and their lambs as the minimum needed for the subsistence of a nomad family. The composition of *bogarnyi* agricultural brigades is not described. Since the work is seasonal, it is possible that some members of the family take care of planting and harvesting while others belong to herding brigades or herd family animals. Cattle, less hardy than the Central Asian breeds of sheep, horses, and camels, do not fit well into the nomadic pattern. Those who care for cattle must remain at the center during the winter and cannot go far afield in summer. Cattle breeding is thus transitional between traditional pastoralism and settled agriculture. No description of a cattle brigade is available, but women are described as doing most of the work on kolkhoz dairy farms. Also, women regularly make up 60 per cent or more of the labor force of the kolkhozes described. Furthermore, it has been reported that in Kazak agricultural kolkhozes, men often seek employment in industry or in the towns, leaving kolkhoz work to their women. It is thus possible that when families are assigned to dairy cattle brigades, some men break with tradition by leaving the kolkhoz entirely, while following tradition in leaving dairy work to their womenfolk.[13]

The yurts, in which most Kazak kolkhozniks live from spring to autumn, and which some recently settled people like the Karakalpaks set up beside their permanent dwellings for summer use, are constructed in the traditional way. As in the old days, women of a family, often working with those of a neighboring family, make the felt, and professional carpenters make the wooden framework. The only differences are that the carpenters are often paid in money or grain instead of in livestock, and some of them have been organized into artels. Setting up the yurts and dismounting them is still the work of women. Permanent dwellings show both Russian and oasis influence. Some, particularly in the eastern mountains where wood is plentiful, are built of timber with gabled roofs; others are of tamped earth with flat roofs. Occasionally, one finds a combination of influences in tamped earth walls with a gabled roof of thatch.[14] Even when Kazaks live in houses a part or all of the year, the interior arrangements and furnishings are like those of a yurt. The principal innovations in yurt furnishings are: some utensils of aluminum and enamelware to supplement the traditional iron kettle, which is still standard equipment, and an iron frying pan for baking bread flaps; and, along with traditional types of wall hangings, embroidered cloths showing Ukrainian or Uzbek influence, and some factory-made ornamental cloths. In permanent dwellings, kerosene lamps are common for illumination. For cooking and heating, some houses have fireplaces like those of the Tajiks; some have iron stoves of European inspiration; in others, stoves of Russian type are built into the wall. In such dwellings, factory-made metal utensils and containers are customary; but although Kazak kolkhozniks use teapots and the Chinese tea bowls adopted in Tsarist times, they seldom have plates or cups of china or pottery. In industrial communities, such as those of Kirghiz coal miners and Turkoman oil workers, china plates and platters have to a large extent replaced the wooden ones still used by pastoralists. Even in those homes possessing European furniture, a majority of people continue to sit and sleep on the floor.[15]

In diet, the most marked change is that bread and meal have become staples. Kazak kolkhozniks receive grain as part of their pay, and although they sell some of this in the open market, they regularly bake bread flaps of the oasis type on frying pans, hot stones or bricks, or, in settlements in the Alma Ata district, in *tandyr* (ovens) like those of the Uighurs. The use of meal in broth and milk dishes, which began in Tsarist times, has been reinforced by the availability of grain. Fruits and vegetables are eaten to some extent, and in winter at the kolkhoz center, potatoes are a welcome addition to dried cheese (*kurt*) in the soup. Some Uzbek and Uighur dishes, such as pilau, have been accepted as tasty but are not often made. Sugar, tea, and confectionery can be purchased at stores in the district centers. In general, the traditional diet persists. In spring and summer, Kazak kolkhozniks live largely on milk products, and probably the average Kazak has more kumiss, the national favorite, than did his ancestors. During this season, meat is not served except on ceremonial occasions and in entertaining guests. Meat, plentiful in autumn, becomes an important part of the diet then and is prepared for winter use in the traditional way. For each family, a cow or horse and two or three sheep are made into sausages and preserved in other ways; those kolkhozniks who have no animals to slaughter buy them. *Kurt* and other kinds of cheese are also made for winter use in time-honored fashion. Even the Kirghiz miners, who have been more strongly influenced by Uzbek and Russian culture than stockbreeding kolkhozniks, take their meals on the floor, with old people and guests seated in the traditional place of honor and solid food served on a platter from which people dip with their hands.[16] Thus, in eating habits the Kazaks have changed but little. They have accepted some additions to the diet but, except for bread, these have been sparing. The chief difference is that they have more food and can indulge their fondness for kumiss more fully than in Tsarist times.

In clothing there have been greater changes. For winter wear, the nomads in particular tend to cling to traditional forms and materials, adapted over the centuries to the rigorous climate of the steppes and mountains. Here, the chief change noted is that leather trousers appear to be going out of use. For summer wear, army uniforms came into use after World War II and were widely worn because of their practicability. Young men often wear clothes of European style, either bought ready-to-wear in a regional center store or made at home by the women. Women are more conservative than men, but even in woman's dress there has been change. The old-style redingote jacket, itself a Russian borrowing, has shortened and lost its redingote. The traditional *khalat* has been replaced by an overcoat made of black velvet or plush, the materials esteemed ever since Kazaks began to receive Russian-manufactured cloth. When women go out in very cold weather, they wear over this the traditional *chapan* of fur. Trousers of cotton cloth are worn by a majority of young women as well as by almost all older ones, and the headdress adopted in Tsarist times persists. While kolkhoznik women make their own clothes and much for their menfolk, they use factory-made cloth (already a pronounced tendency in Tsarist times), and many have sewing machines. The only clothing material prepared by women themselves are the

131

skins for *chapan* and winter caps; felt for summer caps, and woven camels'-hair cloth for the *khalat*s worn by nomads, particularly in winter. In headdress, older traditions persist. Some Kazak kolkhozniks have their footwear made by local craftsmen, others buy factory-made boots at district stores.[17]

Among the coal miners of Kirgizia, those in the south, near Uzbekistan, show more resistance to Russian dress than in the north. The miners are issued European-style clothes for wear in the mines, but when not at work, all the older men wear quilted *khalat*s of Uzbek style as do many of the younger men in the south. In the south, some have their boots made by craftsmen; others, and almost all those in the north, wear factory-made boots. Almost every man has a white felt cap, regarded as the national headdress, although in the south, men also wear skullcaps of Uzbek style, and old men even wear turbans over their skullcaps, a practice that has disappeared in some parts of Uzbekistan. Most older women wear traditional Kirghiz costume; young women in the north wear clothes of European style, while those in the south follow the Uzbek tradition, in which the robe is gathered onto a yoke. Kirghiz women wear not only traditional styles of jewelry made by local craftsmen but also pieces bought in shops. They also retain (or have adopted from the Uzbeks) the practice in which girls wear their hair in many tiny braids, while married women braid their hair into one or two strands. In the south, women henna their nails, an oasis practice.[18]

In the oil fields of Turkmenistan, where work clothes were not issued, men gradually adopted European clothing as being more convenient than the traditional long robes. While some older men cling to the traditional garb, most younger men wear clothes of European style. For headgear they have replaced the shaggy high sheepskin hats of exaggerated size, peculiarly characteristic of the Turkomans, by a similar one of smaller neater design in astrakhan fur which is modeled on the Cossack hat. In woman's dress, there has been less change. Clothes are now made of factory-woven material instead of homespun, but since Turkomans traditionally used cloth woven by Uzbeks, the pattern of employing trade material has not changed. Like their menfolk, Turkoman women wear factory-made boots. They often shorten their skirts and sometimes even run elastic through the lower edge of their sleeves for greater convenience in working. In the main, however, they retain their traditional costume and predilection for reds and purples, as well as their love of jewelry.[19]

In craft work, Kazak women continue to make felts for family use, following traditional motifs in ornamental appliqué and stitchery, and also make cord and rope. About the only innovation is in the use of aniline dyes, which have brought a wider but harsher range of colors to the felts. As in pre-Soviet times, only some women are skilled in weaving. Using the traditional horizontal loom, they weave cloth of camel hair, as well as pileless rugs, bands for reinforcing the yurt, storage bags, and horse blankets of yarn they have spun and dyed—again using aniline dyes. Many women continue to work skins for winter clothing and the bags used for storing liquids. In southeastern Kazakhstan at least, every woman learns to do embroidery at an early age. Except for work on felt, however, their embroidery shows strong Russian and Ukrainian influence. Among Kirghiz coal miners in the south, where they have long been subject to Uzbek influence, women weave pileless wool rugs and cotton wall hangings and also make pile rugs for home use, with four or five women working together on a large rug. Specialized craftsmen survive, though in somewhat changed circumstances. As in the past, woodworkers make yurt frames, saddles, chests, and other traditional objects, and carve and paint them in the traditional way. However, they are usually employed as kolkhoz carpenters or organized into artels and make traditional wares in their free time. Sometimes they fabricate European furniture on order for the kolkhozniks. Blacksmiths employed on kolkhozes to keep tools and implements in repair also make objects to order for the kolkhozniks in the traditional way. A very few silversmiths—these were never very numerous—continue to make jewelry, chiefly rings and bracelets, ornamented with incisions in the old way. Information is not available on the relationship of the craft bootmakers to the kolkhoz, but since many kolkhozniks wear boots and shoes made to order, such craftsmen obviously exist.[20]

Kinship, which was the basis of traditional tribal society, appears to have retained notable vitality despite many Soviet attempts to destroy "feudal-bay" relationships. Kolkhoz nomad brigades regularly consist of a close family unit.[21] Those described seem smaller than a traditional *aul,* but it is possible that some members of the extended family group devote themselves to caring for privately owned animals and are not enrolled as members of the kolkhoz or brigade. Another possibility is that some members of a family belong to a horse or camel brigade and others to a sheep brigade. The traditional *aul* always herded different types of animals separately. Animals continued to *teben*—horses were sent into a new pasture in winter to break through the snow with their hooves and eat the top of the grass, after which sheep were turned in to eat the lower grass stalks. This implies a close co-operation between horse and sheep breeders. There is also co-operation among women of two or more households in making felt. In nomadic pastoralism as practiced in Central Asia, there is a practical minimum as well as a maximum for the number of families and livestock comprising an effective nomadic work unit.[22] The normal sheep brigade has riding horses and a few pack camels; the horse brigade would at least have some privately owned sheep for its own use. Furthermore, if the young are to be born in the spring, when they will have a chance to grow strong before undergoing the rigors of winter, the herds should be separated according to sex in certain seasons of the year. In spring, mother animals with their young must be kept near camp where the females can be milked and the young animals protected. Altogether, several people are needed to watch over the various herds and flocks. For all these reasons, it seems fairly safe to infer that the effective nomadic unit is not much smaller than the old *aul*, although officially it may be subdivided into two or more brigades.

The kolkhoz itself is made up of closely related families of a tribal kin segment. When collectivization took place, families were migrating in the traditional territory of the tribal subdivision to which they belonged, and the small kolkhozes and artels formed in this period naturally consisted of closely related *auls* which normally moved out together in spring and gradually fanned out into nearby pastures. When these early kolkhozes and artels were consolidated to form larger kolkhozes, such a consolidation usually brought together related kin groups by virtue of their traditional sharing of a common territory. In some cases, where one small kolkhoz kin group happened to be rather far afield, it was nevertheless included in the kolkhoz of its closest tribal kin segments rather than in that nearest to it geographically. Thus, the old tribal kin structure has not been destroyed. Indeed, the formation of kolkhozes within the traditional territory has perhaps strengthened kinship ties. In the course of migrations away from winter quarters the modern brigades, like the old *auls*, are often widely scattered. The modern kolkhoz center brings together many kolkhozniks during the winter months, and children, old people, artisans, and others for a longer period each year.

The kolkhoz center thus might be expected to have a more

continuous, and so stronger, effect in reinforcing kin ties than the old occasional meetings at the weddings or funerals of chiefly families; or than the old winter quarters, where the camps of related families were often strung along over a considerable distance in sheltered areas. The identification of the kolkhoz as a kin group is so strong that kolkhoz exogamy has replaced genealogical exogamy. In practice, in the old days, since few people could remember their genealogies for seven generations back, some point in the tribal genealogy was fixed as marking the limit within which marriage could not take place. The kolkhoz has now become this exogamous unit. This substitution might be expected in time to lessen the incentive for remembering the old tribal genealogy, a feat that was difficult for the average tribesman, while reinforcing the feeling, always strong, that families occupying the same territory were related.[23] Such a transfer has not yet occurred to any extent; even Turkoman and Kazak oil workers in Turkmenistan remember their tribal genealogies for five or six generations back, and in the 1950's it was possible to record rather full Kirghiz tribal genealogies. In general, people remember their major tribal and orda affiliations, as in the case of a blacksmith belonging to the Middle Orda who took up residence in a kolkhoz of the Great Orda. They also know who belongs to their own tribal segment and the degree of relationship of closely related segments. This was true in the old days, as well, when the average tribesman had little need to be familiar with the middle ranges of the tribal genealogy. The sense of kinship remains so strong in the kolkhoz that nonkin, who are usually skilled personnel such as bookkeepers and truck drivers, remain outsiders. In the oil fields of Turkmenistan, where Turkoman and Kazak oil workers live in villages near their place of employment, the people settled in kin clusters within the villages. The continued strength of tribal kin ties is attested by newspaper comment. The phenomenon was deemed worthy of notice by the editors of *Izvestiia,* which in 1960 published an article by the secretary of the Central Committee of the Communist Party of Kirgizia. In Turkmenistan, the Party secretary of a kolkhoz was expelled from the Party for allegedly stirring up discord among tribal kin groups.[24]

Tribal chiefs of the old type have disappeared, but they have often reappeared in the guise of district administrators, as in a district of the Alma Ata *oblast,* where all the key positions were held by members of the Alban lineage, the traditional aristocratic lineage of the branch of the Great Orda occupying that area. Elsewhere there are newspaper complaints that administrators give preference to members of their own tribal kin segment in making appointments and decisions. The kolkhoz head is normally also chief of his tribal kin group, and the *aqsaqal*—head of the extended family—is a person of importance. The authority of the *aqsaqal* shows little sign of diminishing, for almost universally children are trained from earliest childhood to respect their elders. In Turkmenistan, indeed, the traditional council of elders has been officially revived by the Soviet administration in the hope that the elders will use their great influence to advance Soviet aims.[25]

The Soviet government made a strong drive to "rescue women from bondage," usually implying that tribal women were as secluded as those of the settled oasis peoples. Although tribal women usually did most of the work, as still seems to be the case, and often saddled the husband's horse, which nomad women still do, they had a good deal of responsibility and even authority. Thus, when women are elected to head kolkhozes or appointed as brigade leaders, their status is not very different from that of some tribal women in the past, such as the plural wives of prosperous pastoralists, each of whom managed one of her husband's *auls*; or of the widows who, declining to remarry under the levirate, acted as head of household until their sons grew up. This status seems to be reflected in the recent attitude toward higher education. In 1960 there were higher percentages of Kazak and Kirghiz women with a specialized education or enrolled as students in VUZ than of any other Central Asian nationality. It would thus appear that the Kazaks and Kirghiz, whose women traditionally had higher status than that of the oasis women, have been most ready to accept the opportunities of higher education.

Turkoman women, on the other hand, although they had traditionally enjoyed more freedom than oasis women, were more subject to Islamic and oasis influences even in Tsarist times. In 1960 there was a lower percentage of Turkoman women with higher education than any people other than the conservative Tajiks, but in that year there was a higher percentage of Turkoman woman students enrolled in VUZ than among the Tajiks.[26] These statistics would suggest that, although there is considerable conflict between the old and the new order—in 1958 a Turkoman father had his daughter murdered because she wished to study in a pedagogical institute and marry a man of her own choice—Soviet policy in emancipating women may be making greater headway among the Turkomans, where it has some support in tribal tradition, than among the Tajiks, where women traditionally have had low status.

The levirate, and polygamy in general, have not disappeared. Since polygamy is a "crime based on tradition," severely punished when proved in court, and is not a state easily kept secret on a kolkhoz, a marked decrease might be expected. Yet, to judge from complaints in Soviet newspapers, the practice is comparatively widespread, taking into consideration the fact that, traditionally, few men could afford more than one wife. In some cases, a divorced first wife remains a member of the household after the husband's marriage to a second wife; in others, later marriages are not recorded. Instances have been reported in which the husband had the several marriages recorded without bothering with the formality of divorce. Kolkhoz presidents, some of them Party members, are said to be the worst offenders. These are the very men who, as heads of lineages, traditionally had more than one wife, and who, because of their prosperity, would have been obligated to marry a relative's widow under the levirate. However, one kolkhoz in the Frunze *oblast* of Kirgizia was said to have eighteen men with two wives each. Unless the kolkhoz was a large one, this would seem excessive by pre-Soviet standards. There are no statistics on polygamy for either the post-World War II period or that before the 1917 Revolution, but such evidence as is available suggests that if the pattern of polygamy has changed at all it may have been in the direction of increase.[27]

Formerly, Kazak women were not secluded. Yet, in the region of Chimkent, an oasis town not far north of the Uzbek city of Tashkent, the secretary of the regional Communist Party was said to keep his wife in seclusion. Such an important official was, of course, not a kolkhoznik living in a yurt, but it is significant that an urbanized Kazak, with no Kazak tradition for the seclusion of women, should, on achieving high position in the Soviet hierarchy, adopt an Uzbek custom as a status symbol.[28]

Two "crimes based on tradition" other than polygamy are marriage of a girl under the age of eighteen and payment of a bride price, both strictures designed to free girls from family pressures and arranged marriages. To judge from complaints about school dropouts of girls at the traditional age of marriage, a useful clue to early marriage, fewer Kazak and Kirghiz girls appear to marry early than in the oases or among the Turkomans. As for bride price, which in tribal society had many important functions and in no sense represented the sale of the woman, Soviet pressures have modified the form but not discouraged the practice to any extent. In the old days, the bride price consisted chiefly of livestock; in 1928 the average *kalym* was reported as consisting of one horse and thirty sheep. Little information is available for later periods, for payment of bride price is not only illegal, but much more readily disguised than polygamy. For some time after collectivization, few families would have had animals to spare, and with the stabilization of collective farms, there was a partial shift to a money economy. By the late 1950's and early 1960's, some year-round nomads had sizeable private herds and flocks from which a bride price might be drawn, but many other Kazaks did not. From the scant data available, it would appear that the bride price is made usually in the form of a gift and that it may consist more of cash than of livestock. Since the reciprocal dowry is not illegal, it has been described: the traditional outfits of clothing and household equipment.[29]

Although the dowry is an essential counterpart of the bride price, it has not been discouraged; indeed, this tradition has at times been exploited as a means of getting European furniture into new homes. While the tribal peoples, like other Central Asians, still prefer to sit, eat, and sleep on the floor. European furniture has become a prestige symbol and thus fits into the Central Asian pattern in which prestige is gained by the size of the bride price and richness of the dowry. In this way, furniture is finding its way into a number of homes —though not, of course into nomadic yurts—and it is possible that in time the owners may begin to sit on the chairs, sleep on the beds, and spread their meals on tables.

Formerly, wedding guests brought animals or kumiss to supplement the wedding feast. Now they sometimes bring money instead, and it is a policy of Soviet activists to try to persuade the guests to make these gifts directly to the bride and groom instead of to the bride's father. When this is done, presumably a smaller dowry is given. While the form of the marriage transactions has changed somewhat, the major elements persist. The bride price and major contributions toward the wedding feast are furnished by the groom's family. A substantial dowry is provided by the bride's family. Supplementary supplies for the wedding feast are given by more distant relatives. Weddings are still very expensive.[30]

It is difficult to compare modern wedding entertainment with that traditionally offered, for nineteenth-century accounts usually describe those of wealthy families. Singing was always an important feature of the nuptial celebration, even when there were horse races, wrestling, and other diversions. Music, together with a feast, may always have been the chief entertainment at the average wedding, as it is today, when sometimes no more than five or six families make up the wedding party. While the guests frequently do the singing, there is a suggestion that in some regions, at least, the oasis practice has been adopted of hiring musicians for the wedding, musicians who, during the day, have some other occupation on the kolkhoz. A notable change in the ceremony is that the bride. who was formerly conducted on a horse to her husband's home, now frequently makes the journey in an open car or truck rented for the occasion. Despite such innovations, however, modern weddings conform to the traditional pattern: a ceremony and feast of several days held at the home of the bride, followed by a feast at the home of the groom. This is observed even among Kirghiz coal miners. Moreover, weddings continue to be held in the autumn, when meat is plentiful.[31]

Little information is available on the present religious practices of the Kazaks and Kirghiz. Funerals are celebrated in the traditional way by the slaughtering of animals for a feast, and many families continue to call in *baqshi* (shamans)

141

to cure sickness.[32] Presumably, traditional Central Asian religious practices, insofar as they survive at all, are strongest among the nomads, who could carry on their rituals far from the prying eyes of alien observers. Of particular interest are indications that Islam has been strengthened among tribal peoples who formerly were little noted for observing the rites of this religion. Circumcision, the Muslim practice most readily accepted by the Kazaks and Kirghiz before the 1917 revolution, appears to be almost universal. Shrines attract pilgrims to an extent not reported before the revolution. Even members of the Academy of Sciences of Kazakhstan were said to visit a certain shrine in Kazakhstan regularly, while a count made at one shrine in Kirgizia recorded some four hundred people visiting the shrine between seven and ten o'clock in the morning, with a much greater number of visitors later in the day. A Kazak worker in Akmolinsk was said to stop his work to perform the daily prayers, and hundreds of Kirghiz attended Friday prayers at mosques. Mullahs hold public prayers in time of drought, and in 1956 a chain letter enjoined recipients to make sacrifices to Allah. A religious resurgence with Islamic flavor is also implied by an intensification of atheist propaganda after World War II. In 1951 the Komsomol organization in the Tien Shan region of Kirgizia arranged nearly three thousand antireligious lectures in a three-month period, and in 1958 a guide was published for propagandists and agitators in Kazakhstan entitled: "What an Atheist Should Know about the Quran." [33]

The Kazaks and Kirghiz have not become as strongly Muslim as the oasis people; a majority probably know little about the tenets of the religion and are unfamiliar with the prayers. Soviet reporters have a tendency to lump under the title of Islam many beliefs and practices that are not basically Islamic and that sometimes may have no religious connotation in the minds of the observers. Many instances cited in the literature

IX. Ancient tomb of Hodja Mashat, a Muslim saint, in a village of Tajikistan. (Sovfoto.)

X. New home of a collective farm head, Uzbekistan. The traditional architectural style has been modified to include such modern elements as windows facing the street. (Sovfoto.)

represent customary rituals in which a mullah is not essential, though one may be invited to officiate if he is present in the locality. Other instances represent the type of belief common to people who seek a supernatural cause of events for which they have no rational explanation. That spirits indigenous to Central Asia have acquired the Arabic appellation of *"jinn"* does not make the Kazaks more devout Muslims. Nevertheless, there does appear to be a trend among Kazaks and Kirghiz toward accepting forms and patterns associated with Islam in oasis culture in counterpoint to the Soviet drive toward atheism. In this context, it is significant that there has been an expansion of Christian protestant sects among Slavic colonists in Central Asia.[34]

In Turkmenistan, where before the 1917 revolution Islam was stronger than in Kazakhstan and Kirgizia, the transition from a free tribal life to settled or semisedentary communities was accompanied by a strengthening of the bonds of Islam and of the religious practices associated with Islam in Central Asia. This was simply a continuation of the process noted just before the Tsarist Russian conquest of the Turkomans. In the period following World War II, fasting during Ramazan has been frequent, despite strong Soviet disapproval of a practice that lessens the efficiency of workers. Funeral feasts also distract people from their work, as does attendance at mosques on religious holidays. Animal sacrifices for Qurban Bayram appear to be frequent, and there is a consistent refusal to eat pork. Circumcision is practically universal. *Jinns* abound, and as in Iran, women in particular avoid places where evil spirits might do them harm. Shamans and *tebibs* (doctors who supplement the resources of their pharmacopoeia with magic) are called in to treat the sick, and many Turkomans make pilgrimages to shrines. Even Soviet-trained doctors sometimes send members of the family to shrines famous for their believed efficacy in curing certain ailments. Soviet observers have noted a marked revival of religious practices following World War II, and an earthquake at Ashkhabad seems also to have stimulated an increase in religious zeal. This trend apparently continues, for during Qurban Bayram in 1959, more than twice as many people attended a shrine near Charjui as in the preceding year.[35]

In Turkmenistan the tendency to indulge in opium, which was noted after the Tsarist conquest of the Turkoman tribes, has continued under Soviet rule. Turkmenistan appears to be the one republic in Central Asia with a recognized problem of drug addiction.[36]

A major goal of the Soviet government in Central Asia as elsewhere in the Soviet Union was the spread of literacy. Before the 1917 revolution, most Central Asians were illiterate, and among the tribal peoples fewer men had had the opportunity to attend a *mekteb* than in the oases. There was, however, a small educated élite. The Crimean Tatar Gaspirali had promoted a Turkic literary language that could be used by Turkic speakers throughout Muslim Russia, but Kazak writers had begun forming a literary language of their own in the nineteenth century and in the early twentieth century Ahmad Baitursun introduced phonetic and other reforms in the Arabic script which made it particularly congenial to Kazak writers. The Kirghiz were also developing a literary language written in the Arabic script but had not produced so extensive a literature as the Kazaks. The Turkoman literature dates back to the eighteenth century, although the only major author writing in Turkoman was the poet Maqdum Quli (?1735–*ca.* 1805). Before the 1917 revolution, most literate Turkomans preferred to write in Persian. Only the Karakalpaks had no literary language of their own before the 1917 revolution.

The Soviet government, when embarking on its program of mass education, had its reasons for not accepting the scripts and literary languages already in use. The Pan-Turkic language of Gaspirali was rejected because of its potential effect of drawing peoples of Turkic speech together in opposition to Russians. The several national literary languages written in Arabic script were rejected because a broad educational program based on that script might be expected to open doors to the thinking of Persians, Arabs, and other Muslims rather than to the ideology of Soviet Russia. The Soviet policy was therefore to develop new literary languages, a different one for each *narodnost,* ethnic group, which would retard or prevent the growth of Pan-Turkic sentiment and would permit an orientation toward Russian ideas. After brief experiments with modified Arabic alphabets, scripts in the Latin alphabet were officially introduced in 1928 (in 1929–1930 for the Turkomans). Kazaks and Turkomans, who already had literary languages, were most resistant to the changes introduced. In 1939–1940, when many Kazaks and members of other nationality groups had learned Russian, the Latin alphabets were replaced by Cyrillic scripts adapted from that employed in writing Russian.[37] Since the Soviet linguistic program was similar for both the tribal and the settled peoples of Central Asia, this program and the response of the Central Asian peoples to it will be discussed in a later section.

In establishing schools, Soviet administrators were faced with much the same problems with tribal populations and with the settled peoples of the oases. At the beginning of the Soviet regime, the literacy rate was low and few individuals among the nationalities concerned were qualified to teach. There were even fewer Russian teachers with a command of Central Asian languages. Textbooks conforming to Soviet standards were lacking. Since the Soviet government did not wish to retain the Arabic scripts employed in the existing literary languages, there were no national languages in which to write suitable texts. Few Central Asians could see any reason for educating women, and it was difficult to establish schools for nomads even when they could be brought to appreciate the value of education for their sons. The Soviet government was thus confronted with a formidable task in implementing its policy of universal literacy and of training skilled administrators and professional and technical workers. Then, just as they were beginning to build up a cadre of native intelligentsia, the purges of 1937–1938 destroyed many of the best educated members of the Central Asian nationalities.[38] Since, as Soviet leaders were keenly aware, schooling is a prime channel for acculturation—in the case of the Soviet Union, for Sovietization—the degree of Soviet success in achieving their program of education is of concern in gauging the degree of culture change.

Something like universal education has been attained for at least the lower grades, although there are some isolated rural communities without schools.[39] Many girls drop out of school at the traditional age of marriage, though this seems to be a less serious problem among Kazaks and Kirghiz than among Turkomans. For girls who leave school after the third or fourth grade, the lasting effect of their schooling is probably slight. In pastoral kolkhozes where families who winter at the kolkhoz center move into yurts in early spring, children held at the kolkhoz school might be expected to give less than their full attention to studies in spring and fall. In addition, a major drag on education is the shortage of properly trained teachers. In Kirgizia, for example, there was an alleged shortage of more than 2,000 teachers in 1963. According to complaints in the Soviet press, not enough people complete the middle school course. Of those who do so, many cannot meet the entrance requirements of pedagogical institutes; of those who enter, many drop out before completion of their training; and, finally, of those who do graduate, a considerable number do not become teachers, often because they object to living in rural communities. As a result of this circular process, the standards in the native language schools are comparatively low and many students who aspire to a higher education are unable to pass the entrance examinations. Graduates of schools giving instruction in the nationality language are further handicapped in that they have an inadequate command of Russian, the language needed for advancement in a career.

The Kazaks have a particular advantage from this point of view in that in Kazakhstan, where Russians constitute a majority of the population, about a quarter of all Kazak children attend Russian-language schools,[40] where the general standards are higher and Russian-language facility is readily acquired. These students, by associating daily with Russian teachers and pupils, have an opportunity to observe and adopt Russian manners and customs. During the academic year 1960–1961, a higher percentage of Kazak students were enrolled in VUZ than of Kirghiz and Turkomans. This appears to represent a recent trend, however, perhaps reflecting a recent large influx of Russians into Kazakhstan and an increase in the number of Russian-language schools. In 1939, Kazaks made up 57.1 per cent of the population of the republic and Russians 19.7 per cent, while in 1959 Kazaks comprised only 30 per cent of the population of the republic named after them, while Russians constituted 42 per cent. In statistics on the number of Central Asians who had completed a higher or specialized secondary school education by 1960, the Kazaks held their lead over Turkomans and Kirghiz. When specialists with a higher education are separated from those with specialized secondary education, however, the picture is rather different. Of Kazaks in the two categories, only 45.7 per cent had a higher education, as compared with 49.2 per cent of Kirghiz and 50.9 per cent of Turkomans. Furthermore, statistics show that in 1960 only 21.4 per cent of the research personnel in Kazakhstan was

Kazak, whereas in Kirgizia 24.7 per cent of research personnel was Kirghiz; and in Turkmenistan, the republic often represented as the most backward of the three republics with a population of tribal origin, 36 per cent of the research personnel was Turkoman.[41]

The Turkoman lead in proportion of research personnel and of those who had attended institutions of higher education rather than specialized secondary schools suggests a value preference for "white collar" learning found also among the Tajiks. The higher proportion of Kazaks with a specialized secondary school education might be interpreted in two ways. It is possible that Kazaks making a transition from pastoralism to an industrial economy preferred the freedom of driving a truck or tractor to the restrictions of a desk or research laboratory. On the other hand, it may be that the Soviet government, in view of the large Slavic population and the important mining and industrial enterprises in Kazakhstan, preferred to employ scientific personnel trained in Moscow and Leningrad and directed Kazak education toward those technical skills needed on the kolkhoz and sovkhoz. In any event, the VUZ enrollment statistics for 1960–1961 suggest a new trend among Kazaks in favor of advanced education.

The 76,100 Kazaks, 19,100 Kirghiz, and 20,400 Turkomans who were specialists in 1960; and the 36,869 Kazaks, 9,054 Kirghiz, and 8,328 Turkomans enrolled in VUZ in 1960–1961 constitute a core of partly Russianized individuals whom Soviet leaders expect to act as transmitters of Russian culture to their people. As intelligentsia, in favored positions, they wear European clothes, have European furniture in at least one room of the home, speak Russian during work hours, and generally avoid an overt show of ethnic practices frowned on by the Russians. Party members, for example, often send their sons off to relatives in the country for cir-

cumcision, and they themselves even eat pork in public dining rooms. Since these cores of intelligentsia, centers of
diffusion of Soviet Russian culture, exist in the oases as well
as among the Central Asian peoples of tribal origin, the im-
plications will be discussed in a later chapter.

Decorative arts have been strongly subject to alien influence under the Soviet regime. Even in felt work, where traditional motifs prevail, the introduction of aniline dyes has
added new colors and harsher tones. In the decorative bands
woven to strengthen the yurt frame, not only aniline dyes but
new motifs often appear. Embroidery on cloth is derived so
fully from Russian, Ukrainian, and Uzbek models in both
techniques and designs that Kazak traditions are almost entirely absent. Only the interest in embroidery as such follows
the traditional pattern. The carving and painting of wooden
chests and yurt doors continue as an art form. Examples
available suggest a greater variety and harshness of color, and
some new motifs. Silverwork, never widely practiced, appears
to be on the verge of extinction among Kazaks and Kirghiz
and on the wane among Turkomans. Many Turkoman
women still wear massive silver jewelry, but some ornament
their clothes by sewing on silver coins, a transitional practice
observed among Kazaks near Alma Ata in 1934. In Turkmenistan, famous for its rugs, weavers in artels are encouraged to abandon traditional motifs in favor of designs illus-
trating Soviet slogans. In tribal Central Asia in general, the
Soviet models offered, both in guidance of work done by
artels and in manufactured decorative objects offered for sale
in stores, have been either propagandist in content or characteristic in subject and style of lower-middle-class Russian
taste. Only among the Kazaks and Karakalpaks of the lower
Amu Darya, the most conservative of the tribal peoples of
Central Asia, do traditional decorative arts show continuing

vitality. Elsewhere, except for felt work among Kazaks and Kirghiz, and the Kazak interest in embroidery, there seems to be little cultural continuity in the decorative arts. Rather, the old forms are disappearing and there is no evidence to suggest a replacement by new forms.[42]

VI

The Oases
under Communism

IN the oases, the evolutionary gropings of the Muslim intelligentsia toward a social and cultural adjustment to the modern world were abruptly cut short by the events of 1916 and 1917. As among the Kazaks, the Tsar's edict of 1916 calling for a draft of native labor for war work resulted in a series of spontaneous popular local uprisings. Directed initially against the district officials responsible for making up conscription lists, they were put down by force, with considerable loss of life and property. Although order had been restored in the oases by the end of the year, there remained a strong undercurrent of bitterness against the Russian government.

When news of the Tsar's abdication in February, 1917 reached Central Asia, Russian railroad workers lost no time in setting up a soviet in Tashkent. Other groups also organized, and a Congress of Turkistan Muslims meeting in Tashkent called for a democratic government of Turkistan within a Russian federal system. Almost at once, however, the Muslim leaders divided into two camps, a Jadid party favoring reform and a conservative "Union of the Clergy." [1] The Russians in Central Asia also split into several political groups, leaving the field to the small but well-organized Bolsheviks who had a specific plan of action and, after the October revolution, the help of Russian troops and German and Austrian war prisoners. In the ensuing civil war, some Muslim leaders joined the Basmachi revolt, which had been started by convicts released from prison at the outbreak of the revolution. (It is likely that these convicts had become so when the obligations of customary law ran counter to the laws of the state.) Others accepted Bolshevik military aid in the hope of thereby achieving their own goals. Such a group was that of the Young Bukharans, who in 1920 set up a reform government after Bolshevik troops had driven the emir into exile. Later, many of these, disillusioned, joined the Basmachi or were executed as counter-revolutionaries.

The Bolsheviks had hoped that the Central Asian peasants would rise spontaneously against their overlords, as happened on many of the great Russian estates, but the Uzbek and Tajik villagers showed remarkably little class feeling. Instead, their hostility turned against Russians of every political stripe, whom they blamed for the political and economic dislocations of the revolution and the ensuing famine. When grain shipments failed to arrive and the market for cotton vanished in the turmoil of the revolution, grain was planted in former cotton fields to the point where cotten culture was in danger of disappearing. While little involved in the Basmachi revolt themselves, the peasants—particularly in Kokand—looked on Basmachi leaders as heroes of a Jihad, holy war, against the infidel Russians. Muslim mullahs and *ishan*s had always opposed the Russian infidels, and after the Tashkent Bolsheviks ruled the Shariat invalid, their opposition increased and was transmitted to townsmen and villagers alike.[2] The restoration of the Shariat in 1921, when the New Economic Policy was put into effect, did little to reassure the mullahs of Bolshevik Russian intentions, and despite the NEP, economic recovery in Turkistan was laggard.

The years 1917–1927 were devoted largely to the re-establishment of Russian rule—this time Soviet instead of Tsarist—over the peoples of Turkistan. The Soviets strove on the one hand to revitalize the stricken economy, on the other to gain acceptance of the Soviet way of life. There was little popular response to Soviet blandishments. The peasants, the native group the Soviet government was most intent on winning over—there was no native "working class" to speak of, and other parts of the population were usually branded as "reactionary" or "bourgeois-nationalist"—had neither understanding of nor interest in Soviet theory. Indeed, because of the violence of the civil war and the miseries of the famine, there was a deep well of hatred against anything Russian. In the drive to obtain native adherents to their cause, the Soviet program attracted chiefly landless workers and very poor peasants who, having nothing to lose, were willing to try anything that might improve their lot. Such a one was Akun Baba, president of the executive committee of Uzbekistan. Also drawn into the Party were individuals like Faizulla Khoja, a rich merchant of Bukhara who, in order to protect his property, first joined the Young Bukhara party and then, when the Soviet government gained control of Bukhara, became president of the Communist Party in that city. He later became first president of the Council of Commissars of Uzbekistan. Several former interpreters in the Tsarist government, suspected of having been in the employ of the Tsarist secret police, also worked their way into high office in the Party. In tribal regions, Party membership was sometimes used as an instrument in tribal feuds. The average peasant was content with his lot—the only one he knew—and had no interest in creating a new form of agricultural economy. Furthermore, he profoundly distrusted the infidel Russian conquerors, whether they called themselves Soviet or Tsarist, and resented their propagandist efforts. The Soviet administration therefore had to backtrack for a time, returning *waqf* lands, recognizing Shariat law anew, restoring Friday as a day of rest, and striving to give the illusion of popular support by placing natives in high government office.[3]

The first problem of the Soviet government after 1917 was to restore the economy in general and, in particular, to bring back into production those items most needed to revive Russia's own economy—cotton, silk, karakul fur, and wool. Water was essential to productivity in arid Turkistan, and it was by expanding irrigation that the Soviet administration was able to bring the peasants under some sort of control. Although land-water reforms had been instituted in Kazakhstan in 1921–1922, it was not considered feasible to initiate these reforms in Uzbekistan until 1925–1929, and then only in certain districts. However, confiscation of lands and redistribution among poor peasants had much the same result as earlier Tsarist redistribution of lands. To finance the growing of cotton, peasants had to borrow from moneylenders at exorbitant rates. In 1926, a survey of 888 cotton farms showed that over two-thirds of the farmers were in debt.

The sovietization of the peasants of Turkistan, combined with an attempt to bring production up to the 1914 level, required almost superhuman efforts. State credits had to be made available so that farmers could afford to grow cotton. Co-operatives were organized to sell the cotton and buy consumers' products. When agricultural machinery was introduced to lighten the heavy burden of cotton production, it was necessary to overcome a conservative resistance to machinery as such, as well as to train peasants in its use. Early attempts at collectivization had been markedly unsuccessful, and it was only when the land-water reforms made choice land available to those willing to accept collectivization that kolkhozes achieved any importance. In 1924, for example, there were only 62 kolkhozes in Uzbekistan, with a shifting membership, while by 1927 there were 832.

The drive for collectivization under the First Five-Year Plan was attended by drastic measures to enforce conformity. To overcome resistance, not only "kulaks"—prosperous peasants—but many middle peasants, who made up over half the rural population of Uzbekistan, had their lands confiscated and were either liquidated or exiled. Poor peasants were given tax advantages. Attempts were made to create a class struggle and winnow out kulaks who had become heads of village soviets. Since the native peoples, government officials as well as kolkhozniks, were largely unresponsive to collectivization efforts, various devices were invented to introduce Russian agitators, organizers, and technical specialists to spur on the program. The turmoil of collectivization was accompanied by a famine which did not abate until 1934. Eventually, however, the Soviet government was successful, and by the end of the Second Five-Year Plan, 99.2 per cent of the peasants in Uzbekistan had been collectivized.[4]

In addition to restoring Russian control over Turkistan and revitalizing its economy, the Soviet government gave high priority to certain social goals. Education—the "liquidation of illiteracy"—was pressed as zealously in Central Asia as in other parts of the Soviet Union. As elsewhere, the separation of church and state was a first step toward the eradication of religion, regarded as an enemy of the new way of life. Given special emphasis in Muslim areas was the drive to emancipate women. To further this, the legal age of marriage was raised to eighteen; polygamy was legally abolished; and it became a crime for parents to arrange a marriage without the approval of the young couple and to pay a bride price. A great effort was made to persuade women to throw off the veil and play an active role in the economic and political life of the community. Another major target of Soviet effort was the "patriarchal" kin solidarity which, whether that of the extended family of the settled people or of the tribal kin organization of the seminomads, was a potent force of resistance to change. The ultimate Soviet goal was Russianization of the peoples of Central Asia, though this was played down in the early years after the revolution in a program that ostensibly encouraged the development of nationality cultures.

Uzbekistan became a socialist soviet republic in 1924, Tajikistan in 1929. Just what cultural changes occurred in the course of forty years of being pushed and prodded toward the Soviet way of life?

Cultural changes were greater in the towns and cities than in rural areas. In any urban center, modern innovations are introduced more readily than in conservative rural areas, and the concentration of population makes feasible a development of educational institutions, of theaters and concert halls, of stores stocked with a wider variety of goods than is possible in the village, and of mechanized public transportation. In Central Asia, in Soviet as in Tsarist times, Russians tended to concentrate in urban and industrial areas, bringing with them the goods and services favored by Russian culture in food, clothing, household furnishings, music, theater, art and architecture, as well as such personal services as hairdressers. The native inhabitants of the towns and cities, in addition to students and workers who reside there temporarily, are thus subject to much stronger acculturative forces than are rural villagers. There is also a class difference in degree of Russianization. Party members and intelligentsia—those ambitious for status and material benefits in the Soviet world in which they live—are under strong pressures to conform to the Russian way of life. To be accepted, they must display at least the outer manifestations of Soviet Russian culture. In rural areas, the intelligentsia make a conscious effort to wear European clothes, for example, eat Russian-style food, and speak Russian in public, while the rest of the community adheres much more closely to the traditional way of life.

Thus, there is a considerable range in the degree of acculturation, both between urban and rural, and between upper and lower classes. Furthermore, it is often difficult to determine from the Soviet literature the extent of culture change, since descriptions tend to emphasize the Soviet ideal rather than the reality. When Soviet accounts state that the intelligentsia do such and such, this writer has inferred that the rest of the population does not. For deviations from the ideal, one is often dependent on letters to the editor in newspaper campaigns of self-criticism. These must be evaluated with caution, for even statistics can be misleading. In Uzbekistan, for example, according to *Pravda Vostoka,* the sale of potatoes and vegetables per person in 1959 was one-half, of fruit one-fifth, that in the other Central Asian republics.[5] Does this mean that the people of Uzbekistan, who had always eaten more fruits and vegetables than their tribal neighbors in Kazakhstan, Kirgizia and Turkmenistan, were eating less than formerly; were they, as always, raising much of what they needed in their own gardens or, in the case of city-dwellers, buying in the private market? In this case, supporting evidence favors the second interpretation. Often, it is only when the Party and government of a Central Asian republic, or of the Soviet Union, finds it necessary to enact a law or make a policy statement, that one can be sure that the problem is widespread. The following analysis of culture change must, because of the nature of the data, be tentative in many cases, interpretive rather than statistical.

Since Soviet writers give ample coverage to major achievements, we will not here go into the vast irrigation projects which have enabled farmers of Turkistan to increase their production of cotton and other crops needed in the Russian economy, though with every new district brought under cotton cultivation, more peasants are bound firmly to the Soviet economic system because of the special requirements of cotton culture and marketing. Nor will we look into the degree of industrialization that has taken place, though for factory workers there is a greater change from the traditional way of life than among cultivators. Here we are concerned with trying to discover the type and degree of "survivals"—those facets of traditional culture that have managed to persist after forty years of a Russian-propelled drive toward change, a drive that has encompassed force, law, economic pressures, hard-sell propaganda, the soft-sell blandishments of making traditional luxuries readily available to the masses, and the economic and psychological rewards of conformity to the ideal Soviet pattern and punishments for nonconformity.

In agriculture, although the cotton acreage has been greatly increased through the extension of irrigation, there has been a reversion to the pre-Russian system of crop rotation, in which soil impoverished by cotton was planted to alfalfa and, also more recently, to maize, to restore its fertility. Since alfalfa is the preferred fodder for horses, still widely used in rural areas for riding and draft, and maize provides fodder for cattle, this pattern is not likely soon to be changed. Little wheat is now grown in irrigated lands, but in the unirrigated areas, which comprise a large part of the acreage of Uzbekistan and Tajikistan, dry farming (*bogarnyi*) continues to produce the wheat that, because of its superior quality, was always preferred by Central Asians to irrigated wheat. Rice, formerly a luxury food, has increased in production, and millet—always an important food grain among poor marginal farmers—has found an additional use as chicken feed on kolkhoz chicken farms.[6] Kolkhozes in the oases, whatever their major crop, usually raise some of the fruits and vegetables that are a traditional part of the oasis diet, and some kolkhozes specialize in producing these foods for the urban market. Furthermore, both kolkhoz and industrial workers usually have private family gardens with the traditional fruit trees, grape arbors, and vegetables. Although the produce of private garden plots is supposed to be for home use, there is indication that many families raise a surplus for sale on the private market. A letter to *Izvestiia* in 1960 complained that in the neighborhood of Ashkhabad in Turkmenistan, home owners had a monopoly on the sale of those harbingers of spring—green onions, garlic, radishes, and cucumbers—for a month before kolkhoz vegetables were ready for market. In addition to traditional vegetables, such introduced vegetables as potatoes, tomatoes, cabbage, and eggplant are raised in kolkhoz gardens. Potatoes are apparently consumed chiefly by Russians or in public dining rooms managed by Russians, but tomatoes seem to be winning acceptance in the diet of the oasis peoples.[7]

The chief changes in the home diet seem to be that cottonseed oil, formerly used by only the poorest people, has become the chief cooking oil; more meat is eaten; and the Uighur method of steaming meat pasties, a novelty in the 1860's, has been rather widely adopted by both Uzbeks and Russians, as has the Chinese type of noodles introduced by Uighurs and Dungans. For workers who take their midday meal in industrial dining rooms, dietary changes are greater. Although Soviet writers state with pride that pilau, formerly a luxury food, is served in every dining room, the diner may more often be served *kotleti* (chopped meat cakes), sausage, or stuffed cabbage; such restaurant patrons probably find borshcht on the menu more frequently than mutton broth and bakery bread rather than bread flaps. In the towns, women are encouraged to open a tin of meat and cook storebought macaroni which, although not characteristically Russian, is available in most food stores and, because it is mass-produced, conforms to the Soviet ideal. Most oasis people, however, appear to take their chief meal of the day in the evening, at home, in the traditional way and with the traditional foods, and can thus avoid many of the Russian dishes provided in dining rooms that follow the Russian pattern of serving the main meal at midday. Pork, regarded as unclean by Muslims, has not been accepted despite Russian encouragement. It has been pointed out that pig breeding in the republics of Central Asia is in direct ratio to the Russian population of these republics; Central Asians have not been won over to the meat Russians prefer. Although consumption of Russian bread baked in mechanized factories is encouraged, most kolkhozes have native bakers producing the traditional bread flaps. For sweets, local confectioners ply their trade in competition with Russian factory-made candies.[8]

Dastarkhan, the offering of sweets, nuts, and fruits traditionally served to guests, continues to be an important institution. The chief innovation is that, with the Islamic strictures against alcohol removed, a special *dastarkhan* for drinking wine is laid out in a separate room at large parties. In this, the oasis people are following a taste that antedates the introduction of Islam into Central Asia. The general pattern of hospitality and of sharing food has not lost force. In even the lowliest home, when sweets and fruits are not available, bread and tea are served to visitors, and anyone who arrives at mealtime must be offered food. On festive or ceremonial occasions, the special dishes prepared are shared with relatives and neighbors, as are the first fruits of the home garden. Among tribal Uzbeks, the entertainment of guests entails killing a sheep, certain parts of which are given the guest of honor in the traditional way. As of old, hands are carefully washed before and after eating, and when there are guests the customary ewer, bowl, and towel are offered as people sit around the spread cloth. Bread is broken—bread flaps are never cut—and passed out by the senior male, and children are trained not to leave the smallest crumb on the floor, for bread should not be defiled. Children also eat the leavings of guests' food as "god-giving"; the leftovers of students and *ishan*s are believed to transmit knowledge and health. The Soviet model is that of people sitting on chairs at a table of European height, with solid food served on individual plates and liquids in individual bowls, and conveyed to the mouth with forks and spoons. This pattern is followed by intelligentsia in public dining rooms. In the home, however, the low table found in aristocratic oasis homes before the 1917 revolution appears to be finding wider acceptance than the high European table which requires sitting on chairs. Actual Soviet educational efforts seem to be directed toward persuading people to use a spoon in taking solid food from the common platter and toward the use of individual bowls, or at least of one bowl for only two people, for drinking liquid foods.[9]

In housing, the first Soviet goal was to bring family life out into the open, thus making the seclusion of women more difficult. Wide, tree-lined avenues of the Tsarist colonial type were cut through the major cities, and in kolkhozes and industrial towns new dwellings were built along similar broad avenues. In the dwelling itself, the prime symbols of change were glazed windows looking on the street, with a door opening onto the street unmasked by courtyard walls. Gabled roofs of slate or iron were regarded as desirable, apparently simply because they were Russian. In cities and industrial communities, the first impulse in planning was to put up apartment houses. At least some windows facing the street appear to be obligatory for anyone building a new house or remodeling an old one, but in general climate and circumstances have modified the early pattern of Russianization. Apartment houses, in which three small rooms are considered adequate for a family of eight, would be less than comfortable in the long Central Asian summers. Furthermore, the government construction program has never been able to keep pace with population growth. As a consequence, people have been able, to a considerable extent, to follow their cultural inclinations in the construction of new dwellings. In industrial communities, workers are given plots of land and often the necessary building materials with which to build their own homes with the help of friends and neighbors. In urban centers also, when apartment-house construction has not kept pace with housing needs, families are given plots of land at the edge of the city where they can build their own homes. In this way, residential suburbs of one-family homes have grown up around the cities.

More and more, walls are being erected around the plot, as in pre-Soviet days, and an *aivan* faces the interior courtyard where grape arbors are planted to give shade from the summer sun. Flat roofs coated with mud seem to be winning out over gabled roofs of iron or slate, both because they are cheaper and easier to build and because mud is a poor conductor of heat and so keeps the house cooler in summer and warmer in winter. For the same reasons, house walls continue to be constructed of sun-dried brick. Thus, often the chief innovations in the newest homes are in details. There is usually a house foundation of kiln-fired bricks, cement, or cobblestones, and wood floors are not infrequent. People are encouraged to whitewash their walls, inside and out, and to ornament interior walls with the painted designs and carved *ganch* formerly found only in wealthy upper-class homes. The ceilings are sometimes faced with plywood painted in bright colors after the fashion of the old painted roof beams. The *mehmankhane* is not completely separated from the living quarters as in older dwellings, but except among young members of the intelligentsia who sometimes daringly hold soirees attended by both men and women, this guest room is still used by men to entertain their friends.[10] While there is a great range in domestic architecture from the Russian to the traditional, one senses that a modern Central Asian form is evolving which is essentially traditional in its inspiration, but which has adopted from the Russian such features as glazed windows, house foundations, and stoves. Soviet leaders now recognize that the Central Asian dwelling, both in the materials used and in the general layout, with its orientation of the house away from the street and toward a walled court-yard with grape arbors and gardens, is better adapted to the climate of Turkistan than are dwellings of Russian type.

For cooking and heating, stoves of brick, tiles, or of cast iron are coming increasingly into use, but the traditional *sandal* has not disappeared. In the conservative Fergana Valley, the open fireplace remains the center of family life even in modern houses. Facilities for gas and electricity are being extended but appear still to be in the luxury class. Kerosene lamps, however, are found in most homes. Members of the intelligentsia, as well as others exposed to Russian influence and prosperous enough to afford European furniture, have a table, straight chairs, and a metal bed, though most people prefer to sit and sleep on the floor. For great prestige, the home should also include a bookcase, a wardrobe for cloth-ing, and, rarest, a buffet or cabinet for dishes. Most people, however, prefer to display their best dishes in wall niches; and even in homes having European furniture, the chest, bound with metal strips in the style introduced from Moscow in the Tsarist period, occupies a large niche and is piled high with quilts. Even the most Russianized intelligentsia have at least one room in the old Central Asian style. Sewing ma-chines have been readily accepted by those who can afford them (they can be purchased on the installment plan), and radios appear to be fairly widespread. Home decorations are traditional in form, but embroidered wall coverings are often machine stitched. The strongest mark of sovietization in a home is the presence in the guest room of photographs of people, either of friends and relatives or of Party leaders. Few Uzbeks or Tajiks have been able to make a break from the Muslim proscription of the representation of living creatures.[11]

In clothing, changes have been greater for men than for women. As elsewhere in Central Asia, the intelligentsia wear European dress and in rural areas particularly, the mackintosh has become the status symbol of this group. Frequently, young men wear European garments combined with those of native tradition, but older men cling to the *khalat*. Among these older men, there is a tendency to wear quilted *khalat*s throughout the year, not in winter only as was formerly the custom. Many have given up the turban, but the skullcap is still worn, even with European dress. Women, more conservative, cling to old forms and regional color preferences, though many make their costumes of factory-woven materials. As among the Kazaks, the redingote jacket introduced from Russia in the late nineteenth century has become shorter. The *paranja*, which Soviet leaders worked so hard to dislodge, has not completely disappeared; it is seen occasionally even on the streets of Tashkent, that most Russianized of Central Asian cities, though it is now chiefly a ritual costume worn by women attending weddings and funerals. Comparable cloaks traditionally worn over the head in other parts of the oases still persist. In some regions, their present use is largely ritual, but in certain conservative rural areas all women wear them when going into the street. The woman's turban, which was already going out of use in the nineteenth century, is now found only among some seminomadic tribes.

In its place, women wear a shawl over the head, while girls are adopting a skull cap of Tatar origin. In hairdress, however, girls and young women continue to braid their hair in the forty tiny plaits associated with the magical generative properties enclosed in the hair; after the birth of a child, women wear two braids. Children's hoods and skullcaps are often adorned with talismans. Both men and women in rural areas frequently wear high skin boots of Russian style, and Soviet shoe factories make footwear characteristic of the area, as well as European shoes.[12]

The crafts of Turkistan had already undergone considerable change during the Tsarist regime. After the 1917 revolution, Soviet authorities undertook to transform craftsmen into "workers" with all possible speed. First, craft guilds were converted into "professional unions," and artels were formed. Craftsmen continued to work in their own shops for a time, but eventually craft members were brought under one roof. Into these co-operative workshops modern equipment and machinery were gradually introduced, beginning in the 1930's, in a process of conversion to factory production. The oasis crafts have not been completely industrialized; many potters, cutlers, saddlemakers, shoemakers, and others continue to work independently on order, as do professionals who adorn homes with *ganch* or murals. Many weavers of cloth and of rugs work in artels, following traditional craft methods. Despite these retentions, however, factory-manufactured goods are gradually crowding out the old crafts. In Tsarist days factory-woven velvet, velveteen, and plush became favorites for women's jackets, and they remain so. The demand for these materials, as well as for factory-woven shawls, is such that sovkhoz and district kolkhoz shops ration them to customers, giving preference to those with good work records. Silks and satins, once reserved for the rich, are made available to everyone in factory-produced replicas of the traditional weaves and colors. China, aluminum, and enamelware are slowly but relentlessly displacing craft pottery.

In the decorative arts, the Soviet government has encouraged such crafts as brass work, wood carving, *ganch* work, rug weaving, and embroidery. However, the brass work appears limited chiefly to large, circular platters which are hung on the walls of teashops and other public places as ornaments. In wood carving, even when a master craftsman is engaged to carve the doors of a public building, the work lacks the delicacy of nineteenth-century doors for upper-class private homes, and master craftsmen are rewarded for embarking on such subjects as portraits of Lenin. Rug weaving has continued the decline in artistry already noted at the turn of the century, and machine looms have to some extent replaced hand-weaving. The richly embroidered wall hangings every Sart girl used to make for her dowry, with perhaps one or more less ambitious ones done for sale, are now often embroidered on a sewing machine and commercial production has been taken over by men working in artels. The jeweler's craft seems to be nearing extinction. While the Central Asian arts languish, stores stock objects that can best be described as the Russian version of Edwardian lower-middle-class art forms, such as cushions embroidered with sequin-eyed kittens. There are two conflicting trends in the decorative arts. On the one hand, people prefer to decorate their homes in the traditional fashion; and the Soviet government has encouraged the retention of certain art forms by hiring surviving master craftsmen to instruct young people in their crafts and to decorate public buildings. On the other hand, the general effects of industrialization and the influence of culture-bound Russian administrators have led to the debasement of the old arts.[13]

Bazaars are no longer the center of city activity. Many goods are sold through consumers' co-operatives and state-owned stores facing on broad avenues which have been cut through the congested centers of the old cities. Yet, away from the main streets, craftsmen making the same type of goods cluster together in a neighborhood as in the old days. Since there is still a good deal of free trading in fruits, vegetables, livestock, and other products of private initiative, and of grain received by kolkhozniks as part of their wages, there are market places where such commodities can be bought and sold. Nevertheless, the old bazaar, with its teashops and strolling entertainers, appears to have well-nigh disappeared. A European traveler in 1954 remarked of the bazaars of Samarkand that they were "clean" but "colorless." In Bukhara he found teashops where customers sat "cross-legged on the tables, sipping tea, pulling on home-made hookahs and gossiping with all the East's supreme contempt for the passage of time," and he even observed an occasional strolling minstrel and storyteller. By 1958 the authorities were "driving great boulevards through the middle of the old city" of Bukhara "and cementing everything in sight." Replacing the leisurely commerce of the old bazaar, there seems to have been on the one hand a partial reversion to a direct trade between producer and consumer; and on the other, a modern type of free enterprise in which alert entrepreneurs ship fruit and vegetables by bus or train to cities outside the oases, sometimes as far as Moscow, or buy up scarce factory-made goods for resale in the local market. The oasis peoples' cultural interest in trade has retained its vitality, but the forms have been greatly modified.

In transportation, the slow-paced camel has been largely replaced by trains and by motor vehicles running along paved roads. In rural areas, however, the riding horse has not lost its usefulness and kolkhoz produce is moved from the fields in the traditional *arba*. The automobile, still a luxury, is a prestige symbol that can be put to practical use, and the more easily obtainable bicycle serves the same function at a less ambitious level. On the Amu Darya, modern steamers have replaced the old river boats. There appears to have been no cultural resistance to mechanized transport once the people became familiar with the idea of machinery. Unlike the pastoral tribes, the oasis people had no particular cultural commitment to the animals they used for transportation. In the old days they had depended on tribesmen to conduct their caravans and breed most of the camels and horses used in the oases. As speedier and more comfortable means of transportation are made available to them, these are accepted readily enough.[14]

In social organization, the extended joint family of tradition has been under steady attack under the Soviet regime. The concept of joint ownership of property runs counter to the Soviet policy of collectivizing the means of production, and the payment of wages to individuals has upset the balance of a traditional family economy in which the family head controlled income and decided its allocation. The law setting the age of marriage at eighteen, when a girl might have ideas of her own about choice of mate, was intended to lessen parental authority, as did that forbidding the payment of bride price which made a son dependent on his parents. When young people marry, it is now the practice for local administrators to try to provide a separate apartment or the means of building a separate house in order to break the pattern of common residence. These external policies are reinforced by a tendency that in traditional tribal society often led to the fractionization of an *aul,* but which had never been allowed to break up an oasis household in the old days: quarrels and jealousies among daughters-in-law. When such quarrels occur now, the daughter-in-law has administrative support in moving with her husband to a single unit residence. Yet, despite these forces favoring the disruption of the extended joint family, family solidarity has not been destroyed.

In rural areas there are still many joint family households in which sons bring their brides to the paternal residence and all employed members turn over their earnings to the family head. Even when a son establishes a separate residence after marriage, family ties remain strong. Among apartment dwellers the young couple normally obtains an apartment in the same building as that of the man's parents. When a couple obtains a separate house, on the other hand, it is usually in a new part of town, some distance from the old section where the parents live. Nevertheless, very close ties are maintained between the two households, and sons remain responsible for the support of parents in their old age. Parents are gradually becoming adjusted to the idea that it is not a mortal insult for a son to set up his own household on marriage, but it will be a long time before Soviet leaders achieve their ideal of nuclear family units independent of broader family ties. Children are brought up from infancy to respect their fathers and senior members of the family and to reflect in their behavior the relative status of various members of the family, male and female. Such family training is not easily overcome, and while Soviet administrators may support young people against their parents, the local community is not likely to do so. The Soviet government has not yet provided substitutes for all the functions traditional to the Uzbek and Tajik family.[15]

In marriage, members of the intelligentsia, who have been exposed to Russian cultural orientation, sometimes select their own mates, but even these ask for parental approval. Girls particularly are subject to parental wishes. Traditionally, a girl was expected to marry a man of her own social status or higher, and her status was also dependent on the value of the bride price paid for her and on the dowry she received from her parents. Apparently, girls today almost never go counter to the wishes of the parents. In one case where an Uzbek opera singer wished to marry a Russian, she was murdered by her brother. It is possible that educated young women use persuasion or even the threat of elopement to obtain parental permission for marriage to a preferred male, but few cases have been encountered of a girl marrying outside the social class or ethnic group that would traditionally receive family approval. In rural areas, even among intelligentsia and Party members, many girls drop out of school at the traditional age of marriage, an age when they would have little opportunity to form preferences of their own. Even the most Russianized intelligentsia insist that a girl be a virgin until she marries. In the marriage ceremony itself, civil registration is obligatory, and a new Soviet marriage form has been hopefully introduced. Most young people go through the traditional ceremony "to please their parents." The financial exchanges between families of bride and groom have been transformed into "gifts," and the bride's dowry sometimes includes European furniture, which satisfies the traditional pattern in that it is expensive and prestige-giving. The length of the marriage feasts at the homes of bride and groom has been curtailed, and the traditional ritual has become attenuated and changed. Details of the old rites are often forgotten, and in their place new elements have often crept in, such as modern songs or those borrowed from other ethnic groups. The old professional entertainers have either disappeared or become "People's Artists," but in their place parttime musicians, who work at some other trade during the day, are hired to perform at weddings, and families who can afford it employ a "People's Artist" to the tune of several thousand rubles for an evening's entertainment. Marriages are still very expensive.[16]

The emancipation of women was a major goal of Soviet

policy from the time Soviet power was established in Central Asia. In the late 1920's and early 1930's, emotional public meetings were organized in which women were exhorted to throw off their veils and cast them into bonfires. Such a gesture required great courage, particularly among the Tajiks, for during the Basmachi revolt of the 1920's the assassination of "emancipated" women was not infrequent. Special women's artels were formed and women's brigades were organized in the kolkhozes to bring women into the labor force. Much has been achieved in this direction. Many women walk along the streets unveiled and do not turn away at sight of a strange man. Girls attend coeducational schools, women work on kolkhozes, and some have entered the arts and professions. For women to perform in public, as do opera singers and film actresses, is a radical change from traditional attitudes which made *déclassée* any woman who performed professionally, even before an audience of women only.

For the most part, however, oasis women lag behind their tribal sisters, the Kazaks and Kirghiz, in progress toward emancipation. In the field of education, there are statistics to support an impression derived from other data. In the academic year 1960–1961, for example, the enrollment of Uzbek woman students in VUZ (13,219) was only some 300 more than of Kazak women (12,900), although the total Uzbek population was almost double that of the Kazaks (5,038,000 to 2,795,000 in 1959). Kirghiz women students outnumbered Tajiks 2,878 to 1,900 despite a considerably larger Tajik population (837,000 to 1,051,000 in 1959). Among students in VUZ, 32 per cent of Kazak students were women, 29 per cent of Kirghiz, 25 per cent of Uzbeks, and only 16 per cent of Tajiks. Even the culturally conservative Turkomans and Karakalpaks made a better showing than the Tajiks, with 21 per cent and 19 per cent of women students.[17]

This contrast between progressive tendencies among

women of tribal origin and conservatism among those of the oases is also brought out in a Karakalpak community that had settled in the Fergana Valley in the eighteenth and early nineteenth centuries. There, customs associated with the former inferior position of women were disappearing much more quickly among the Karakalpaks than among their Uzbek neighbors.[18] That Uzbek women make a much better showing than Tajiks in education is due perhaps partly to the presence of Tashkent, long the chief center for the diffusion of Russian culture in Uzbekistan, perhaps partly to the fact that many Uzbeks are of tribal origin. Such Uzbek regions as Samarkand, Surkhan Darya, and Khiva appear to be as conservative as Tajikistan. In these regions polygamy is widespread, women cover their faces in the presence of men, and husbands often refuse to allow their wives to be treated by a male doctor. Even in Tashkent some *paranja*s are seen on the streets, while in Fergana, according to reports, active Party members often go into seclusion after marriage.

It is not only among the poor and ignorant in remote villages that old customs persist. In one of the most prosperous districts of Fergana, kolkhoz presidents and members of village soviets are most inclined to seclude their wives, women who, though formerly active in the Party, are not demonstrably averse to being secluded. Polygamy and the rigid seclusion of women, which could be practiced most extensively only by the upper classes in old oasis society, appear to have been adopted as status symbols by the new upper class—Party members and kolkhoz and Soviet officials. In 1963, plenums of the Central Committee of all the Central Asian republics expressed concern over the persistence of such "feudal-bay" attitudes toward women.[19]

Old social ties beyond the family also appear to persist with considerable vitality. The kolkhoz comprises essentially the old local group of the *qishlaq* (village), and young people who leave for special training usually return to the natal village on completion of their studies. It is the Soviet hope that they will act as agents in the dissemination of Russian culture, introducing to their fellow villagers the ideas and patterns of behavior they have acquired in the cities. This they undoubtedly do to a certain extent, but it is also possible that on returning to the village they are drawn anew into the old way of life.

In the towns and cities, the Soviets have used ward associations as centers for the propagation of the Soviet way of life, with committees to police the life of the ward and to organize such activities as meetings, lectures, exhibits, and projects that will bring women out of seclusion. In the wards as in the villages, however, Soviet efforts appear to run into quiet resistance. The older people continue to exert considerable influence on public opinion, since children are still brought up to respect their elders. Thus, despite Soviet efforts, the ward system, like that of the *qishlaq*-turned-kolkhoz, tends to support the retention of traditional customs and attitudes. Among Uzbeks of tribal origin, tribal kinship ties remain so strong that in the 1950's a program was instituted of forming new, small villages in order to break up the traditional population patterns. Even the craft guilds have shown remarkable persistence in the face of industrialization. Indeed, new guilds have been formed on the traditional pattern for such modern occupations as those of chauffeur and riverboat crews. The history and secrets of the craft that had been written out in the old guild *risola*s can no longer be replaced or, perhaps, even be read since they were written in the Arabic script. Nevertheless, the contents are now transmitted orally from generation to generation.[20]

Religion, almost from the beginning, was a major target of Soviet policy in Central Asia. In Russia, where the Greek Orthodox Church had been a dominant force for conservatism among the masses, atheism became a basic tenet of Soviet dogma. In Central Asia also the mullahs and *ishan*s were potent forces for conservatism. Beyond this, they had used religion as a rallying point for resistance to Russian encroachment, both Tsarist and Soviet. In the early years after the 1917 revolution, Soviet leaders utilized the mosque, which traditionally had been the social center for the men of a ward or village, as a center for the organization of kolkhozes and for general indoctrination. However, as soon as was feasible, mosques were closed, and the property of dervish orders expropriated. The *medresseh*s which had trained religious leaders were also closed, and pilgrimages to Mecca and Medina were forbidden. It was made clear by Party organizers and officials that adherence to Muslim practices was not the way to advancement in the Soviet order; attendance at a mosque was noted and during Ramazan people were tested by offers of cigarettes or food. Finally, during the purges of 1932–1938, a majority of the religious leaders were liquidated. Thus, by the beginning of World War II much of the formal organization of the Muslim religion had disappeared, including facilities for education. Except for a comparatively few old men trained before the revolution, who had to remain in hiding, there was no one to transmit Muslim learning to new generations. Many members of the intelligentsia did not know how to perform the daily prayers.

With World War II there was a change in Soviet policy. In order to win the sympathy of Muslim countries to the south, Islam was given some semblance of respectability within the Soviet union. Muslim spiritual directorates were established in 1941, one for Central Asia and Kazakhstan with headquarters in Tashkent. These directorates were given permission to publish the Koran as well as some religious calendars, but in Tashkent facilities for printing the Koran were not made

XI. Uzbek master craftsman displays a carved slab of *ganch*—plaster made from gypsum and loess. (Sovfoto.)

XII. Tajik pensioners enjoy *dastarkhan* at a collective farm rest home. Architecture and furnishings combine modern and traditional forms. (Sovfoto.)

available until 1958. In that year, a visitor to Central Asia observed that the mosque in Samarkand had "an enormous and obviously devout congregation," and was told by the Grand Mufti of Tashkent that far more people were then worshipping at the mosques then ever before. Just where the mullahs who preside at these mosques were trained is not clear. The one or two *medressehs* reported could not begin to train enough mullahs and other Muslim officials to serve the needs of the oasis population. Yet, a 1945 visitor to Central Asia reported his impression that there were many more candidates to become mullahs in Central Asia than in Turkey. One is inclined to believe the rumors heard by a visitor in the late 1950's that a number of clandestine Koran schools existed. Certainly the officially recognized *medressehs* have no difficulty in enrolling students—young men who have completed their secondary school studies in the Soviet educational system and presumably realize that by their entry into a *medresseh* they are closing the door to advancement in the Soviet system. Perhaps they make this choice in expectation of respect and honor among their own people.[21]

While the Soviet government was introducing a semblance of religious tolerance as a part of foreign policy, wartime stresses were creating a popular need for the psychological security that religion offers. Actually, much of the folk religion of Central Asia has roots that long antedate Islam in the area and that were associated with Islam only through the participation of mullahs and *sheikhs* in the ceremonies. These rituals and beliefs, deeply embedded in the folkways of the people, could continue without formal Islamic training, and they appear to have done so. However, because Soviet antireligious propagandists have treated such folk religion as a part of Islam, there is some suggestion that "Islam" may have become a rallying point for nationalism, or at least for a

175

sentiment of non-Russian ethnic identity. As an Uzbek Party official expressed this feeling, "the Muslim religion is the Mother of the Uzbek people." [22]

For an indication of the persistence of specifically Muslim practices, one may first consider the "five pillars." 1. No information is available on the profession of faith, *la ilah illa Allah; Muhammad rasul Allah* (no god but Allah; Muhammed is the messenger of Allah). It has been written of Muslims that "these are the first words to strike the ear of the newborn Moslem babe; they are the last to be uttered at the grave. Between these two episodes no other words are more often repeated." [23] Since the profession can be made at any time and the formula is simple and easily remembered, this could have persisted, unnoted or unreported by Soviet or Western observers. 2. Even in the days of the khanates, the five daily prayers were not strictly observed in rural areas, and in Tashkent, prayers in public fell off noticeably after the office of *reïs* was abolished by the Tsarist government. Although there is an occasional newspaper complaint of some individual taking time off from work to say his prayers, it seems likely that comparatively few know how to perform the prayers. Prayers are no longer held obligatory by the Soviet-sponsored spiritual directorate. 3. Almsgiving in the khanates took the form of paying *zakat* as a state tax, but it was popularly believed that if a part of a man's earnings were not given for religious purposes, his income would suffer. In the high Pamirs, Tajiks of the Ismaili faith are said to pay *zakat* to collectors for the Aga Khan from Pakistan. The Grand Mufti of Central Asia, though appointed by the Soviet government, receives no subsidy from that authority. His funds, which are said to be ample, come from the people. The popular shrines of local saints, which by all accounts have many visitors, are also supported by the gifts of the people. 4. Fasting during the month of Ramazan has been a particular target of Soviet activists because it reduces the efficiency of workers. In pre-Soviet days, it was strictly observed in the towns and cities, less often observed in rural areas. No precise data are available on the present distribution of fasting, but informants who had left Central Asia around 1941 and who for the most part did not know how to perform the daily prayers were all familiar with fasting; they reported both the efforts of officials to spy out and deter the practice and the compromises made by people unable to fast for the full twenty-eight days of Ramazan. According to more recent information, children in many families begin fasting at the age of eight or nine, and the practice continues to be a source of Soviet complaint. 5. Pilgrimages to Mecca were always limited to such a small number that the title *hajji* gave great prestige. These have now been reduced to token parties. While the interruption of pilgrimages to the city held holy by all Muslims hinders communication with the Muslim world outside the Soviet Union, this is not necessarily a criterion of lapse of Muslim faith in Central Asia. Before the introduction of the railroad in Tsarist times, the pilgrimage to Mecca had been an arduous one in the course of which many pilgrims died. Most people fulfilled the requirement of the fifth pillar by making the tour of local saints' shrines which Central Asian mullahs accepted as an equivalent to the journey to Mecca. Visits to local shrines have increased greatly since World War II, but there is no clue as to whether these are regarded as pilgrimages in this sense.[24]

Of other practices immediately associated with Islam, circumcision remains practically universal. Among many it continues to be accompanied by the ritual and feasting characteristic of an important family rite of passage. For Khwarizm it has been described as "the formal admittance of a child into the Muslim community." [25] Among some Central Asians it is explained as a health measure, and when no

177

special itinerant Muslim practitioner is available, the operation is performed by a barber or anyone else with the skill. Circumcision appears to have become a symbol of ethnic identity; one of the reasons advanced for forbidding the marriage of Uzbek and Tajik girls with Russian and other European men is their uncircumcized state.[26] Qurban Bayram, commemorating Abraham's sacrifice, has perforce lost its character of a public celebration. Up to the outbreak of World War II, it was usually a close family affair, observed "with windows shut and the doors locked." [27] At that time, it was difficult to obtain sacrificial animals, but with the increase in privately owned animals sold in the free market, this is no longer a problem. There is no way of discovering what proportion of the population still observes the sacrifice, but Qurban Bayram is still celebrated, apparently rather widely. For the festival at the end of Ramazan, which in pre-Soviet days was not as important as Qurban Bayram, it was reported that in 1960 many members of one Uzbek kolkhoz absented themselves from work to attend a ceremony at the neighborhood shrine.[28]

Folk religion maintains a strong hold on the people. Important are the family rites that mark the passage of an individual through life. Many women still go through the traditional cradle ritual for a daughter's first-born son, although in the cities a crib or perambulator is sometimes substituted for the cradle. Girls change their style of hairdress on marriage. Circumcisions and weddings continue to be major occasions for most families, though changes in the traditional ritual have been noted. Funeral and memorial ceremonies also are reported to be both impressive and expensive. Midwives, who play an important role in various rituals of infancy, command a fund of traditional lore and magical recipes and in rural areas are still frequently called in to treat women's illnesses in preference to doctors with modern training. A belief in evil eye and nature spirits persists among many, and even in such cities as Tashkent, small children wear decorative amulets on their caps. During World War II, people consulted fortune tellers in their anxiety for absent members of the family. Most noticeable of religious survivals is the cult of saints' tombs. These shrines, always popular, appear to have become centers of religious activity in the oases, perhaps taking over former functions of the mosques as well as continuing their own. It is at such shrines that public ceremonies are celebrated, and even highly educated Central Asians visit them.[29]

"Mullahs" not only preside at those mosques now open, but are frequently called in to officiate at circumcisions, weddings, funerals, and other ceremonies. As of yore, *sheikhs* serve at the shrines, receiving sacrificial offerings as well as other payments for their services. Yet, from the establishment of Soviet power until 1941 there were no officially recognized schools where clergy could be trained, and after that date there have been only one or two *medressehs*. Many men trained before the revolution were liquidated during the purges of the 1930's. Who, then, are these mullahs and *sheikhs* who serve the religious needs of the people? Traditionally, Muslim education was based on memorization. At the *mektebs*, schoolboys memorized passages of the Koran by rote, and comparatively few learned to read, much less to write. Many of the mullahs who officiated at family ceremonies in the old days performed the ritual from memory. While some learned men who escaped the purges have secretly taught students in book learning—one such school has been reported in Kirgizia—it seems probable that, at the very time when most Central Asians have become literate, their mullahs may have reverted to the practices of illiterate or nonliterate peoples and transmit religious lore orally. Certainly, mullahs and *sheikhs* there are, far more than could have survived the purges or been trained in the one or two post-1941 *medressehs*.[30]

The *sheikh*s who presided at saints' shrines were traditionally members of dervish orders who administered the shrine for the benefit of the order. Almost no information is available on the present organization of the shrines. It is possible that many of the *sheikh*s are now independent. Some orders or brotherhoods still exist, however, though those mentioned in the literature were in Kazakhstan and Kirgizia, not in the oases. There has been an interesting development in Khwarizm and perhaps other parts of Uzbekistan. Shamanistic possession, in which the shaman characteristically works himself into a dissociational state to the rhythm of a tambourine and, frothing at the mouth, is believed to be possessed by a spirit control who speaks through him, was widespread among the Kazaks and other tribal peoples of Central Asia, but was not reported for the settled peoples of the oases. One Soviet ethnographer wrote that by the end of the nineteenth century only women were shamans in most parts of Uzbekistan, but the author offers no evidence to support this statement. Another ethnographer reported that in Khiva and some other districts of Khwarizm both male and female shamans are still fairly numerous and are frequently called in to cure illness. There, shamanesses have formed a "sisterhood" on the pattern of the oasis brotherhoods, who traditionally reached an ecstatic dissociational state of an entirely different kind. In Khwarizm, the region for which some detailed information on shamanism is available, tribal Uzbek culture was much more pronounced in the late nineteenth century than in Bukhara or Tashkent, where most of the people had a long sedentary tradition. In Khiva, we seem to have a tribal pattern of women shamans organizing themselves on the model of oasis brotherhoods who traditionally never admitted women.[31]

Soviet authorities have attempted to combat persistent folk

beliefs and practices in several ways. First, new rituals have been introduced in the hope of replacing the old ones which had been such a vital part of traditional family and community life. Instead of the cradle ceremony for the first-born child, in which only women participate, a family party is encouraged at which husband and wife play host to friends and relatives of both sexes. Such a party is sometimes given on the birth of each child, with birthdays celebrated annually thereafter. According to one source, birthday celebrations are becoming popular in rural areas as well as in the towns.

"Red wedding" ceremonies have been introduced as an ideal model, as well as civil funerals patterned on Russian mortuary customs with religious aspects deleted. Much is done to encourage family parties celebrating graduation from school or receipt of Soviet honors, and in one region of Kazakhstan, a program was introduced to plant a fruit tree for every birth and marriage. Christmas trees are displayed in the schools, and in schools and places of work, New Year's Eve parties are given in the hope of displacing the traditional Nau Ruz celebration which takes place in March. Because major Muslim festivals such as Qurban Bayram often come during a period of agricultural activity, an attempt has been made to substitute new festivals held before spring planting and after the harvest. A cotton picking festival, with *ulaq* (*baïga*) and other contests on horseback (indigenous to Uzbeks of tribal origin) and "folk" dancing (not indigenous), was introduced in 1951, but this seems to have been less than successful. In 1964, it was announced that new "Hammer and Sickle" festivals were to be introduced in Uzbekistan. These were to be held in rural areas before the spring planting, and after the harvest in the towns and cities.[32] These substitute ceremonies, which are essentially Russian in form, do not appear to have been taken up to any extent by the peoples of Central Asia.

Some of these ceremonies and celebrations are admittedly

limited to schools and places of work where they are organized by Soviet administrators or activists. Others, such as birthday parties, Red weddings, and civil funerals, appear to be observed chiefly by members of the intelligentsia who, under the pressures of both Soviet activists and their own community, often go through both the Soviet and traditional ceremonies. The hold of religion, both folk and formal, on the people is illuminated by the antireligious activities of the Soviet government. The League of Militant Atheists, which had been responsible for antireligious propaganda during much of the 1920's and 1930's, became inactive in 1938 or 1939, but immediately after World War II a new organization was founded, the Association for the Propagation of Political and Scientific Knowledge, for the purpose of counteracting the religious resurgence of the war years. Attached to the Communist Party, it organizes antireligious lectures (in 1951, 10,000 were given in Uzbekistan) and furnishes articles for publication in kolkhoz and other local newspapers.

Since much of the Central Asian folk religion is associated with beliefs concerning the cause and cure of disease, religion is attacked from another direction by Soviet-trained medical practitioners who are supported by the findings of research institutions in Central Asia. In all Central Asian republics, women of the local nationalities are encouraged to study medicine. Since in many homes only women can treat women and infants, women medical workers alone can hope to break the influence of the traditional midwife.[33] But progress appears to be slow.

In one aspect of Islam—a taboo on the drinking of alcoholic beverages—the Soviet administration has been unintentionally effective in overcoming religious restraints. In pre-Islamic times, the oasis peoples were noted for their wine, and there is ample evidence that under Islam the art of wine making was not lost. Thus, the Soviet removal of restrictions on the partaking of alcohol may simply have made oasis people less secretive in their wine bibbing. It is also possible that when a special *dastarkhan* for wine drinking is laid out on the occasion of large family festivals, there is an element of imitating the drinking practices of khans and high officials in pre-Russian days, just as Soviet officials of Central Asian birth imitate the behavior of the former upper classes in taking plural wives and keeping them in seclusion. Beyond this, however, the Russians have introduced the Russian pattern of vodka drinking. Because of the high profit to be made from the sale of vodka, some restaurants, food and soft-drink shops, and teahouses sell wine and vodka as an easy way of achieving their sales target. While drunkenness appears to be particularly prevalent in localities where the Russian population is large, a heavy sale of alcoholic beverages is reported for Khwarizm, one of the most culturally conservative parts of Uzbekistan. Cigarettes appear to have replaced the *chilim* or water pipe to some extent, but the continued use of *nos,* a mixture of powdered tobacco, lime, and flavoring placed under the tongue, is widespread. The comparatively high incidence of cancer of the mouth among oasis people has been attributed to this practice.[34]

In the realm of popular entertainment, the informal appears to have survived better than that requiring organization. Many traditional children's games are played with only minor adaptations to changing culture, and in rural villages, groups of men of the same age meet as of old in the home of each in turn for convivial conversation on winter evenings. The institution of the *chaikhane* (teahouse), traditionally a favorite gathering place for oasis men, has been encouraged by the Soviet government as useful for the informal dissemination of information. Chess remains a favorite diversion at the teahouses; whether the patrons still indulge in gambling is not recorded. For the rest, Russian influence is strong. Gone are the dancing boys. The troops of professional entertainers who formerly performed in the bazaar on market days, on the *maidan* for public festivals, and at weddings and other family celebrations, have been broken up, though some of them were still active in the late 1930's, and "an occasional strolling minstrel" was observed in Bukhara as late as 1954. The popular puppet theater has become the concern of museums preserving records of extinct culture. Some performers, such as clowns and tightrope walkers, have joined Soviet circuses, while other clowns and storytellers perform in theaters and on the concert stage. The often mordant satire of the old comics has been harnessed and directed against targets designated by the Soviet regime. If they manage to give a double edge to their satire, as they often did under the khans, this has not been recorded, though satire directed toward administrative abuses and misapplication of directives appears in oasis newspapers. A satirical monthly, *Khorpushtak* ("The Hedgehog"), published in Tajikistan was said to have a circulation of 10,000. Apparently the traditional entertainers most successful in adjusting to changed times have been the musicians, particularly singers. Once established as "People's Artists," they are assured of steady employment and income derived from performing at state-organized concerts; in addition, they are much in demand at weddings and other private parties where the most famous are paid enough to support a private automobile, plural wives, a large private dwelling, and other luxuries accorded the new Soviet upper class.[35] During World War II, Tashkent became a haven for Russian and Ukrainian film producers, and after the war, a native film industry was developed. Its films are often shown during the summer in the Russian-style parks of culture and rest which have sprung up at the edge of Central Asian cities and industrial towns. Much earlier, the Soviets had introduced the performing art forms regarded as most important in Russian culture: opera, theater, and ballet. Since the oasis peoples had no tradition in these arts, visiting Azerbaijani and Tatar troupes served as models for the Turkistan style, which is subject to the influence of Russian tastes and techniques,[36] just as the traditional professional entertainers, where they survived at all, have had to adapt to the Russian pattern of circuses, variety shows, and concerts.

The oasis peoples were always essentially sedentary in their entertainment. Other than playing such games as chess or gambling, their cultural preference was to watch and listen to the entertainment provided by professional entertainers, animal fights, or the random diversions of *tamasha*. Such active sports as horse racing were indulged in chiefly by Uzbeks who had not forgotten their tribal traditions. The Soviet government has introduced active sports of the European type and stadiums, swimming pools, and gymnasiums have been constructed in the cities and larger, more Russianized towns. There is physical culture training, with gymnastics, football, volleyball, and basketball, and competitive matches between the football teams of large factories. This sports program, with rewards for achievement comparable to those in other parts of the Soviet Union, has produced some Uzbek "master" sportsmen and sportswomen, but they seem to be drawn from communities under strong Russian influence. The conservative Tajiks appear to have very few sportsmen and it seems unlikely that the average Uzbek of oasis origin has been diverted from the sedentary pleasures of sitting, talking, and watching others.[37]

The introduction of Soviet education in the oases met the same difficulties as among tribal peoples: lack of textbooks and of teachers qualified in the vernacular. In addition, the sedentary peoples of the oases displayed a particularly strong resistance to the education of girls. Girls in the oases now attend school for the elementary grades, but this is just an extension of the age at which little girls were traditionally allowed to play with boys. There is still strong resistance to sending them to middle school, particularly among Tajiks and rural Uzbeks. In the Panj district of Tajikistan, for example, of 3,944 girls who entered school in 1952, only 25 completed six grades and of these only 14 finished the full ten-year course. In the Hissar district, of 2,000 girls entering the middle school, only six graduated. In the Uzbek village of Niiazbashi, with a population of 10,000, 38 girls were enrolled in secondary school in 1956–1957.[38] It is clear that most oasis families resist allowing their daughters the freedom of school associations when they reach marriageable age.

The Tajiks, most conservative in their attitude toward the education of women, reacted with equal conservatism to the program of vocational training initiated in 1958. In this, students in secondary schools were expected to devote part of their time to vocational training, which in effect meant working in industry or on kolkhozes, and to go to work after completion of the middle school education, either postponing advanced training or undertaking this in evening school or by correspondence courses. Tajik parents objected to this, feeling that their sons should be allowed to go directly from middle school to VUZ or at least to a proper technical school. This vocational program might be expected to keep more secondary school graduates in the home locality after completion of their studies. In one Uzbek community, out of forty-three graduates in 1959, thirty remained on the kolkhoz.[39] At about the same time that the vocational training program was instituted, the total time devoted to elementary and middle school courses was reduced from eleven to ten years. The Soviet purpose of the shift to vocational training, which applied to all parts of the Soviet Union, was to increase the labor force and also to impress students with the idea that manual labor was not demeaning to people of education. How effective this program will be in its second goal among the oasis people remains to be seen, for they share with the peoples of southern Asia the notion that educated people should not soil their hands with manual labor.

The most immediate effect of the program of vocational training might be to reduce the number of students who go on to higher education. For those who wished to continue their education, there would be an additional problem. Either it would be necessary to lower the standards of the universities and other institutions of higher learning, which Central Asian students already have difficulty entering because of poor preparation, or the number capable of meeting the entrance requirements would have to be diminished. In either event, the result would be to reduce the already inadequate number of qualified teachers in the schools offering instruction in the nationality language. If, as might be supposed, the vocational training program kept more students on the kolkhoz after graduation, it could retard acculturation. Children are under the influence of the home until they reach school age; the Russian system of crèches has had little success in Turkistan. During their school years, the children receive some ideas alien to their home environment, but they continue to receive cultural indoctrination in the home. If their schooling is curtailed by a "vocational training" which, according to reports, consists of augmenting the labor force by performing traditional work instead of acquiring, as was envisaged when the program was set up, new technical skills; and if, further, they continue to do such work in the home locality after completion of the middle school course, then the cultural influence of home and locality would be much greater than that exerted by a few teachers and administrators who had had some experience in the larger Soviet world. The vocational training program and the retreat to the ten-year school is undoubtedly a zag in the zigzag of Soviet policy, but like other such shifts in Soviet policy made to meet some all-Union rather than specifically Central Asian need, it could have the effect of reinforcing Central Asian culture.

VII

Russian Influence on Central Asian Languages

IT has been written that "every language reflects, and is in some of its features linked up with, the culture of the people speaking it, and is liable to undergo changes in these particular features in accordance with changes in the culture of the people." [1] A consideration of what has happened to the languages of Central Asia may thus give a clue to the degree and kind of change in other aspects of culture.

Before the 1917 revolution, all the peoples of Central Asia had employed the Arabic alphabet in writing. Although the Arabic lack of interest in vowel sounds contrasted strongly with the emphasis placed on vowels in Turkic vocalic harmony, these limitations of the Arabic alphabet had the effect of obscuring to some extent dialectal differences among the Turkic languages. [2] Thus, literate Central Asians of Turkic speech could, without too much difficulty, read the literature of other Turkic peoples. This permitted communication not only among the Turks of Central Asia but also with other Turks in the Russian Empire, notably the Kazan and Crimean Tatars, and with Turkey, which in the nineteenth century was a gateway for Islamic thought and for new European political concepts. The use of the same alphabet for Turkic, Persian, and Arabic also facilitated the borrowing and comprehension of Persian and Arabic terms among Turkic speakers. In addition, it encouraged multilingual scholarship. All Central Asian students received training in Arabic, and many educated Uzbeks read Persian and found pleasure in the classic poets of Persia. So many educated Tajiks read Uzbek that after the 1917 revolution they questioned the need of a separate Tajik literary language. The Arabic script was thus something all the Central Asian peoples had in common, both as a familiar system of writing and as a symbol of religious and cultural ties with the larger Islamic world. A few scattered attempts to introduce the Cyrillic alphabet in the nineteenth century had been ineffective.[3]

Following the 1917 revolution, the first impulse of Soviet leaders was to modify the Arabic script universally used by educated Central Asians in writing the languages traditional to the area. In 1923, an improved Arabic alphabet was adopted for Uzbek, and at about the same time, similar alphabets were introduced for Kazak and Kirghiz. However, to a Soviet government that had had to establish its control over Central Asia by force, the dangers soon became obvious of allowing its people to continue the use of an alphabet that at once separated them from Russians and gave them a common mode of expression with Muslim neighbors outside the Soviet Union. In 1925 the importation of materials printed in the Arabic alphabet was forbidden by decree. As early as 1924, a Latin alphabet had been introduced into Soviet Azerbaijan just across the Caspian Sea from Central Asia. In 1926, at a Turcological Congress at Baku, it was proclaimed that a Latin alphabet was to be adopted for all the Turkic languages of the Soviet Union. A year later, a Unified Turkic Latin Alphabet was presented for propagation, with a few symbols added to represent special Turkic phonemes. This modified Latin alphabet, officially introduced for use in writing Central Asian languages in 1928 (in 1929–1930 for

Turkomans), did not arouse great resistance among Central Asian scholars. Like the Arabic alphabet it replaced, it provided a common script for all Turkic speakers. It was better adapted to the Turkic phonetic system than was Arabic, and many Central Asian scholars were aware of the move toward a Latin alphabet in Turkey. As it happened, the Latin alphabet adopted in November, 1928 under the leadership of Kemal Atatürk was almost identical with that officially introduced in Central Asia in the same year.[4] Tajik scholars were less pleased with the Latin alphabet adopted for the writing of Tajik, for it emphasized dialectal differences between Tajik and standard Persian.

The adoption of the Latin alphabet coincided with the campaign undertaken throughout the Soviet Union to eradicate illiteracy. By 1930, all the languages of Central Asia had been provided with Latin alphabets, and these were used in the textbooks prepared for the new schools being set up, and in the newspapers, journals, and books published by newly established presses. Many hundreds of thousands of adults and school children learning to read for the first time knew only the Latin alphabet. Unfamiliar with the Arabic script, they were cut off from the classic works that comprised the literary tradition of Central Asia. The Koran and its commentaries became closed books, as did the Persian poetry of Sa'di, Firdausi, and Hafiz and the scholarly works produced during the golden days of learning in Samarkand and Bukhara. For the generations beginning their education in Soviet schools and adult education classes, the literary blackboard was wiped clean, ready for new writing.

But Turkey's adoption of a similar Latin alphabet aroused new fears in Soviet leaders. There was a potential danger that a new Pan-Turkic literature might develop in the Latin alphabet and that this new script, like the Arabic one before it, might attract the Central Asian peoples toward Turkey and away from Russia. Confronted with this possible danger, Soviet policy-makers and linguists turned to the literary languages of Central Asia. The alphabet was after all only a system of symbols created to record languages. The fact that the Latin alphabet introduced into Central Asia was particularly attuned to the phonetic needs of the Central Asian languages offered possibilities for emphasizing differences among the several languages. This had already been demonstrated in Tajik, where phonetic differences between Tajik and standard Persian had been brought out by the introduction of the Latin alphabet.

As for the language, the Uzbeks had a literary language that had begun to take form in the seventeenth century and had evolved further during the period of Tsarist rule. After the 1917 revolution, Soviet scholars sought to develop from this base a national literary language. Uzbek scholars had favored retention of the Arabic alphabet to which they were accustomed but, whatever the alphabet, they hoped to achieve a literary language that would serve the Uzbek people by incorporating grammatical and vocabulary peculiarities of all Uzbek dialects. Furthermore, they drew on rural dialects that retained the vowel harmony characteristic of Turkic speech rather than on the Iranicized dialects of Tashkent and other cities where this element had been largely lost. As new European terms entered the Uzbek language on the wave of political change and industrialization, Uzbek scholars attempted to replace them with words of Arabic or Persian origin, or by forming new Turkic words to fill new terminological needs. Their goal was to aid the development of a vehicle of communication for all the Uzbek people. Kazak scholars also were eager to further the growth of the literary language that had been developed by Kazak writers during the Tsarist period not only for poetry, a traditional literary form, but also for novels, a new form for

Kazaks. Turkoman scholars, with a limited literary tradition, argued over whether the new Soviet literary language should be developed from older forms or based on Anatolian Turkish, while Tajik scholars were quite content with the literary language they shared with their Persian neighbors across the border.

The goals of Central Asian scholars received little attention from Russian linguists working under Soviet directive. In a first move, the Tashkent dialect, which under Persian influence had almost entirely lost the vowel harmony characteristic of Turkic, was chosen as the base for grammar and vocabulary of the Uzbek literary language, while the phonetics were drawn from the dialect of Turkestan, an oasis town in southern Kazakhstan, which retained vowel harmony. This language, which could be read and usually understood by Kazaks, Karakalpaks, and Turkomans, showed promise of becoming a lingua franca for the peoples of Central Asia. In 1937 the Uzbek literary language was changed to conform phonetically with the Iranicized dialects of Tashkent, Samarkand, Bukhara, and other cities that had lost vocalic harmony.[5] In other Central Asian republics also, the trend of Soviet policy was toward the adoption, for the literary language of the republic, of the dialect of a large urban or administrative center. Such a policy has support in history. In many parts of the world, the standard language of the country developed from that of the administrative center. The French language, for example, evolved from the dialect of the region where the French kings held their courts, but the *langue d'oïl* became standard throughout France only after many centuries. The Soviet government sought to establish such a standard language within a generation through the use of modern industrial methods of communication. In Central Asia of the 1930's, the new would-be standard languages were employed in textbooks, newspapers, and books, but they often differed considerably from the regional dialects used in conversation.

As it turned out, these new standard languages did not have a generation, or even a decade, to become established. The use of the Latin alphabet for the Central Asian languages made more difficult the learning of Russian, written in a different alphabet, and impeded the reception of Russian vocabulary into the native languages. By the end of the 1930's, there was a generation of Central Asians who had learned to speak and read Russian and who had come to appreciate the importance of a competence in Russian for attaining economic and political status under the Soviet regime. Furthermore, the purges of 1932–1938 had liquidated many of the Central Asian scholars who had made one transition from Arabic to Latin script and might have objected strongly to another. With memory of these purges strong, those who survived had little spirit to resist. In 1939–1940, therefore, the Soviet government replaced the Latin alphabet with new scripts based on the Cyrillic alphabet. By such a substitution, it was explained, students would be spared the labor of learning two different alphabets. This change in alphabet made it possible to introduce diverse symbols for Turkic sounds not found in the Cyrillic alphabet. Whereas in the Unified Turkic Latin Alphabet one symbol was employed for the same phoneme throughout the Turkic languages, with the introduction of the Cyrillic alphabet, a different symbol was introduced for each language in which the phoneme was found. The application of this policy to Karakalpak to differentiate it from Kazak resulted in such phonetic ineptnesses that reforms in Karakalpak orthography had to be initiated in 1954.[6]

While Soviet administrators were making changes in the alphabets, the political, economic, and social changes introduced by the Soviet government had been accompanied by an influx of new words and concepts. Many of these were Russian; others were international terms which had entered the Russian language in the course of its own industrialization. This latter category included not only such standard international terms as *telegraf,* but very specialized ones like the American trade name Vaseline which this writer encountered in 1934 in the Kazak rendition of *böselin.* New concepts were incorporated into the recipient language in various ways. Sometimes the Russian term was translated into the equivalent Turkic, as in "five-year plan" which was rendered as *beshiyllyq* (*besh,* "five"; *iyl,* "year"; and *lyq,* a Turkic suffix denoting abstraction). During the 1920's, Persian words were often adopted for concepts introduced by the Russians, such as *inqilob,* which the Uzbeks preferred to the Russian *revoliutsiia,* and *shaitan arba* ("devil cart"), the term devised by the Karakalpaks for bicycle.

This tendency to translate concepts introduced by the Russians into more familiar Turkic, Persian, or Arabic words was gradually overcome by constant reiteration of the Russian terms in school, speeches, and newspapers. The introduction of the Cyrillic script facilitated the adoption of Russian vocabulary. In these ways, some terms already present in the native vocabularies have been replaced by the Russian term for the same or a similar concept. The Russian term *universitet,* for example, is gradually replacing the Uzbek *dorulfunun* (literally, "gateway of the sciences"). The adoption of foreign terms to express new concepts is normal to the linguistic process. The Persian and Iranicized Arabic terms that abound in Uzbek and are frequent in Kazak represent, for the most part, concepts that had been unfamiliar to Turkic pastoralists. For nomads who had never known writing, for example, it was natural to adopt the terms for book, paper, and pen from the Arabs and Persians from whom they acquired these concepts. In the same way, Central Asian peoples are now adopting Russian terms for the multitude of new concepts which have been introduced under the Soviet regime.

A study of Tajik vocabulary shows that Russian loan words are prevalent for concepts and forms that have entered Tajik culture through Russia: the vocabulary of Marxism and of the Soviet political structure; and that of the newly industrialized economy and of modern communication. The largest number of Russian loan words are found in the realm of science. An analysis has been made of several specialized Russian-Tajik dictionaries. In a dictionary of mathematical terms published in 1940 and listing 2,800 words, 1,545 of these were Tajik and 680 more were combinations of Russian and Tajik. The Tajiks had comparatively little need to borrow in the field of mathematics, given their cultural legacy from such illustrious scholars of the past as the ninth-century mathematician al-Khwarizmi, native of Khiva, and Avicenna (ibn Sina) of Bukhara (980–1037), who wrote on geometry and astronomy as well as philosophy and medicine. A dictionary of biology published in 1941 and containing 3,724 words also shows a Tajik predominance; the 2,264 Tajik terms included almost the entire agricultural vocabulary. In the fields of chemistry and physics, where great research advances have been made internationally, Russian and international terms introduced through Russian are in a majority. Of 3,724 words listed in a dictionary of physics published in 1948, only 1,058 were Tajik, and in the chemical dictionary, only 550 Tajik words and 640 hybrid Tajik-Russian terms appeared in a total listing of 3,240. However, these dictionaries are designed for specialists. In the domestic vocabulary of Tajik life, loan words are comparatively few, limited to such concepts as potatoes, tomatoes, chairs, and tables, none of which have made much impact on Tajik culture.

Another study of general Russian-Tajik and Tajik-Russian

dictionaries published in 1933–1934, 1946, 1949, 1954, and 1957, showed that there has been a progressive increase of Russian terms in the Tajik vocabulary, including replacements of Tajik terms by Russian equivalents.[7] In Turkmenistan, the influx of Russian vocabulary is so great that in newspapers one may find whole sentences in which all the nouns are Russian. The vocabulary of dictionaries and of published works written in the Central Asian languages is of course subject to policy editing and thus does not necessarily reflect general usage. Most people continue to employ their regional dialects in conversation. In speech, the "standard" language appears to be limited to the intelligentsia, who use it perhaps for the same reasons that they eat pork in public restaurants and wear mackintoshes. The gap between the standard and the spoken language is indicated by the fact that some Uzbek authors provide glossaries for the benefit of would-be readers of their works. A good many Russian words have, nevertheless, entered the vocabulary of speech. The concept of collective farm or kolkhoz has come within the experience of every peasant and nomad, and with it the Russian terms have entered his speech. The oasis peasant who has found tomatoes to be good uses the word *pomidor* because he knows no other. Similarly, the nomad accepts *brigad* because he draws his pay as a member of this now familiar organization. It is presumably the hope of Soviet planners that more and more concepts requiring Russian terminology will come within the experience of peasant and nomad, and that the reiterative effect of the use of Russian terms in school textbooks, kolkhoz wall bulletins, and radio broadcasts will hasten the day of acceptance of the Russian terms for these concepts.

It is the Soviet thesis that the introduction of Russian terms and concepts has the effect of enriching the nationality languages. This seems to be the case. While thousands of terms have entered the vocabularies of the Central Asian languages, comparatively few "archaic" terms have been lost despite the hopes of Soviet planners to the contrary. Rather, often the Russian loan word is accepted for one meaning while the native word continues in use for other meanings. In Tajik, for example, *sovet* is employed only for purely Soviet councils, while the old *majlis* continues to be used in the general sense of "assembly," and *maslihat* for advice. Thus, borrowing from the Russian has increased and enriched the vocabularies of the Central Asian languages in much the same way that the vocabularies of Western languages, and of Russian itself, have been enriched by modern developments in science, technology, political ideology, and, above all, by an expansion in the facilities of communication. Many of these loan words, if transliterated into a familiar alphabet, would be recognizable to Europeans, Americans, Japanese, and peoples in many other parts of the world. On the other hand, it is probable that many of the terms listed in the Tajik technical dictionaries studied were as alien to the speech and nonscientific writing of Tajiks as would be the vocabulary of comparable American or European dictionaries to most Americans or Europeans. The real gap between the standard written and the spoken languages in Central Asia may perhaps lie in two areas: one, where peoples of Tajik or Turkic speech have culturally satisfactory terms for the concepts expressed by proffered Russian words; and two, where the newly introduced concepts themselves are little understood or accepted. That there is a real gap is suggested by the cries against "pollution" of their language with foreign words made by Central Asian scholars and writers and the reiteration of Soviet spokesmen that the Central Asian languages are being enriched.[8]

Borrowing words is a first step in linguistic change. However, the loan word, if it is to survive, must then be fitted into the phonetic and grammatical structure of the recipient language. The Russian sound *ts* has apparently caused little difficulty to Central Asian speakers, but this is not true of all new sounds. In the early years of the Soviet regime, Turkic speakers changed Russian loan words to conform to the rules of vowel harmony, but as the number of loan words increased, the effort apparently became too great, and loan words of recent introduction are seldom changed to conform to this Turkic phonetic system. The dialects of the large oasis cities had already lost much or all of their impulse toward vowel harmony even for words in their own language, under the influence of Persian. The other dialects appear to be going in the same direction under the influence of Russian, though rural Turkic speakers, both villagers and nomads, who are required to assimilate fewer new concepts—and so fewer loan words—may more readily adjust these loan words to the phonetic pattern of vowel harmony, just as they retain vowel harmony more strongly in their Turkic speech. Turkic speakers continue to cling to the pattern of syllabification that calls for vowels before or between certain consonants, so that *stanitsa,* for example, is pronounced *estanitsa.* For the most part, Central Asians change the pronunciation of loan words to conform to their own phonetic systems, at most perhaps altering the tonal patterns of recent loan words. A majority speak Russian "badly," that is, they find it difficult to adapt to the Russian phonetic system. Even when they learn to speak Russian fairly well, they continue to pronounce Russian loan words according to their own phonetic systems. This continues to be true, though it has been obligatory since about 1952 to write Russian loan words in the Central Asian languages as they are written in Russian. However, changes in the orthography of the Central Asian languages have not led to phonetic changes. In Turkoman, for example, long vowels are retained in speech even though they are no longer reflected in the written language.

In grammar, almost all loan words enter the Central Asian

languages as nouns. Some adjective forms are gradually becoming established and a very few conjunctions (as is also happening in Osmanli Turkish under the impact of Western European languages), but for the most part, loan words are treated as nouns, to be modified according to the grammatical system of the language. In the Turkic languages, this means by the addition of suffixes. To the Russian loan word *kolkhoz,* for example, the Karakalpaks add the suffix *la* to form *kolkhozla,* "to act collectively," and *ly* to form *kolkhozly,* "having collective farms." Tajiks treat Russian loan words according to their own grammatical patterns. Verbs are formed by the suffixes *an* and *dan* as *elektrikonidan,* "to electrify," or by the addition of the auxiliary verbs *mondan* and *kardan* as in *remont kardan,* "to repair." Nouns, adjectives, and adverbs are formed by characteristic prefixes and suffixes. The Russian noun *partiia* is thus transformed into a negative adjective by a prefix and suffix, *bepartiiavi,* "non-Party." [9]

In sum, linguistic changes do not suggest any disintegration of Central Asian culture or any wholesale acceptance of Russian culture. The accretions in vocabulary are considerable, but many of these are international terms the Russians themselves acquired from abroad not many decades ago in the course of their own industrialization. Some of them, Russian in origin or in special meaning, such as "soviet" and "kolkhoz," have spread to many languages outside the Soviet Union. Still others are employed in the standard written languages, with the vehemently expressed objection of Central Asian writers who feel obliged to use them or to accept their editorial insertion, but are ignored in normal conversational usage. In speech, loan words are modified to conform to Central Asian phonetic patterns, whether Turkic or Tajik, and both in writing and speech, the loan words are subject to the grammatical patterns of the recipient languages. The frequent complaints of Soviet commentators on Central Asian literature, that it is too ethnographic, too prone to descriptions of "the old national way of life" or of "ugly features in everyday life," may reflect not only dissatisfaction with the content of novels and short stories but with the fact that such subjects justify the use of native Turkic or Tajik terms to the exclusion of Russian loan words.[10]

Since language characteristically changes slowly, there is no way of predicting the course of the Central Asian languages in the future. It would be illuminating, though probably impossible, to make a detailed comparative study of a Central Asian language under the Soviet policy of planned Russianization; of the language of Turkey under a policy of planned rejection of foreign loan words; and of that of a country that, after isolation, had entered the modern world with its international technological, social, and political concepts without language planning. Without such a study, one can only hazard a guess that linguistic changes in Central Asia may differ from the other cases hypothesized chiefly in that Central Asian scholars and writers object more strongly to the changes which they feel are forced on them. The great mass of the Central Asian population at most has completed the equivalent of a junior high school education and is thereafter exposed to the limited Russianized vocabulary of kolkhoz bulletins and activist speeches. Those who live within bus travel of towns and cities have new experiences that encourage the acquisition of new vocabulary. Those who live in isolated villages or who follow their herds far from the kolkhoz center have few experiences to call for new vocabulary and little opportunity to learn the loan words that abound in literary publications.

VIII

Central Asian Cultures as of 1965

GREAT changes have occurred in Central Asian cultures within the last century, and there is no possibility of their reverting to the ways of the khans. Nevertheless, the Central Asian peoples have not lost their sense of ethnic identity, nor are they likely to become merged with the Russian people. There has been an evolution of the traditional cultures, with selective borrowing of new elements and modifications congenial to the traditional patterns and interests of the area.

The peoples of Central Asia have shown a strong tendency to cling to their traditional occupations. Pastoral nomadism has survived vicissitudes that seemed certain to extinguish it, and as of 1965, it flourished with the blessing of the Soviet government. A larger proportion of the pastoral population than formerly is semisedentary, engaging in some dry farming and dairying as well as the breeding of horses, sheep, and camels, and alternating between permanent dwellings in winter and yurts in summer, but the transitional pattern itself is as old as the history of Central Asia. The oasis peoples also have for the most part continued their traditional occupations. As always, a majority of Uzbeks and Tajiks are village-dwelling cultivators. By the 1950's, Soviet theory had come to accept the principle that Kazaks, Kirghiz, and some

Turkomans had a cultural aptitude for stockbreeding and that Tajiks and Uzbeks had a special gift for cultivating irrigated fields. Stockbreeders and cultivators have benefited from technological and scientific innovation, but they have also demonstrated the efficacy of traditional methods. Crafts have suffered under Russian dominion, as have crafts in other parts of the world under the impact of industrialization. Trade, on the other hand, has not been destroyed by a Soviet policy of government control. The machinery and channels of trade have changed somewhat in adjustment to new circumstances, but oasis merchants and entrepreneurs have displayed marked ingenuity in devising ways to follow their traditional cultural predilection for trade.

Central Asian dietary habits have changed very little during the century of their association with Russians. The greatest change has been the Kazak and Kirghiz acceptance of bread as a staple food, but the bread is of the oasis type such as has traditionally been adopted by pastoral nomads in western Asia as a result of contact with village-dwellers. Industrial and other institutional workers avoid the Russian food served in public dining rooms by taking their main meals at home in the evening. In clothing, women have been conservative to the point where ready-made clothing in Central Asian styles are being offered in urban department stores. The chief change occurred in the nineteenth century, when both pastoral and oasis women adopted the Russian redingote jacket. At the same time, they acquired a lasting preference for plush and velours, and the Kazak women for flower prints. Men have been more ready to adopt clothing of European cut, but have not accepted Russian headgear. Where changes have occurred, they have been for non-Russian forms. In dwellings, the oasis people have evolved an architectural style that combines traditional forms and materials with such innovations as house foundations, windows, and stoves. For pastoral nomads, no adequate substitute has been found for the yurt. The winter dwellings of pastoralist are of the oasis type except in the eastern mountains where wood is plentiful and snow fairly heavy; there, Russian influence is found in log walls and gabled roofs. European furniture has found its way into many homes, but as a status symbol. Most Central Asians continue to sit, eat, and sleep on the floor. It is in household utensils that the effect of industrialization is most evident.

In social organization, old patterns persist. The kolkhoz has the form of a tribal genealogical kin group among the pastoral peoples, of a traditional village in the oases. In the towns, the ward has retained its vitality as a functioning social unit. The *aqsaqal* retains his position of respect and authority. Among the pastoralists, the extended family *aul* appears to persist in the guise of associated brigades, but in the oases the traditional joint family is slowly being broken up into conjugal family households. Family ties remain strong, however. The Soviet program of crèches to take care of small children had little success in Central Asia. Children are brought up in the home, where traditional values and patterns of behavior are instilled in them before they come under Soviet cultural influence in the schools. The early training in respect for elders and in the importance of kin relationships counteracts, to a large extent, the outside forces that might operate to weaken family and kin ties. Nepotism, an admirable practice by Central Asian standards, is a constant source of concern to Soviet administrators. Respect for elders is a potent force for social conservatism.

The status of women has changed to the extent that some girls are allowed to attend middle school or technical high schools and even, on occasion, institutions of higher learning. The extent to which they do so often reflects traditional cultural attitudes as much as it does Russian influence; among Kazaks and Kirghiz, where women's status was always relatively high, a larger percentage of girls go on to advanced training than among Uzbeks and Tajiks, where woman's life was formerly very constricted. The Tajiks, generally most conservative of the Central Asian peoples in their resistance to change, are also most unwilling to allow their daughters to attend school beyond the traditional age of marriage. There is a small nucleus of educated women in Central Asia who, as mothers, might be expected to make some break with tradition in bringing up their children. However, there is a counterforce at work. The seclusion of women appears to have become a prestige symbol among those who have risen to positions of authority in the Party or the Soviet administrative system. Not only in the oases do some educated women go into seclusion on marriage, but also among the Kazaks and Kirghiz, who formerly did not practice seclusion. Particularly in the oases, the number of school dropouts in the fourth and fifth grades suggests that many girls are married at the traditional though now illegal age, too young to make any real choice of mate. Even those girls who attend school for a longer period apparently do not marry without parental consent. The bride price, though illegal, is still paid in some guise, and the reciprocal dowry, not illegal, is displayed with pride. Polygyny, also outlawed, is frequent and may even have become a status symbol, as has the seclusion of women.

Religious beliefs and practices have shown great persistence despite prolonged Soviet efforts to destroy this "opiate of the people." Mosque attendance, forbidden for a decade in the 1930's, rose to impressive numbers in the 1950's, and much of the folk religion remains strongly entrenched. The traditional rituals and ceremonies that mark the progress of the individual from birth to death continue in force though with changes in detail. The cult of saints' shrines flourishes; even Party members and university professors visit such shrines. Doctors trained in modern medicine compete with shamans and midwives, and they sometimes send their children to shrines for cures. Soviet attempts to introduce new festivals as substitutes for Nau Ruz and the major Muslim festivals have been unsuccessful; and many people, even children, observe the fast of Ramazan. There have been some transferences. The mosque is apparently no longer a meeting place for the men of a town ward or country village. Instead, this function appears to have been transferred to the teahouse, an alternative Central Asian institution which has been encouraged by the Soviet administration. Similarly, the ceremonial center seems to have become the saint's shrine that, usually standing a distance from the village, is less exposed than the mosque to unfriendly observation.

Decorative arts, like the crafts, suffer from industrialization and also from pressure on the artists to adopt Soviet or Russian themes and styles. Yet, ethnographic descriptions of house furnishings are almost unanimous in affirming a preference for traditional forms of decoration, even in rooms set with European furniture. The floors are characteristically spread with felt or double-face pileless rugs, which were always the product of home industry, made by tribal or rural village women, partly for home use, partly for sale. As always, piles of quilts and cushions with ornamental colored bindings constitute a major household furnishing. These were traditionally made by the housewife, as were the embroidered wall hangings. One might infer that while professional craft art is deteriorating, Central Asian housewives continue to make the traditional decorative objects, with some changes in style or technique, for their own use and for sale through unofficial channels to other Central Asians.

Central Asian culture has undergone many changes in the century that has passed since the peoples of the steppes and oases came under Russian rule. The Russian governments, both Tsarist and Soviet, envisaged eventual Russianization of the peoples of Central Asia. The drive of the latter government to impose a Soviet political and economic system on the people, as well as Soviet Russian social values, implied an expectation that the process of Russianization would be speedy. Yet, many of the changes that have occurred are not specifically Russian but rather of the kind that have occurred in many countries exposed to the forces of modern industrialization and technology. In country after country newly opened to the influence of the modern world, the traditional crafts have been weakened in competition with mass-produced wares. In bazaars and trading posts in all parts of the world, there are displayed factory-made utensils and textiles. Men who have acquired some status in the new world adopt the European style of clothing, and artistic work deteriorates when artists cater to the tastes of foreigners. Except for the Soviet system itself, which at the local level is often adapted to culture patterns indigenous to Central Asia, there is comparatively little in modern Central Asian culture that is specifically Russian.

This is not to decry what has been accomplished, particularly under the Soviet regime, to bring the Central Asian peoples nearer the standard of life that has come to be regarded as desirable by the states and philosophers of the modern world. Whereas a hundred years ago illiteracy was prevalent and even khans were often unable to read and write, everyone now has had some schooling and most people can read at least the simple messages presented in kolkhoz bulletins. Considering the fact that Central Asia has been exposed to Western educational concepts for only a hundred years, the number who have gone on to higher education and entered professional occupations is impressive. The oasis people have undoubtedly benefited from the new technology that has brought new lands under irrigation, as have the pastoralists from new veterinary practices and new wells in arid grazing lands. The people as a whole appear to have more food and more creature comforts than ever before, and for those who have aspirations beyond the material, there are opportunities for education and careers in science and the arts. The peoples of Russian Central Asia are inclined to regard with pity their Muslim neighbors to the south who do not enjoy their advantages.

Nevertheless, the peoples of Central Asia have retained the patterns and values of their own traditional cultures. They have been selective in their borrowing of new elements and have modified these to fit into their own way of thinking and behaving. Such proffered elements as do not fit into their own patterns are rejected. The peoples of Central Asia have learned from the liquidations of the 1920's and the purges of the 1930's not to resist with violence innovations they find unacceptable. They have, however, learned to follow quietly their own cultural inclinations despite legal enactments and the urging of agitators. Count K. K. Pahlen, the perceptive official who made a study of Turkistan for the Tsarist government in 1908–1909, remarked on the attitude of the Central Asians toward Russians: "I had my first glimpse of that peculiar subtlety with which the Asian regards the European. What I believe to be genuine contempt is veiled by an appearance of outward submission that somehow suggests inner awareness of a culture and an outlook on life vastly older than our own." [1] To judge from recent information, this attitude of veiled contempt persists. The oasis peoples, with a legacy of countless centuries of experience in submitting to irresponsible rulers, appear to be more adept at giving "an appearance of outward submission" than the Kazaks and Kirghiz, whose literati are sometimes outspoken in their objections to Soviet policy.

Many of the elements introduced by Russians and accepted

into Central Asian culture are actually international in character rather than specifically Russian. It is true that the Russian samovar was widely accepted in the Tsarist Russian period, but this fitted into the pattern of tea drinking that came in from China at about the same time. Even today, Central Asians drink their tea from handleless tea bowls of the Chinese type. Of the elements introduced by the Russians, sometimes with forceful attempts to obtain acceptance, there has been as much rejection as acceptance. The free cultural borrowings have been among the several peoples of Central Asia or from non-Russian neighbors in the Soviet Union. The oasis people have adopted Chinese noodles and the Chinese method of steaming pasties introduced by Uighurs and Dungans, but not Russian cooking. When Soviet authorities wished to introduce opera, an art form much esteemed by Russians, into Uzbekistan, it was visiting Azerbaijani opera troupes who set the pattern of Uzbek opera. The Central Asian intelligentsia have adopted the Tatar skullcap for summer wear, and Turkoman workers chose Cossack hats to replace their own unwieldy headgear.

In cultural borrowing among Central Asian peoples, two main trends may be discerned. First, patterns of behavior associated with the upper classes in the khanates have become prestige status symbols for the new Soviet upper and upper-middle class of Party and government officials. The low tables that were coming into fashion in upper-class oasis homes in the late nineteenth century appear to be more widely used for eating in present upper-class Uzbek homes than are the tables of European height also found in these homes as status symbols. This preference might be due to the fact that Central Asians, habituated to sitting on the floor, are not comfortable on the chairs required by European tables. Most Central Asians continue to spread their tablecloths on the floor. Physical comfort is, of course, not an issue when prosperous families have the walls of new homes ornamented with *ganch* and murals of the type found in wealthy homes in the late nineteenth and early twentieth centuries, and have plywood ceilings painted in the fashion of ceiling beams in the days of the khanates. This ornamentation does not run counter to Soviet policy. In the matter of plural wives and the seclusion of women, however, there is direct conflict with Soviet law. Yet, to judge by available reports, these practices are most widespread among Party and government officials—the new upper class. Furthermore, women who were active in the Party and in community affairs before marriage appear to accept seclusion and the sharing of a husband with co-wives.

The second trend is the diffusion of cultural elements from the oases into the steppe, a process that has been active since prehistoric times. When former nomads build permanent dwellings, they are likely to follow oasis models rather than Russian, except in regions where climate and materials favor the Russian model. When they adopt bread, as most tribesmen have, it is bread flaps of the oasis type and not Russian loaves. When Kazaks and Kirghiz become prosperous urban dwellers, they begin to seclude their wives in the oasis fashion. The extent to which oasis patterns have been accepted is illustrated by a Kazak novel published around 1950 in which the Russian hero had become so completely Kazak that his Kazak wife still wore the *paranja* and lived secluded in an *ichkar*.[2] In the old days, of course, the *paranja* was worn only by women of the oasis cities, and Kazak women were not secluded.

Soviet leaders had expected that through education the peoples of Central Asia would become Russianized. Undoubtedly, some individuals have been drawn into Russian society, just as in Tsarist times the sons of Kazak khans became isolated from their people as a consequence of Russian education. For the most part, however, members of the

210

intelligentsia trained under the Soviet regime have not lost their ethnic identity. They speak Russian, wear European-style clothes, and generally conform in public to the behavior expected of them by Russian officials, but they remain a part of their own community. During World War II, when the Soviet government encouraged an interest in national heroes as a psychological stimulant to the war effort, the Central Asian peoples acclaimed their epic heroes with a fervor that shocked Russian leaders. To counteract a trend regarded as dangerously nationalistic, there was an official purge in 1951 and 1952 of the epic poems of Turkomans, Uzbeks, Kazaks, and Karakalpaks. The Kirghiz were less ready to accept the suppression of their heroic poem *Manas,* and it was only after heated controversy that Kirghiz scholars bowed before official condemnation by the Academy of Sciences in Moscow.[3]

Central Asian scholars also took advantage of the relaxation of the war years to express their cultural nationalism in another direction. During the 1930's, Communist doctrine had held, first, that the Tsarist Russian conquest of non-Russian territories was "an absolute evil," then, after 1937, that these conquests were "a lesser evil" in that the people conquered were saved from the worse fate of domination by the khanates of Central Asia or conquest by Britain or other foreign powers. During the 1940's, Central Asian scholars interpreted this as allowing them to glorify the leaders who had struggled against Russian conquest and to describe the conquest in terms scarcely flattering to the Russians. The dangers of this trend were met by a Soviet enunciation of the doctrine of "absolute good." After reinforcement of this doctrine by purges of the universities of Tashkent and Samarkand in Uzbekistan and of Stalinabad (now Dushanbe) in Tajikistan, the Russian conquest was depicted as a beneficent one.[4]

Writers of poetry and fiction are less easily regimented by edict, and complaints about Central Asian authors continue over the years—that they write of nightingales and gazelles instead of railways, that they are tediously ethnographic, that they describe the "ugly features of everyday life." [5] There are also objections from the Russian side that the Uzbek theater draws too much on folklore and legend and that painters depict "outmoded" scenes. Native scholars, in their turn, decry the squandering of the riches of folk music by the use of folk melodies in operas, and the pollution of their literary languages with Russian loan words.[6] Interest in native history was not destroyed by the abrupt measures of 1951. In 1958 the Kazakhstan Ministry of Education yielded to popular desire and introduced the study of Kazak history in the secondary schools of the republic; and Tajiks were complaining that Central Asian history was not taught in their schools, attributing this lack to too close imitation of the Russian school system. It has been suggested that the suppression of their history from the school curriculum actually stimulated Central Asians to imagine glories that their history had seldom attained in fact. Furthermore, the Soviet zigzag policy of ignoring the Central Asian cultural heritage in the 1930's, encouraging exaltation of ancestral heroes in the 1940's, then calling a halt to this enthusiasm in 1951, may have had the cumulative effect of strengthening Central Asian resistance to Soviet policy as it related to ethnic attitudes. To quote a Kazak newspaper, it "encouraged anti-Russian sentiments among the University youths." [7]

There is no evidence of anti-Russian political activity. Such would be difficult under Soviet conditions, and the Central Asians must have learned the futility of overt resistance during the fighting of the 1920's and the purges of the 1930's. Most of them do not appear to be opposed to Communism as such. The masses are more prosperous than ever before, and the life of the new upper classes, with automobiles, radios, and sometimes even television sets, compares favorably in comfort and interest with that of the khans. The peoples of Soviet Central Asia are inclined to look down on the poverty and backwardness of the "free" peoples south of the Soviet border, but they consider themselves superior to the Russians. They have developed a sense of pride in their culture and ethnic being and through a hundred years of living with Russian rulers have learned to manage with these overlords, as their ancestors contrived to get along with the corrupt officials of the khanates. The Kirghiz, who traditionally placed a high value on independence and who were last to feel the weight of Russian power, are most prone to voice their disapproval of unpopular policies. Kazak leaders, with their memory of the short-lived Alash Orda, have the clearest vision of autonomy. The oasis peoples quietly adhere to their own culture unless the advantages of change are obvious. Few Central Asians have any desire to become Russian.

Soviet leaders appear doomed to disappointment in their hope that the intelligentsia they had educated would lead the masses toward Russianization. The most highly educated Central Asians are also the most skilled in communicating the cultural values of their own ethnic group to those around them. Party members and administrators are inclined to react according to the values of their own culture rather than work toward Russianization. It is taken for granted that they will use their position and influence to help their relatives and friends. The secondary-school graduate, who represents the intelligentsia at the kolkhoz level, is likely to have little understanding of Russian culture. He wears Russian clothes; he speaks Russian, but with no great facility unless he attended a Russian school; he has acquired certain skills that give him social and economic status. He will make some contribution to change in kolkhoz life, but on becoming a member of the community, he is likely to lose much of what he tentatively learned at school, for his associations outside work hours will be with those of his own ethnic group and not with Russians.

Although the Russian governments, both Tsarist and Soviet, envisaged eventual Russianization of the native peoples, Russian colonists and administrators themselves posed a serious deterrent to such acculturation. Like settlers in most colonial areas, they established their own cultural islands within the sea of the native population. Under the Tsarist regime, they set up separate towns on the outskirts of native cities. Agricultural colonists also had separate communities. In Kazakhstan they displaced nomads. In Turkistan, where they were not allowed to settle until 1911, they were given lands newly brought under irrigation. Whatever the circumstances, they lived in cultural enclaves, not interspersed with the native inhabitants. With some notable exceptions, they did not bother to learn the native language, let alone try to understand the local culture. The picture did not greatly change under the Soviet regime. In the towns and cities, a third quarter was added, inhabited by members of the new intelligentsia, both Russian and native, but even in these mixed quarters, there seems to have been little mixed social life beyond the requirements of employment. This social barrier was not due solely to Russian ethnocentricity. The native peoples were equally aloof, and in the oases the seclusion of women precluded any normal social intercourse between Russian and native.[8]

Ethnic separation is particularly noticeable in marriage, and here the Central Asian peoples show themselves more aloof than the Russians. While Russian women sometimes marry Central Asian men, Central Asian women almost never take Russian husbands. In the few such instances recorded, the woman was either an orphan or a divorcée, with no family to prevent the match. In Tsarist times, when a

Central Asian man married a Russian woman, she was converted to Islam and adopted the ways of her husband's people. In similar mixed marriages under the Soviet regime, the woman more frequently exerts a dominant cultural influence in the home and on the children. Among the peoples of Central Asia, there has always been some intermarriage among those living along the borders of ethnic territories, such as between Kazaks and Karakalpaks near the Aral Sea, but many small groups have avoided such intermixture. The Dungans still marry only within their own group, but the Arabs, traditionally proud of their "purity of lineage," have begun to take wives from other Muslim groups. Tatar women are regarded as desirable brides by both Uzbeks and Tajiks, while at a lower status level there is some intermarriage with Gypsies. The high bride price asked for Kirghiz and Kazak women acts as a deterrent to marriage with oasis men, though men of these groups occasionally marry Tajik or Uzbek women, particularly as second or third wives. It has been observed that mixed marriages usually occur in families where there are several children. One child, particularly a son, is expected to marry a kinsman, but for other children the parents are sometimes more lenient in permitting marriage outside the group. In general, mixed marriages among Central Asians appear to be increasing, but are still infrequent except along ethnic boundary lines. Available data suggest that once an ethnic break has been made, the children of a mixed marriage are likely to contract mixed marriages. In one Kirghiz mining family, for example, the father was Kirghiz, the mother Uzbek. The daughter was married to a Tajik, one son to a Kirghiz, another to a Tatar, while the third wished to marry a Russian.[9]

When the Soviet government came into power, the peoples of Central Asia had little sense of ethnic nationality except for the Kazak intelligentsia who had organized the Alash

Orda. The Uzbeks, divided politically among the khanates, identified themselves with the region and class to which they belonged rather than as Uzbeks. Educated Tajiks, trained in both Uzbek and Persian, had so little sense of nationality that they questioned the need for creating a Tajik literary language. Turkomans were divided into often hostile tribes. Throughout Central Asia, regional and tribal separatism was reinforced by dialectal and cultural differences. The Soviet policy of setting up separate republics for each of the major ethnic groups of Central Asia, and of developing an alphabet and literary language for each of these peoples, was designed to thwart the ferment of ideas, often labeled Pan-Islamic or Pan-Turkic, that were working among the intelligentsia of Central Asia at the time of the 1917 revolution. It was successful in this aim. It also had the effect of creating a feeling of nationality.

Although most rural people are still primarily conscious of subtribal or regional identity, there is a new sense of *narodnost'* identity. (*Narodnost'* is usually translated as "nationality," meaning an ethnic group, such as Uzbek, Turkoman, or Tajik.) During more than forty years of Soviet rule, there has been a drawing together (*sblizhenie*) of subgroups to create some feeling of nationality. In the 1926 census, for example, 143,500 tribal Uzbeks reported themselves as Turks, Kipchaks, or Kuramas, while in 1959 only about a hundred Kipchaks and slightly over four thousand Turks give their tribal name instead of Uzbek. The Soviet government has shown concern over signs of "cultural nationalism" which have been manifest since World War II. To counter it, there has been a *sblizhenie* program under which multinationality kolkhozes have been organized in the hope that cultural barriers will be broken down when members of many nationalities live and work together. Intermarriage is encouraged, and emphasis is given to the theme "boy meets girl" in school or at work, where attachments could be formed divergent from the traditional pattern of matches arranged by parents. There has been some drawing together within the ethnic groups of Central Asia and, to a smaller extent, among the peoples of Central Asia, but there has been little *sblizhenie* between Central Asians and Russians.

Notes

Preface

1. Wilhelm Radloff, *Opyt Slovaria Tiurkskikh Narechi* (*Versuch eines Wörterbuches der Türk-Dialecte*) (St. Petersburg, 1893–1911).

Chapter I

1. Herodotus, *The Histories,* trans. Aubrey de Sélincourt (Baltimore: Penguin Books, 1954), pp. 95, 257–266; R. Ghirshman, *Iran* (Baltimore: Penguin Books, 1954), pp. 154, 215; W. Barthold, *A Short History of Turkestan,* trans. V. and T. Minorsky (Vol. I: "Four Studies on the History of Central Asia," [Leiden: E. J. Brill, 1956]), p. 3.

2. Barthold, *Histoire des Turcs d'Asie Centrale* (Paris: Librairie d'Amérique et d'Orient, 1945); Babur, *The Babur-nama in English* (*Memoirs of Babur*), by Zahiru'd-din Muhammad Babur Padshah, trans. Annette Susannah Beveridge (London: Luzac & Co., 1921), I, 155–156.

3. S. P. Tolstov *et al.,* eds., *Narody Srednei Azii i Kazakhstana* (Moscow: Akademiia Nauk SSSR, 1962), I, 159–164.

4. Francis Henry Skrine and Edward Denison Ross, *The Heart of Asia* (London: Methuen, 1899), pp. 182–210; Barthold, *A Short History of Turkestan,* pp. 64–65; Barthold, "Kazak," *Encyclopaedia of Islam* (Leiden: E. J. Brill, 1929), II, 836; A. Samoilovich, "O Slove 'Kazak,'" in *Kazaki: Antropologicheskie Ocherki* (Leningrad: Akademiia Nauk SSSR 1927), pp. 5–16.

In Russian the name Kazak is also applied to the Cossacks. It was in 1936, when Stalin accidentally mispronounced Kazak in a public address, that the Turko-Mongol people of Central Asia became Kazakh, and their republic, Kazakhstan.

5. A. Woeikof, *Le Turkestan russe* (Paris: Librairie Armand Colin, 1914); L. Dudley Stamp, *Asia: A Regional and Economic Geography*

(9th ed.; London: Methuen & Co., 1957); François Bourlière *et al.*, *The Land and Wildlife of Eurasia* (New York: Time Inc., 1964), pp. 81–103.

6. Tolstov *et al.*, *Narody Srednei Azii*, I, 149–153.

7. Barthold, *A Short History of Turkestan*, p. 63; Richard A. Pierce, ed., *Mission to Turkestan: Being the Memoirs of Count K. K. Pahlen 1908–1909*, trans. N. J. Couriss (London: Oxford University Press, 1964), footnote, p. 10; Alexandre Bennigsen and Chantal Quelquejay, "Le problème linguistique et l'évolution des nationalités musulmanes en U.R.S.S.," *Cahiers du monde russe et soviétique*, III, (1960), 456.

8. Stefan Wurm, *Turkic Peoples of the USSR* (London: Central Asian Research Centre, 1954), p. 8.

9. T. A. Zhdanko, "Karakalpaki Khorezmskogo Oazisa," in *Arkheologicheskie i Etnograficheskie Raboty Khorezmskoi Ekspeditsii 1945–1948* (Moscow: Akademiia Nauk SSSR, 1952), pp. 466–467; B. V. Andrianov, "Etnicheskaia Territoriia Karakalpakov v Severnom Khorezme (XVIII–XIX vv.)," in *Materialy i Issledovaniia po Etnografii Karakalpakov* (Moscow: Akademiia Nauk SSSR, 1958), pp. 8, 12–13, 52–60, 94–96; Bennigsen and Quelquejay, "Le problème linguistique," p. 457.

10. Tolstov *et al.*, *Narody Srednei Azii*, II, 582–584; Bennigsen and Quelquejay, "Le problème linguistique," footnote 106, p. 457.

11. Barthold, *A Short History of Turkestan*, p. 16; Walter J. Fischel, "The Leaders of the Jews of Bokhara," in *Jewish Leaders (1750–1940)*, ed. Leo Jung (New York: Bloch Publishing Company, 1953), pp. 533–547; Fischel, "Israel in Iran (A Survey of Judeo-Persian Literature)," in *The Jews: Their History, Culture, and Religion*, ed. Louis Finkelstein (3rd ed.; New York: Harper & Brothers, 1960), pp. 1174–1176; Rudolph Loewenthal, *The Judeo-Muslim Marranos of Bukhara* (Washington, D.C.: 1958), pp. 1-3; Bennigsen and Quelquejay, "Le problème linguistique," p. 457; Tolstov *et al.*, *Narody Srednei Azii*, II, 610–614.

12. Eugene Schuyler, *Turkistan* (3rd ed.; New York: Charles Scribner's Sons, 1885), II, 41, 58; Tolstov *et al.*, *Narody Srednei Azii*, II, 597–609.

13. Bennigsen and Quelquejay, "Le problème linguistique," footnote 106, p. 457.

14. Tolstov *et al.*, *Narody Srednei Azii*, II, 488; Bennigsen and Quelquejay, "Le problème linguistique," pp. 458–459.

15. Tolstov, *et al.*, *Narody Srednei Azii*, II, 527, 529; Bennigsen and Quelquejay, "Le problème linguistique," p. 459.

16. Alexander Bennigsen and Chantal Quelquejay, *Les Mouvements nationaux chez les musulmans de Russie* (Paris and The Hague: Mou-

ton & Co., 1960), pp. 26–33; Lt. Colonel Geoffrey Wheeler, "Race Relations in Soviet Muslim Asia," *Royal Central Asian Journal*, XLVII (1960), 99.

17. "The Size of the German Population in Kazakhstan and Central Asia," *Central Asian Review*, X (1962), 372–373; Eric Downton, "Soviet Central Asia," *Royal Central Asian Journal*, XLII (1955), 133.

18. Wurm, *Turkic Peoples*, pp. 25–27.

19. Wurm, *Turkic Peoples*, pp. 11–16.

Chapter II

1. Alexis Levshin, *Déscription des hordes et des steppes des Kirghiz-Kazaks ou Kirghiz-Kaissaks*, trans. Ferry de Pigny (Paris: Imprimerie Royale, 1840), pp. 341–342, 348–349, 408–409; S. S. Krivtsov, ed., *Kazakstan i Kirgiziia* (Moscow: Moskovskoi Oblastnoe Otdelenie Gosizdat RSFSR, 1930), p. 66; Wilhelm Radloff, "Die Hausthiere der Kirgisen," *Zeitschrift für Ethnologie*, III (1871), 301–306, 309; G. Meyendorff, *Voyage d'Orenbourg à Boukhara, fait en 1820* (Paris: Dondey-Dupré, 1826), pp. 45–46; Henri Moser, *À travers l'Asie Centrale* (Paris: Librairie Plon, 1885), pp. 26, 35; Thomas Witlam Atkinson, *Oriental and Western Siberia* (New York: Harper & Brothers, 1858), pp. 220, 223; S. I. Rudenko, "Ocherk Byta Severo-vostochnykh Kazakov," in *Kazaki: Sbornik Statei Antropologicheskogo Otriada Kazakstanskoi Ekspeditsii Akademii Nauk SSSR, Issledovanie 1927 g.* (Leningrad: Akademiia Nauk SSSR, 1930), p. 22; P. S. Pallas, *Voyages de m. P. S. Pallas en différentes provinces de l'empire de Russie, et dans l'Asie septentrionale*, trans. Gauthier de la Peyronie (Paris: Maradan, 1789–1793), I, 623; B. A. Kuftin, *Kirgiz-Kazaki: Kul'tura i Byt* (Moscow: Tsentral'nogo Muzeia Narodovedeniia, 1926), p. 13.

2. Levshin, *Déscription*, pp. 311–312; Kuftin, *Kirgiz-Kazaki*, pp. 14–19; Richard Karutz, *Unter Kirgisen und Turkmenen* (Leipzig: Klinkhardt & Biermann, 1911), p. 49; Alfred E. Hudson, *Kazak Social Structure* (New Haven: Yale University Press, 1938), p. 26; Elizabeth E. Bacon, *Obok* (New York: Wenner-Gren Foundation for Anthropological Research, 1958), pp. 70–71; N. I. Grodekov, *Kirgizy i Karakirgizy Syr'-Dar'inskoi Oblasti* (Tashkent: S. I. Lakhtin, 1889), p. 110; Wilhelm Radloff, *Aus Sibirien* (2nd ed; Leipzig: T. O. Weigel Nachfolger, 1893), I, 513; Henry Lansdell, *Russian Central Asia* (Boston: Houghton Mifflin, 1885), I, 319; Bronislas Zaleskie, *La Vie des steppes kirghizes* (Paris: J.-B. Vasseur, 1865), p. 10; A. N. Samoilovich, "Kazaki Kosha-

NOTES

gachskogo Aimaka Oïratskoi Avtonomnoi Oblasti," in *Kazaki* (Leningrad: Akademiia Nauk SSSR, 1930), pp. 311–312; Rudenko, "Ocherk Byta," p. 10.

3. Levshin, *Déscription*, pp. 312, 412; Pallas, *Voyages*, II, 303–305; Krivtsov, *Kazakstan i Kirgiziia*, p. 64; Thomas G. Winner, *The Oral Art and Literature of the Kazakhs of Russian Central Asia* (Durham, N.C.: Duke University Press, 1958), p. 3; I. V. Zakharova, "Material'naia Kul'tura Kazakhov-kolkhoznikov Iugo-vostochnogo Kazakhstana," in *Trudy Instituta Istorii, Arkheologii i Etnografii*, III, *Etnografiia* (Alma Ata: Akademiia Nauk Kazakhskoi SSR, 1956), p. 110; Zaleskie, *La Vie des steppes*, p. 10.

4. F. A. Fiel'strup, "Molochnye Produkty Turkov-kochevnikov," in *Kazaki* (Leningrad: Akademiia Nauk SSSR, 1930), pp. 263–301; Levshin, *Déscription*, pp. 321–322; Radloff, "Die Hausthiere der Kirgisen," pp. 308–309; Atkinson, *Oriental and Western Siberia*, pp. 226, 405–406; Ch. E. de Ujfalvy de Mezö-Kövesd, *Expédition scientifique française en Russie, en Sibérie et dans le Turkestan* (Paris: E. Leroux, 1879), II, 29: Zaleskie, *La Vie des steppes*, pp. 10–11, 13; Zakharova, "Material'naia Kul'tura," pp. 174–176, 178; Arminius Vambéry, *Sketches of Central Asia* (London: W. H. Allen, 1868), p. 293; Krivtsov, *Kazakstan i Kirgiziia*, p. 66; Kuftin, *Kirgiz-Kazaki*, p. 20; Karutz, *Unter Kirgisen und Turkmenen*, p. 77.

5. Pallas, *Voyages*, I, 362, 628; Levshin, *Déscription*, pp. 322, 416–418; Edward Nelson Fell, *Russian and Nomad* (New York: Duffield and Company, 1916), p. 196: Lansdell, *Russian Central Asia*, I, 149; Zaleskie, *La Vie des steppes*, p. 30; Ujfalvy de Mezö-Kövesd, *Expédition scientifique*, II, 110.

6. Kuftin, *Kirgiz-Kazaki*, pp. 20–25, 31; E. R. Shneider, "Kazakskaia Ornamentika," in *Kazaki: Antropologicheskie Ocherki* (Leningrad: Akademiia Nauk SSSR, 1927), p. 139; Rudenko, "Ocherk Byta," pp. 12, 30–32; Levshin, *Déscription*, pp. 211–412; Zaleskie, *La Vie des steppes*, p. 9; Tolstov *et al.*, *Narody Srednei Azii*, II, 715.

7. Levshin, *Déscription*, pp. 310, 420–421; Lansdell, *Russian Central Asia*, I, 337; Atkinson, *Oriental and Western Siberia*, p. 226; Moser, *À travers l'Asie Centrale*, p. 19; Zaleskie, *La Vie des steppes*, p. 11; Karutz, *Unter Kirgisen und Turkmenen*, pp. 47–48; Kuftin, *Kirgiz-Kazaki*, pp. 34–35.

8. Pallas, *Voyages*, I, 612, 614; Levshin, *Déscription*, pp. 327, 420–421; Radloff, "Die Hausthiere der Kirgisen," p. 295; Zaleskie, *La Vie des steppes*, p. 25; Kuftin, *Kirgiz-Kazaki*, pp. 37–42; Shneider, "Kazakskaia

222

Ornamentika," pp. 136–141; Tolstov *et al.*, *Narody Srednei Azii*, II, 367–368; V. V. Vostrov, "Kazakhi Dzhanybekskogo Raiona Zapadno-kazakhstanskoi Oblasti," in *Trudy Instituta Istorii, Arkheologii i Etno-grafii*, III, *Etnografiia* (Alma Ata: Akademiia Nauk Kazakhskoi SSR, 1956), pp. 21–25; Zakharova, "Material'naia Kul'tura," pp. 184–185; Lansdell, *Russian Central Asia*, I, 364; Karutz, *Unter Kirgisen und Turkmenen*, pp. 55–56, 63–64; Rudenko, "Ocherk Byta," p. 44.

9. Pallas, *Voyages*, II, 289–291; Levshin, *Déscription*, pp. 324–327; Moser, *À travers l'Asie Centrale*, pp. 15–18, 99; Atkinson, *Oriental and Western Siberia*, pp. 217–220, 227; Lansdell, *Russian Central Asia*, I, 312; Ujfalvy de Mezö-Kövesd, *Expédition scientifique*, II, 28–29; Vam-béry, *Sketches*, pp. 289–290; Zaleskie, *La Vie des steppes*, pp. 11–12, 23–24; Samoilovich, "Kazaki Koshagachskogo Aimaka," p. 315; I. V. Zakharova and R. D. Khodzhaeva, "Muzhskaia i Zhenskaia Odezhda Kazakhov XIX–Nachala XX Vekov," in *Materialy Issledovania po Et-nografii Kazakhskogo Naroda* (Alma Ata: Akademiia Nauk Kazakhskoi SSR, 1963), pp. 51–86.

10. Bacon, *Obok*, p. 69.

11. Bacon, *Obok*, pp. 66–70; Vostrov, "Kazakhi Dzhanybekskogo Raiona," pp. 9–10; Levshin, *Déscription*, pp. 302–304; A. N. Kharuzin, *Kirgizy Bukeevskoi Ordy* (Moscow, 1889), pp. 26-27; N. A. Aristov, "Opyt Viiasneniia Etnicheskogo Sostava Kirgiz-Kazakov Bolshoi Ordy i Karakirgizov," *Zhivaia Starina*, Vyp. III–IV, Vol. 4 (1894), 394–397; Hudson, *Kazak Social Structure*, p. 20; A. M. Margulanov, "Naimany," in *Kazaki* (Leningrad: Akademiia Nauk SSSR, 1930), pp. 329–354 and tables; Grodekov, *Kirgizy i Karakirgizy*, pp. 16, 110; Radloff, *Aus Si-birien*, I, 513; R. C. F. Schomberg, *Peaks and Plains of Central Asia* (London: M. Hopkinson, 1933), p. 98; Lansdell, *Russian Central Asia*, I, 303; Schuyler, *Turkistan*, I, 34.

12. Grodekov, *Kirgizy i Karakirgizy*, pp. 7–8, 27–28; Bacon, *Obok*, p. 75; Hudson, *Kazak Social Structure*, pp. 43–45; Rudenko, "Ocherk Byta," p. 59; Karutz, *Unter Kirgisen und Turkmenen*, p. 99; Levshin, *Déscription*, p. 364; A. N. Samoilovich, "Zapretnie Slova v Iazyke Kazak-kirgizskoi Zamuzhnoi Zhenshchiny," *Zhivaia Starina*, XXVI (1915), 162–163.

13. W. Barthold, *Istoriia Turetsko-Mongolskikh Narodov* (Tashkent: Izdanie Kazakskogo Vysshogo Pedagogicheskogo Instituta, 1928), p. 26; Tolstov *et al.*, *Narody Srednei Azii*, II, 327, 329; Benjamin von Bergmann, *Voyage de Benjamin Bergmann chez les Kalmuks*, trans. M. Moris (Chatillon-sur-Seine: C. Cornillac, 1825), p. 313; Meyendorff,

Voyage, pp. 47–48, 53–54; Bacon, *Obok,* pp. 71–72; Levshin, *Déscription,* pp. 373–374, 393–397, 402; Radloff, *Aus Sibirien,* I, 513–514; V. G. Shakhmatov, "The Basic Characteristics of the Kazakh Patriarchal Feudal State Organization," *Central Asian Review,* IX (1961), 126–132.

14. V. Grigorief, "The Russian Policy regarding Central Asia," Appendix IV in Schuyler, *Turkistan,* II, 405. See also Levshin, *Déscription,* pp. 304–305; Grodekov, *Kirgizy i Karakirgizy,* pp. 4–5, 30; Moser, *À travers l'Asie Centrale,* p. 24; Radloff, *Aus Sibirien,* I, 515.

15. S. J. Asfendiarov, *Istoriia Kazakstana* (Alma Ata: Kazakstanskoe Kraevo Izdatel'stvo, 1935), p. 97; Pallas, *Voyages,* I, 623; Levshin, *Déscription* pp. 304–305, 351; Grodekov, *Kirgizy i Karakirgizy,* p. 46; Lansdell, *Russian Central Asia,* I, 357; Radloff, *Aus Sibirien,* I, 526; Kharuzin, *Kirgizy Bukeevskoi Ordy,* pp. 31–33; W. Jochelson, *Peoples of Asiatic Russia* (New York: American Museum of Natural History, 1928), p. 130; Rudenko, "Ocherk Byta," p. 60; Hudson, *Kazak Social Structure,* pp. 55-57.

16. Levshin, *Déscription,* pp. 358–362; Grodekov, *Kirgizy i Karakirgizy,* p. 54; Radloff, *Aus Sibirien,* I, 477; Lansdell, *Russian Central Asia,* I, 322–325, 329–330; Zaleskie, *La Vie des steppes,* p. 24; Moser, *À travers l'Asie Centrale,* p. 21; Rudenko, "Ocherk Byta," p. 48.

17. Thomas G. Wiener, "The Kazak Heroic Epos," *Royal Central Asian Journal,* XXXVIII (1951), 289. See also Levshin, *Déscription,* pp. 353–354, 363–364; Schuyler, *Turkistan,* I, 41, 43; Moser, *À travers l'Asie Centrale,* pp. 28, 31–35; Lansdell, *Russian Central Asia,* I, 327–329.

18. Levshin, *Déscription,* p. 333.

19. Levshin, *Déscription,* pp. 332, 356–366; Pallas, *Voyages,* I, 629–630; Meyendorff, *Voyage,* pp. 30–31; Moser, *À travers l'Asie Centrale,* p. 66; Zaleskie, *La Vie des steppes,* pp. 24, 33; Ujfalvy de Mezö-Kövesd, *Expédition scientifique,* II, 30; Lansdell, *Russian Central Asia,* I, 311, 336, 366–367; Karutz, *Unter Kirgisen und Turkmenen,* p. 85.

20. Rudenko, "Ocherk Byta," pp. 22–24; J. Castagné, "Magie et exorcisme chez les Kazak-Kirghizes et autres peuples turks orientaux," *Revue des études islamiques,* IV (1930), 53–156; N. I. Dyrenkova, "Polychenie Shamanskogo Dara po Vozzreniiam Turetskikh Plemen," in *Sbornik Muzeia Antropologii i Etnografii,* IX (Leningrad: Akademiia Nauk SSSR, 1930), pp. 267–291; Pallas, *Voyages,* I, 619–621; Levshin, *Déscription,* pp. 325–339; Vambéry, *Sketches,* p. 291; Karutz, *Unter Kirgisen und Turkmenen,* pp. 129–130.

21. Levshin, *Déscription,* pp. 332–335, 365–366; Zaleskie, *La Vie des*

steppes, pp. 27, 59; Ujfalvy de Mezö-Kövesd, *Expédition scientifique,* II, 30; Grodekov, *Kirgizy i Karakirgizy,* p. 109; Radloff, *Aus Sibirien,* I, 492.

22. Levshin, *Déscription,* pp. 318, 368–372; Vambéry, *Sketches,* p. 293; Moser, *À travers l'Asie Centrale,* pp. 33–34; Fell, *Russian and Nomad,* p. 152.

23. Levshin, *Déscription,* pp. 371–372, 378-383; Meyendorff, *Voyage,* p. 44; Winner, *Oral Art and Literature,* pp. 25–83.

24. Shneider, "Kazakskaia Ornamentika," pp. 135–171; Karutz, *Unter Kirgisen und Turkmenen,* p. 148; Kuftin, *Kirgiz-Kazaki,* pp. 35–37; Rudenko, "Ocherk Byta," pp. 45–48; V. V. Vostrov, "Nekotorye Voprosy Etnografii Kazakhov Kzyl-ordinskoi Oblasti," in *Materialy i Issledovaniia po Ethnografii Kazakhskogo Naroda* (Alma Ata: Akademiia Nauk Kazakhskoi SSR, 1963), pp. 30–50; Zakhovara and Khodzhaeva, "Muzhskaia i Zhenskaia Odezhda," pp. 74–75; E. A. Klodta, *Kazakhskii Narodnyi Ornament* (Moscow: Iskusstvo, 1939). Compare with Berthold Laufer, *The Decorative Art of the Amur Tribes* ("Memoirs of the American Museum of Natural History," Vol. VII [New York: The Museum, 1902]).

25. W. Barthold, "Kirgiz," in *Encyclopaedia of Islam* (Leiden: E. J. Brill, 1927), II, 1025–1026.

26. Schuyler, *Turkistan,* II, 137–140; Grodekov, *Kirgizy i Karakirgizy;* Radloff, *Aus Sibirien;* Gustav Krist, *Alone through the Forbidden Land,* trans. E. O. Lorimer (New York: Harcourt, Brace, 1938); E. Delmar Morgan, "Recent Geography of Central Asia: From Russian Sources," *Royal Geographical Society: Supplementary Papers,* I (1882), 208, 239–240; O. Olufsen, *The Emir of Bokhara and his Country* (London: William Heinemann, 1911), p. 295; Captain John Wood, *A Journey to the Source of the River Oxus* (2nd ed.; London: John Murray, 1872), pp. 210, 212, 215, 221; Major T. G. Montgomerie, "Report of 'The Mirza's' Exploration from Caubal to Kashgar," *Journal of the Royal Geographical Society,* XLI (1871), 146, 149; Barthold, "Kirgiz"; IA. R. Vinnikov, "Rodo-plemennoi Sostav i Rasselenie Kirgizov na Territorii Iuzhnoi Kirgizii," in *Trudy Kirgizskoi Arkheologo-etnograficheskoi Ekspeditsii,* I (Moscow: Akademiia Nauk SSSR, 1956), pp. 136–181; K. Usenbaev, "K Voprosu o Prisoedinenii Iuzhnoi Kirgizii k Rossii," in *Trudy Instituta Istorii,* I (Frunze: Akademiia Nauk Kirgizskoi SSR, 1955), pp. 39–42; Tolstov *et al.,* *Narody Srednei Azii,* II, 170–177.

27. T. A. Zhdanko, *Ocherki Istoricheskoi Etnografii Karakalpakov: Rodo-plemennaia Struktura i Rasselenie v XIX–Nachale XX Veka* (Mos-

cow: Akademii Nauk SSSR, 1950); B. V. Andrianov, "Ak-Dzhagyz (k Istorii Formirovaniia Sovremennoi Etnicheskoi Territorii Karakalpakov v Nizov'e Amu-Dar'i)," in *Arkheologicheskie i Etnograficheskie Raboty Khorezmskoi Ekspeditsii 1945–1948* (Moscow: Akademiia Nauk SSSR, 1952), pp. 567–584; Andrianov, "Etnicheskaia Territoriia Karakalpakov," pp. 7–132.

28. S. Kamalov, "Narodno-osvoboditel'naia Bor'ba Karakalpakov protiv Khivinskikh Khanov v XIX v.," in *Materialy i Issledovaniia po Etnografii Karakalpakov* (Moscow: Akademiia Nauk SSSR, 1958), p. 137.

29. Kamalov, "Narodno-osvoboditel'naia Bor'ba Karakalpakov," pp. 137–138; Tolstov *et al., Narody Srednei Azii,* I, 450–452, 466–468, 485–489; T. A. Zhdanko, "Narodnoe Ornamental'noe Iskusstvo Karakalpakov," in *Materialy i Issledovaniia po Etnografii Karakalpakov* (Moscow: Akademiia Nauk SSSR, 1958), pp. 373–410; B. V. Andrianov and A. S. Melkov, "Obraztsy Karakalpakskogo Narodnogo Ornamenta," in *Materialy i Issledovaniia po Etnografii Karakalpakov* (Moscow: Akademiia Nauk SSSR, 1958), pp. 411–412 and plates.

30. For a discussion of this transitional process, see Bacon, *Obok,* pp. 108–110, 161–163, 180–181.

31. Zhdanko, *Ocherki Istoricheskoi Etnografii Karakalpakov;* Zhdanko, "Karakalpaki Khorezmskogo Oazisa"; Andrianov, "Etnicheskaia Territoriia," pp. 77–112; Tolstov *et al., Narody Srednei Azii,* I, 409, 418, chart facing 412, 466–485, 510–513, 520; Kharuzin, *Kirgizy Bukeevskoi Ordy,* pp. 39–40; Olufsen, *The Emir of Bokhara,* p. 296; Zhdanko, "Narodnoe Ornamental'noe Iskusstvo"; Andrianov and Melkov, "Obraztsy Karakalpakskogo Narodnogo Ornamenta."

32. W. Barthold, *A History of the Turkmen Peoples,* trans. V. and T. Minorsky (Leiden: E. J. Brill, 1962); Alexander Burnes, *Travels into Bokhara* (London: J. Murray, 1834), II, 259; Arminius Vambéry, *Travels in Central Asia* (New York: Harper & Brothers, 1865), pp. 95, 98, 147, 272; Edmond O'Donovan, *The Merv Oasis* (London: Smith, Elder, & Co., 1882), I, 119, 129–130, 192–193, 203–204; II, 91–92, 309, 324–326, 352; Moser, *À travers l'Asie Centrale,* pp. 274–275; Tolstov *et al., Narody Srednei Azii,* II, 49.

33. Vambéry, *Travels,* pp. 60, 82–83, 89–93, 100, 147; Moser, *À travers l'Asie Centrale,* pp. 275, 283–285, 320–328; O'Donovan, *The Merv Oasis,* II, 31, 33–35, 55, 314–315, 324–326.

34. Vambéry, *Travels,* p. 147; O'Donovan, *The Merv Oasis,* I, 80–81, 147–149, 212–214; II, 78–79, 100, 179, 235–237, 274–275, 310, 312, 324–328, 338–343.

35. Vambéry, *Travels*, p. 75; O'Donovan, *The Merv Oasis*, I, 41–43, 48, 129–130, 146–147, 208–210, 213–214, 217, 222–223, 232–233, 237, 239, 247–248; II, 97, 120–121, 138–142, 148–149, 178, 261–262, 265, 308–311, 325, 351; Tolstov *et al.*, *Narody Srednei Azii*, II, 80–99.

36. O'Donovan, *The Merv Oasis*, I, 97, 128; II, 36–37, 134, 159–164, 235, 404; G. P. Vasil'eva, "Turkmeny-nokhurli," in *Sredneaziatskii Etnograficheskii Sbornik* (Moscow: Akademiia Nauk SSSR, 1954), pp. 84–105; G. P. Vasil'eva, "Itogi Raboty Turkmenskogo Otriada Khorezmskoi Ekspeditsii za 1948 g.," in *Arkheologicheskie i Etnograficheskie Raboty Khorezmskoi Ekspeditsii 1945–1948* (Moscow: Akademiia Nauk SSSR, 1952), pp. 430–436; Vambéry, *Travels*, p. 102; Tolstov *et al.*, *Narody Srednei Azii*, II, 18–20.

37. O'Donovan, *The Merv Oasis*, II, 350.

38. Tolstov *et al.*, *Narody Srednei Azii*, II, 109–110; Vambéry, *Travels*, p. 85; O'Donovan, *The Merv Oasis*, I, 234; II, 350–351, 412; Moser, *À travers l'Asie Centrale*, pp. 329, 331, 353.

39. O'Donovan, *The Merv Oasis*, I, 130, 239, 243–244, 251; II, 161, 179–180; Vambéry, *Travels*, pp. 74–75; Olufsen, *The Emir of Bokhara*, p. 385.

40. Tolstov *et al.*, *Narody Srednei Azii*, II, 115–116; O'Donovan, *The Merv Oasis*, I, 198–199, 251; II, 92, 301–303.

41. Tolstov *et al.*, *Narody Srednei Azii*, I, 221–224; II, 90, 142–144; Maurice S. Dimand, *Peasant and Nomad Rugs of Asia* (New York: Asia House Gallery, 1961), pp. 34–39, 66–71; Morgan, "Recent Geography," pp. 229–237; Schuyler, *Turkistan*, I, 309, 325.

Chapter III

1. Moser, *À travers l'Asie Centrale*, p. 24; Tolstov *et al.*, *Narody Srednei Azii*, I, 209–212, 217–218; Olufsen. *The Emir of Bokhara*, pp. 271, 495–501; Annette M. B. Meakin, *In Russian Turkestan* (London: George Allen & Unwin, 1903), pp. 23–27.

2. Moser, *À travers l'Asie Centrale*, pp. 99, 235; Olufsen, *The Emir of Bokhara*, pp. 356–361; Tolstov, *et al.*, *Narody Srednei Azii*, I, 221–225.

3. Olufsen, *The Emir of Bokhara*, pp. 336, 458, 464; Tolstov *et al.*, *Narody Srednei Azii*, I, 305, 308–312; Schuyler, *Turkistan*, I, 125, Meakin, *In Russian Turkestan*, pp. 149–151.

4. Moser, *À travers l'Asie Centrale*, pp. 101, 134; Schuyler, *Turkistan*, I, 120–121; Olufsen, *The Emir of Bokhara*, pp. 452–455, 461–464;

Meakin, *In Russian Turkestan*, pp. 151–154; Vambéry, *Travels*, p. 161; Tolstov *et al., Narody Srednei Azii*, I, 307–310.

5. Moser, *À travers l'Asie Centrale*, pp. 69, 98, 114, 234; Meakin, *In Russian Turkestan*, pp. 52–53, 112–113; Olufsen, *The Emir of Bokhara*, pp. 307–316, 319–322, 330–331; Tolstov *et al., Narody Srednei Azii*, I, 278–282.

6. Schuyler, *Turkistan*, I, 118–119; Meakin, *In Russian Turkestan*, pp. 107–111; Tolstov *et al., Narody Srednei Azii*, I, 278–279.

7. Schuyler, *Turkistan*, I, 119–120; Meakin, *In Russian Turkestan* pp. 114–117; Olufsen, *The Emir of Bokhara*, pp. 325, 328, 330–332, 454; Tolstov *et al., Narody Srednei Azii*, I, 282, 311.

8. Moser, *À travers l'Asie Centrale*, pp. 70–71, 73, 144, 153, 234, 236; Schuyler, *Turkistan*, I, 122–124; Meakin, *In Russian Turkestan*, pp. 55, 128–132; Olufsen, *The Emir of Bokhara*, pp, 328–330, 467–472, 479–485; Tolstov *et al., Narody Srednei Azii*, I, 294–298, 300–302.

9. Vambéry, *Sketches*, p. 164; Schuyler, *Turkistan*, I, 174–175, 257; Moser, *À travers l'Asie Centrale*, pp. 98–105, 111–112, 144–145, 172, 249; Olufsen, *The Emir of Bokhara*, pp. 334–336, 338, 516, 518; Meakin, *In Russian Turkestan*, p. 56; Tolstov *et al., Narody Srednei Azii*, I, 262–266, 269–376.

10. Schuyler, *Turkistan*, I, 174–178, 183–188; Moser, *À travers l'Asie Centrale*, pp. 22–23, 98–105, 144–145, 173; Meakin, *In Russian Turkestan*, pp. 210–215; Olufsen, *The Emir of Bokhara*, pp. 210–215; Tolstov *et al., Narody Srednei Azii*, I, 222–224, 226, 233–244, 255–259, 264–265, 276, 303, 306–307, 310.

11. Meakin, *In Russian Turkestan*, p. 145; Tolstov *et al., Narody Srednei Azii*, I, 323–324, 612.

12. Schuyler, *Turkistan*, I, 142–144; Moser, *À travers l'Asie Centrale*, p. 73; Meakin, *In Russian Turkestan*, pp. 137–142; Tolstov *et al., Narody Srednei Azii*, I, 325–326.

13. Schuyler, *Turkistan*, I, 124, 188, 194; Meakin, *In Russian Turkestan*, pp. 100–102; Moser, *À travers l'Asie Centrale*, pp. 106, 114, 144, 270.

14. S. M. Mirkhasilov, "Kul'turnoe Razvitie Uzbekskogo Kishlaka Niiazbashi," *Sovietskaia Etnografiia* (1962), No. 1, p. 14; Meakin, *In Russian Turkestan*, pp. 139, 143–146, 284; Schuyler, *Turkistan*, I, 146–147; Moser, *À travers l'Asie Centrale*, p. 252; Tolstov *et al., Narody Srednei Azii*, I, 323–324.

15. Tolstov *et al., Narody Srednei Azii*, I, 266–268, 276, 314.

16. Moser, *À travers l'Asie Centrale*, pp. 122–123; Olufsen, *The Emir of Bokhara*, pp. 491–492.

17. Rev. Joseph Wolff, *Narrative of a Mission to Bokhara* (6th ed.; Edinburgh: William Blackwood & Sons, 1852), pp. 147, 186; Moser, *À travers l'Asie Centrale*, pp. 156, 206, 212; Tolstov *et al.*, *Narody Srednei Azii*, I, 175–177.

18. Wolff, *Narrative*, pp. 147, 152, 180; Schuyler, *Turkistan*, I, 136; Vambéry, *Travels*, pp. 152, 166; Moser, *À travers l'Asie Centrale*, pp. 140, 247; Olufsen, *The Emir of Bokhara*, p. 399.

19. Schuyler, *Turkistan*, I, 191–197; A. L. Troitskaia, "Ferganskaia Teatral'naia Ekspeditsiia," *Sovetskaia Etnografiia* (1937), No. 1, p. 163; Tolstov *et al.*, *Narody Srednei Azii*, I, 178–179, 243–244.

20. Wolff, *Narrative*, pp. 116, 153; Vambéry, *Travels*, pp. 73–74, 152, 155, 158–160, 162–164, 166, 173, 178–179, 183–184, 203–205, 210–212, 220, 222–223; Meyendorff, *Voyage*, pp. 253–254, 262–263; Schuyler, *Turkistan*, I, 122, 158–161, 165–168, 173, 235, 257; II, 32; Moser, *À travers l'Asie Centrale*, pp. 75–76, 171–172; Olufsen, *The Emir of Bokhara*, pp. 383–384, 391–399; Tolstov *et al.*, *Narody Srednei Azii*, I, 318, 322; Meakin, *In Russian Turkestan*, pp. 66–68, 70–71; O. A. Sukhareva, *Islam v Uzbekistane* (Tashkent: Akademiia Nauk Uzbekskoi SSR, 1960), pp. 52–54, 58, 84.

21. Vambéry, *Travels*, pp. 140, 198, 232–234, 240; Moser, *À travers l'Asie Centrale*, pp. 118–119; Schuyler, *Turkistan*, II, 44–45, 113–114; Meakin, *In Russian Turkestan*, pp. 75–76, 244; Olufsen, *The Emir of Bokhara*, pp. 373, 392; Tolstov *et al.*, *Narody Srednei Azii*, I, 319–321; Sukhareva, *Islam v Uzbekistane*, pp. 19–20.

22. Schuyler, *Turkistan*, I, 140–142, 150–152; II, 31–32; Meakin, *In Russian Turkestan*, pp. 172–175; Olufsen, *The Emir of Bokhara*, pp. 404–405; Tolstov *et al.*, *Narody Srednei Azii*, I, 320, 325, 329–330, 616-636; Sukhareva, *Islam v Uzbekistane*, pp. 20–21, 83.

23. Schuyler, *Turkistan*, I, 330; II, 79–80; Meakin, *In Russian Turkestan*, pp. 159–160, 252–253; Olufsen, *The Emir of Bokhara*, pp. 367, 384–385; O. Olufsen, *Through the Unknown Pamirs* (London: William Heinemann, 1904), p. 161; Tolstov *et al.*, *Narody Srednei Azii*, I, 318–320, 627–629; Sukhareva, *Islam v Uzbekistane*, pp. 21–23.

24. Meakin, *In Russian Turkestan*, pp. 84–86, 99–100; Mirkhasilov, "Kul'turnoe Razvitie," p. 9.

25. Vambéry, *Travels*, p. 272.

26. Burnes, *Travels*, I, 305–307; Wolff, *Narrative*, pp. 146, 162; W.

Barthold, *Ulugh-Beg* (Vol. II, "Four Studies on the History of Central Asia" [Leiden: E. J. Brill, 1958]), p. 119; Meakin, *In Russian Turkestan*, pp. 77–81, 251.

27. Schuyler, *Turkistan*, I, 165; Meakin, *In Russian Turkestan*, pp. 87, 145, 200–201; Olufsen, *The Emir of Bokhara*, pp. 474–475.

28. Meakin, *In Russian Turkestan*, p. 221.

29. Schuyler, *Turkistan*, I, 128, 234–235; II, 88; Olufsen, *The Emir of Bokhara*, pp. 336, 434–436; Tolstov et al., *Narody Srednei Azii*, I, 315–317; Moser, *À travers l'Asie Centrale*, p. 261.

30. Moser, *À travers l'Asie Centrale*, pp. 175–177, 200, 259–260; Schuyler, *Turkistan*, I, 132–137, 140–141; II, 41, 58–59, 66, 70; Meakin, *In Russian Turkestan*, pp. 159–164, 217–220, 283; Olufsen, *The Emir of Bokhara*, pp. 331, 334, 433–434, 436–439; Troitskaia, "Ferganskaia Teatral'naia Ekspeditsiia," pp. 163–164; Tolstov et al., *Narody Srednei Azii*, I. 318–320, 627, 649–650; Sukhareva, *Islam v Uzbekistane*, p. 23.

31. Meyendorff, *Voyage*, pp. 283–284; Clavijo, *Embassy to Tamerlane 1403–1406*, trans. Guy Le Strange (New York: Harper & Brothers, 1928), pp. 261–262, 266–267; Vambéry, *Travels*, pp. 178–179, 183–184; Moser, *À travers l'Asie Centrale*, pp. 171, 259; Schuyler, *Turkistan*, I, 127; Meakin, *In Russian Turkestan*, p. 68; Olufsen, *The Emir of Bokhara*, pp. 331, 392, 439, 465–466, 520; Mirkhasilov, "Kul'turnoe Razvitie," p. 14; Tolstov et al., *Narody Srednei Azii*, I, 310–311.

32. A gypsum plaster which is carved while still plastic.

33. Meakin, *In Russian Turkestan*, pp. 109–110, 212–213; Olufsen, *The Emir of Bokhara*, pp. 322, 324, 525, 532; Tolstov et al., *Narody Srednei Azii*, I, 242.

Chapter IV

1. Richard A. Pierce, *Russian Central Asia, 1867–1917* (Berkeley and Los Angeles: University of California Press, 1960), pp. 43, 106–135; Zakharova, "Material'naia Kul'tura," p. 107; U. Shalekenov, "Byt Karakalpakskogo Krest'ianstva Chimbaiskogo Raiona v Proshlom i Nastoiashchem," in *Materialy i Issledovaniia po Etnografii Karakalpakov* (Moscow: Akademiia Nauk SSSR, 1958), p. 275.

2. Meyendorff, *Voyage*, p. 38; Levshin, *Déscription*, p. 418; Vostrov, "Kazakhi Dzhanybekskogo Raiona," p. 32.

3. Levshin, *Déscription*, pp. 312, 321–413; Meakin, *In Russian Turkestan*, pp. 225–226, 233; Radloff, "Die Hausthiere der Kirgisen," p. 290; Rudenko, "Ocherk Byta," pp. 3, 18, 20, 24, 30–42; Vostrov,

"Kazakhi Dzhanybekskogo Raiona," pp. 16–18, 21, 26–27; Lansdell, *Russian Central Asia*, I, 314; Moser, *À travers l'Asie Centrale*, p. 56; Ujfalvy de Mezö-Kövesd, *Expédition scientifique*, II, 110; Olivia Fell Vans-Agnew, "A British Family in the Kazakh Steppe," *Central Asian Review*, X (1962), 7, 9; Pierce, *Russian Central Asia*, pp. 160, 191; Zakharova, "Material'naia Kul'tura," pp. 109–112; Tolstov *et al.*, *Narody Srednei Azii*, I, 36, 255–256; John W. Wardell, "An Account of the Happenings at Spasskiy in Kazakhstan between 1914 and 1919," *Central Asian Review*, XII (1964), 110.

4. Atkinson, *Oriental and Western Siberia*, p. 451.

5. Ujfalvy de Mezö-Kövesd, *Expédition scientifique*, II, 112; Vostrov, "Kazakhi Dzhanybekskogo Raiona," p. 15; E. A. Masanov, "Usloviia Truda i Bytovoi Uklad Kazakhskikh Remeslennikov (Vtoraia Polovina XIX i Nachalo XX v.)," *Izvestiia Akademii Nauk Kazakhskoi SSR*, I (XV) (Alma Ata, 1961); Schuyler, *Turkistan*, I, 34. For trade, see Pallas, *Voyages*, I, 356, 359–361, 420–421, 614, 618; III, 375–377; IV, 219; Moser, *À travers l'Asie Centrale*, pp. 22–23, 25–26, 54, 59–60; Radloff, *Aus Sibirien*, p. 114; Vambéry, *Travels*, pp. 184, 208–209, 266; Lansdell, *Russian Central Asia*, I, 53–54; Meakin, *In Russian Turkestan*, p. 225; Olufsen, *The Emir of Bokhara*, p. 359; Vans-Agnew, "A British Family in the Kazakh Steppe," p. 8; Rudenko, "Ocherk Byta," p. 44; Zakharova, "Material'naia Kul'tura," p. 112; G. P. Vasil'eva and N. A. Kisliakov, "Voprosy Sem'i i Byta Narodov Srednei Azii i Kazakhstana v Period Stroitel'stva Sotsializma i Kommunisma," *Sovetskaia Etnografiia* (1962), No. 6, p. 4; T. A. Zhdanko, "Problema Polyosedlogo Naseleniia v Istorii Srednei Azii i Kazakhstana," *Sovetskaia Etnografiia* (1961), No. 2, pp. 53–54; Pierce, *Russian Central Asia*, pp. 158–161.

6. Meyendorff, *Voyage*, pp. 48, 53–54; Levshin, *Déscription*, pp. 374–377, 393–396, 402; Schuyler, *Turkistan*, I, 31–33; Pierce, *Russian Central Asia*, pp. 46–63.

7. Schuyler, *Turkistan*, I, 166–167; Lansdell, *Russian Central Asia*, I, 346–348; Levshin, *Déscription*, p. 400; Grodekov, *Kirgizy i Karakirgizy*, p. 15.

8. Grodekov, *Kirgizy i Karakirgizy*, p. 12; Schuyler, *Turkistan*, II, 140–142.

9. Grodekov, *Kirgizy i Karakirgizy*, p. 16; Levshin, *Déscription*, p. 344; Pierce, *Russian Central Asia*, pp. 119, 156–157; Rudenko, "Ocherk Byta," pp. 3, 20; Radloff, *Aus Sibirien*, I, 410, 416; Bacon, *Obok*, pp. 69–70; Zakharova, "Material'naia Kul'tura," p. 110.

10. Vostrov, "Kazakhi Dzhanybekskogo Raiona," pp. 44–49; Pierce,

Russian Central Asia, pp. 203–211, 219–220; Hélène Carrère d'Encausse, "Tsarist Educational Policy in Turkestan, 1867–1917," *Central Asian Review,* XI (1963), 374–394.

11. Winner, *Oral Art and Literature,* pp. 101–120.

12. Winner, *Oral Art and Literature,* pp. 120–132.

13. Schuyler, *Turkistan,* II, 139; Krist, *Alone through the Forbidden Land,* pp. 118–121; "The Social, Economic and Political Effects of Russian Influence in Kirgizia (1855–1917)," *Central Asian Review,* V (1957), 242–243.

14. "The Development of Kara-Kalpakia after Union with Russia,' *Central Asian Review,* VI (1958), 40–43; "Tsarist Policy towards Islam· The Soviet Version," *Central Asian Review,* VI (1958), 250–251.

15. Moser, *À travers l'Asie Centrale,* pp. 275–278, 314–316, 329, 334–335; O'Donovan, *The Merv Oasis,* II, 55, 65–70, 83–84; Richard Karutz, *Unter Kirgisen und Turkmenen* (Berlin: Verlag Ullstein, n.d.), pp. 32–35; Krist, *Alone through the Forbidden Land,* pp. 37–44; A. Karryiev and A. Rosliakov, *Kratki Ocherk Istorii Turkmenistana 1868–1917* (Ashkhabad, 1956), summarized in *Central Asian Review,* VI (1958), 134–137.

16. William Eleroy Curtis, *Turkestan. "The Heart of Asia"* (New York: Hodder & Stoughton, 1911), p. 121.

17. Pierce, *Russian Central Asia,* p. 137.

18. Pierce, *Russian Central Asia,* pp. 163–166; Meyendorff, *Voyage,* pp. 216–217, 241.

19. Tolstov *et al., Narody Srednei Azii,* I, 182–184.

20. Tolstov *et al., Narody Srednei Azii,* I, 181, 186–188.

21. O'Donovan, *The Merv Oasis,* II, 4; Meakin, *In Russian Turkestan,* pp. 114–115, 211–214; Olufsen, *The Emir of Bokhara,* pp. 465, 471, 520; Curtis, *Turkestan,* p. 36; Tolstov *et al., Narody Srednei Azii,* I, 179, 184–185, 236–237, 240.

22. Meakin, *In Russian Turkestan,* pp. 102–103, 214–215, 290–292. For the effect of the Western market on tribal rug-making in general, see G. Wilfrid Seager, "Oriental Carpets Today," *Royal Central Asian Journal,* LI (1964), 122.

23. Meakin, *In Russian Turkestan,* p. 281.

24. Meakin, *In Russian Turkestan,* pp. 108–109, 132; Moser, *À travers l'Asie Centrale,* p. 251; Olufsen, *The Emir of Bokhara,* p. 343.

25. Tolstov *et al., Narody Srednei Azii,* I, 184–185, 269.

26. Tolstov *et al., Narody Srednei Azii,* I, 184; Schuyler, *Turkistan,* I, 124–125.

27. Schuyler, *Turkistan*, I, 115–116, 158, 161–162, 168–169, 258–259; Moser, *À travers l'Asie Centrale*, p. 118; Meakin, *In Russian Turkestan*, pp. 64–65, 69, 71–72, 75–76; Guillaume Capus, *À travers le royaume de Tamerlan (Asie Centrale)* (Paris: A. Hennuyer, 1892), pp. 314–315; Pierce, *Russian Central Asia*, pp. 223–233; Pierce, *Mission to Turkestan*, pp. 47–48; "Tsarist Policy towards Islam," p. 250.

28. Bennigsen and Quelquejay, *Les mouvements nationaux*, pp. 26–40; Hélène Carrère d'Encausse, "La Politique culturelle du pouvoir tsariste au Turkestan (1867–1917)," *Cahiers du monde russe et soviétique*, III (1962), 374–407; "Tsarist Policy towards Islam," p. 243; Geoffrey Wheeler, *Racial Problems in Soviet Muslim Asia* (2nd ed.; London: Oxford University Press, 1962), p. 11; Woeikof, *Le Turkestan russe*, p. 332.

Chapter V

1. Pierce, *Russian Central Asia*, pp. 161–162, 293.

2. Joseph Castagné, "Les Organisations soviétiques de la Russie musulmane," *Revue du monde musulman*, LI (October, 1922), 178–181; Elizabeth Bacon, "Soviet Policy in Turkestan," *The Middle East Journal*, I (1947), 390–392.

3. S. M. Abramson, "Preobrazovaniia v Khoziaistve i Kul'ture Kazakhov za Gody Sotsialisticheskogo Stroitel'stva," *Sovetskaia Etnografiia* (1961), No. 1, pp. 59–61; Zakharova, "Material'naia Kul'tura," pp. 120–121; Vasil'eva and Kisliakov, "Voprosy Sem'i i Byta," pp. 6–7; D. Kshibekov, *O Feodal'no Bayskikh Perezhitkakh i ikh preodolenii* (Alma Ata, 1957), p. 62.

4. Tsentral'noe Statisticheskoe Upravlenie pri Sovete Ministrov SSSR, *Chislennost', Sostav i Razmeshchenie Naseleniia SSSR. Kratkie Itogi Vsesoiuznoi Perepisi Naseleniia 1959 Goda* (Moscow: Gosstatizdat, 1961), p. 48; Tsentral'noe Statisticheskoe Upravlenie pri Sovete Ministrov SSSR, *Chislennost' Skota v SSSR. Statisticheskii Sbornik* (Moscow, 1957), pp. 30–31; Russia (1923–U.S.S.R.) Tsentral'noe Statisticheskoe Upravlenie, *The National Economy of the USSR in 1960; Statistical Yearbook* (Washington, D.C.: U.S. Joint Publications Research Service, 1962), p. 921.

5. Abramson, "Preobrazovaniia v Khoziaistve i Kul'ture Kazakhov," pp. 58–61; Tsentral'noe Statisticheskoe Upravlenie pri Sovete Ministrov SSSR, *Chislennost' Skota v SSSR*, pp. 30–31, 46–47; "Some Statistics on Higher Education in the Muslim Republics," *Central*

Asian Review, X (1962), 229–238; V. K. Gardanov, B. O. Dolgikh, and T. A. Zhdanko, "Osnovnye Napravleniia Etnicheskikh Protsessov u Naradov SSSR," *Sovetskaia Etnografiia* (1961), No. 4, p. 21.

6. *Kazakhstanskaia Pravda,* October 13, 1962; *Pravda Vostoka,* November 1, 1962, and *Sovetskaia Kirgiziia,* December 22, 1962, in *Central Asian Review,* XI (1963), 45; *Turkmenskaia Iskra,* November 21, 1963, in *Central Asian Review,* XII (1946), 39.

7. Tolstov et al., *Narody Srednei Azii,* I, 36–37, 200, 221–226, 428, 442–445; II, 54–59; "Irrigation in Central Asia," *Central Asian Review,* VIII (1960), 47, 145–148; *Kazakhstanskaia Pravda,* August 20, 1962, in *Central Asian Review,* X (1962), 364; "Irrigation: Progress since 1960," *Central Asian Review,* XI (1963), 146, 149, 151.

8. *Pravda,* June 12, 1961, in *Central Asian Review,* IX (1961), 388.

9. Gardanov et al., "Osnovnye Napravleniia," pp. 21–22; *Pravda,* May 24, 1962, in *Central Asian Review,* X (1962), 248.

10. "Private Property Tendencies in Central Asia and Kazakhstan," *Central Asian Review,* X (1962), 153–156; *Sovetskaia Kirgiziia,* October 1, 1961, in *Central Asian Review,* X (1962), 60; *Pravda Vostoka,* December 12, 1962, in *Central Asian Review,* XI (1963), 59; "The Tashkent Oblast," *Central Asian Review,* VI (1958), 56–57; Theodore Shabad, "Moscow, Reversing Policy, Will Spur Private Farming," *New York Times,* November 7, 1964; Zakharova, "Material'naia Kul'tura," pp. 130, 135–136.

11. Zakharova, "Material'naia Kul'tura," pp. 135–137; Downton, "Soviet Central Asia," pp. 132–133.

12. Rudenko, "Ocherk Byta," pp. 4–10.

13. Vostrov, "Kazakhi Dzhanybekskogo Raiona," pp. 50–61; Zakharova, "Material'naia Kul'tura," pp. 120–137; O. A. Korbe, "Kul'tura i Byt Kazakhskogo Kolkhoznogo Aula," *Sovetskaia Etnografiia* (1950), No. 4, pp. 68–77; IA. R. Vinnikov, "Sotsialisticheskoe Pereustroistvo Khoziaistva i Byta Daikhan Maryiksoi Oblasti Turkmenskoi SSR," in *Sredneaziatskii Etnograficheskii Sbornik,* I (Moscow: Akademiia Nauk SSSR, 1954), 33–35; Shalekenov, "Byt Karakalpakskogo Krest'ianstva," p. 274; Vasil'eva and Kisliakov, "Voprosy Sem'i i Byta," p. 11.

14. Zakharova, "Material'naia Kul'tura," pp. 138–154, 160–161; Zhdanko, "Karakalpaki Khorezmskogo Oazisa," pp. 531–541; Tolstov et al., *Narody Srednei Azii,* I, 466–472; T. A. Zhdanko, "Byt Kolkhoznikov Rybolovetskikh Arteley na Ostravakh Iuzhnogo Arala," *Sovetskaia Etnografiia* (1961), No. 5; Vostrov, "Kazakhi Dzhanybekskogo Raiona," pp. 25–28; Korbe, "Kul'tura i Byt," p. 77.

15. Zakharova, "Material'naia Kul'tura," pp. 155–160, 174, 180–181; Shikhberdy Annaklychev, "Nekotorie Storony Byta Rabochikh-neftianikov Nebit-Daga," *Sovetskaia Etnografiia* (1959), No. 1, pp. 59–60; K. Mambetali'eva, *Byt i Kul'tura Shakhterov-Kirgizov Kamennougal'noi Promyshlennosti Kirgizii* (Frunze, 1963), summarized in "The Life of the Kirgiz Miner," *Central Asian Review,* XII (1964), 119.

16. Zakharova, "Material'naia Kul'tura," pp. 174–181; Vostrov, "Kazakhi Dzhanybekskogo Raiona," pp. 78–81; Mambetali'eva, *Byt i Kul'tura,* p. 119.

17. Zakharova, "Material'naia Kul'tura," pp. 166–172; Vostrov, "Kazakhi Dzhanybekskogo Raiona," pp. 81–82.

18. Mambetali'eva, *Byt i Kul'tura,* pp. 118–119.

19. Annaklychev, "Nekotorie Storony Byta," pp. 62–63.

20. Zakharova, "Material'naia Kul'tura," pp. 161, 168, 172, 181–186; Klodta, *Kazakhskii Narodnyi Ornament;* Mambetali'eva *Byt i Kul'tura,* p. 121.

21. Zakharova "Material'naia Kul'tura," p. 129; Vostrov, "Kazakhi Dzhanybekskogo Raiona," pp. 54–55, 58.

22. Herbert Harold Vreeland, III, *Mongol Community and Kinship Structure* (New Haven: Human Relations Area Files, 1954), pp. 34–35.

23. Bacon, *Obok,* pp. 66–68.

24. Vinnikov, "Rodo-plemennoi Sostav," pp. 136–181; Korbe, "Kul'tura i Byt," pp. 71, 86; Vostrov, "Kazakhi Dzhanybekskogo Raiona," p. 54; Zakharova, "Material'naia Kul'tura," p. 129; Irene Winner, "Some Problems of Nomadism and Social Organization among the Recently Settled Kazakhs," *Central Asian Review,* XI (1963), 355–359; "Stabilization of the Nomads," *Central Asian Review,* VII (1959), 225–227; Gardanov *et al.,* "Osnovnie Napravleniia," p. 20; Annaklychev, "Nekotorie Storony Byta," pp. 58, 63–64; Shikhberdy Annaklychev, *Byt Rabochikh-neftianikoe Nebit-Daga i Kum-Daga* (Ashkhabad, 1961), reviewed by V. Krupianskaia in *Sovetskaia Etnografiia* (1962), No. 1, pp. 115–117; Zhdanko, *Ocherki Istoricheskoi Etnografii Karakalpakov,* pp. 37–94.

25. Alexandre Bennigsen, "The Muslim Peoples of Soviet Russia and the Soviets," *The Islamic Review,* XLIII (1955), No. 4, p. 28; *Komsomolskaia Pravda,* January 12, 1961 and *Pravda,* May 25, 1962, in *Central Asian Review,* X (1962), 155, 266; Mambetali'eva, *Byt i Kul'tura,* p. 120.

26. "Some Statistics on Higher Education," pp. 232, 234.

27. Bennigsen, "The Muslim Peoples of Soviet Russia," p. 29;

Sovetskaia Kirgiziia, September 19, 1961, in *Central Asian Review,* XI (1963), 225; Gardanov *et al.,* "Osnovnye Napravleniia," p. 20; speech by I. R. Rezzakov, First Secretary of the Central Committee of the Kirghiz Communist Party, in "Conference of Kirgiz Intelligentsia," *Central Asian Review,* VIII (1960), 289; Korbe, "Kul'tura i Byt," p. 86; N. S. Sabitov, "Obshchestvennaia Zhizn' i Semeinyi Byt Kazakhov-kolkhoznikov," *Trudy Instituta Istorii, Arkheologii i Etnografii,* III, *Etnografiia* (Alma Ata: Akademiia Nauk Kazakhskoi SSR, 1956), p. 206; "The Peoples of Central Asia: Social Customs," *Central Asian Review,* VII (1959), 214.

28. Bennigsen, "The Muslim Peoples of Soviet Russia," p. 29.

29. Vostrov, "Kazakhi Dzhanybekskogo Raiona," p. 85; "Crimes against Women in the 1961 Turkmen Criminal Code," *Central Asian Review,* XIII (1965), 227–231

30. Vostrov, "Kazakhi Dzhanybekskogo Raiona," pp. 84–87; Korbe, "Kul'tura i Byt," p. 85; Vasil'eva and Kisliakov, "Voprosy Sem'i i Byta," pp. 13–14; Annaklychev, "Nekotorie Storony Byta," p. 68; Gardanov *et al.,* "Osnovnye Napravleniia," p. 20; Irene Winner, "Some Problems of Nomadism," pp. 361–362.

31. S. M. Abramson, "Otrazhenie Protsessa Sblizheniia Natsii na Semeino-bytovom Uklade Narodov Srednei Azii i Kazakhstana," *Sovetskaia Etnografiia* (1962), No. 3, p. 23; Mambetali'eva, *Byt i Kul'tura,* p. 120.

32. Vasil'eva and Kisliakov, "Voprosy Sem'i i Byta," p. 9; Mambetali'eva, *Byt i Kul'tura,* p. 120; "The Peoples of Central Asia: The Survival of Religion," *Central Asian Review,* VII (1959), 110–111.

33. Bennigsen, "The Muslim Peoples of Soviet Russia," pp. 28–31; Richard Pipes, "Muslims of Soviet Central Asia: Trends and Prospects," *The Middle East Journal,* IX (1955), 153; "The Peoples of Central Asia: The Survival of Religion," pp. 111–113; *Sovetskaia Kirgiziia,* December 28, 29, 1963, in *Central Asian Review,* XII (1964), 57; L. Klimovich, "What an Atheist Should Know about the Quran," *Kazakhstan* (1958), No. 6, summarized in *Central Asian Review,* VI (1958), 368–377.

34. "Christian Churches and Sects in Central Asia and Kazakhstan," *Central Asian Review,* XI (1963), 343–354.

35. Nedir Kuliyev, *Anti-nauchnaia Sushchnost' Islama i Zadachi Ateisticheskogo Vospitaniia Trudiashchikhsia v Usloviiakh Sovetskogo Turkmenistana* (Ashkhabad: Akademiia Nauk Turkmenskoi SSR, 1960),

summarized in *Central Asian Review,* X (1962), 105–111; Annaklychev, "Nekotorie Storony Byta," pp. 63–64.

36. "Medical Services in Central Asia and Kazakhstan," *Central Asian Review,* XI (1963), 119.

37. Wurm, *Turkic Peoples of the USSR,* pp. 14–16; T. G. Winner, *Oral Art and Literature,* pp. 130, 139–141; G. K. Dulling, *An Introduction to the Turkmen Language* (St. Anthony's College, Oxford: Central Asian Research Centre, 1960), p. 1.

38. Nicholas A. Hans and Sergius Hessen, *Educational Policy in Soviet Russia* (London: P. S. King & Son, 1930), pp. 175–180; Walter McKenzie Pintner, "Initial Problems in the Soviet Economic Development of Central Asia," *Royal Central Asian Journal,* XL (1953), 287; Azamat Altay, "Kirgiziya During the Great Purge." *Central Asian Review,* XII (1964), 97–107.

39. *Sovetskaia Kirgiziia,* July 3, 1963, in *Central Asian Review,* XI (1963), 397.

40. N. Dzhandil'din, "Some Problems of International Education," *Kommunist* (1959), No. 13, translated in *Central Asian Review,* VII (1959), 338.

41. "Some Statistics on Higher Education" pp. 229–240

42. Tolstov *et al., Narody Srednei Azii,* II, 95–96, 141–152, 305–312, 458–464; Zakharova, "Material'naia Kul'tura," pp. 184–187; Vasil'eva, "Turkmeny-nokhurli," pp. 170–175; Zhdanko, "Karakalpaki Khorezmskogo Oazisa," pp. 554–565; Klodta, *Kazakhskii Narodnyi Ornament;* Mambetali'eva, *Byt i Kul'tura,* p. 121; "Fine and Applied Arts in Central Asia," *Central Asian Review,* IX (1961), 265–268.

Chapter VI

1. Pierce, *Russian Central Asia,* pp. 271–278, 283–286, 292–301.

2. Joseph Castagné, *Les Basmatchis* (Paris: E. Leroux, 1925); Castagné, "Les Organisations soviétiques"; Castagné, "Les Majorités musulmanes et la politique des Soviets en Asie Centrale," *Revue du monde musulman,* LIX (1925), 147–211; Castagné, "Le Turkestan depuis la révolution russe (1917–1921)," *Revue du monde musulman,* L (1922), 28–71. See also "The Basmachis. The Central Asian Resistance Movement, 1918–24," *Central Asian Review,* VII (1959), 236, 240–242; Tolstov *et al., Narody Srednei Azii,* I, 191–194; "Dzhunaid–Khan, 'King of the Karakum Desert'," *Central Asian Review,* XIII (1965), 216–226.

3. Castagné, *Les Basmatchis*, pp. 31, 74; Castagné, "Les Majorités musulmanes," pp. 32–33; Castagné, "Les Organisations soviétiques," pp. 7, 176–177, 245–247; Castagné, "Le Turkestan depuis la révolution russe," p. 70.

4. "The Collectivization Campaign in Uzbekistan," *Central Asian Review*, XII (1964), 40–52; Tolstov *et al.*, *Narody Srednei Azii*, I, 196.

5. "Food Trade and Public Catering in Central Asia," *Central Asian Review*, VIII (1960), 153.

6. Tolstov *et al.*, *Narody Srednei Azii*, I, 212–217; "The Tashkent Oblast," pp. 54–55; Shalekenov, "Byt Karakalpakskogo Krest'ianstva Chimbaiskogo Raiona," p. 269.

7. *Izvestiia*, November 11, 1960, quoted in "Private Property Tendencies," pp. 151–152; *Kommunist Tadjikistana*, July 12, 13, 1962, in *Central Asian Review*, X (1962), 381; Tolstov *et al.*, *Narody Srednei Azii*, I, 217; L. S. Tolstova, "The Kara-Kalpaks of Fergana," *Central Asian Review*, IX (1961), 50; M. A. Bikzhanova, *Sem'ia v Kolkhozakh Uzbekistana* (Tashkent, 1959), summarized in "Family Life in the Kolkhozes of Uzbekistan," *Central Asian Review*, IX (1961), 17.

8. Vambéry, *Travels*, p. 218; Tolstov *et al.*, *Narody Srednei Azii*, I, 304–312, 317; Pipes, "Muslims of Soviet Central Asia," p. 157; "Food Trade and Public Catering," pp. 151–154; Vasil'eva and Kisliakov, "Voprosy Sem'i i Byta," pp. 8, 11; Wheeler, "Race Relations in Soviet Muslim Asia," p. 100; John Parker, "Impressions of the Soviet Middle East," *Royal Central Asian Journal*, XXXIII (1946), 350.

9. Tolstov *et al.*, *Narody Srednei Azii*, I, 305–313.

10. Tolstov, *et al.*, *Narody Srednei Azii*, I, 270–292; Mirkhasilov, "Kul'turnoe Razvitie," p. 16; Vasil'eva and Kisliakov, "Voprosy Sem'i i Byta," pp. 7–10; "Domestic Housing," *Central Asian Review*, IX (1961), 360, 365, 368; "Private Property Tendencies," pp. 147–151; "Town Planning," *Central Asian Review*, X (1962), 269–270; "New Settlements in Central Asia and Kazakhstan," *Central Asian Review*, XI (1963), 241; Bikzhanova, *Sem'ia v Kolkhozakh Uzbekistana*, p. 17; Parker, "Impressions of the Soviet Middle East," pp. 349–350.

11. Tolstov *et al.*, *Narody Srednei Azii*, I, 288–292; "The Peoples of Central Asia: Cultural Development, Part II: The Soviet Period since 1945," *Central Asian Review*, VIII (1960), 12–13; Mirkhasilov, "Kul'turnoe Razvitie," p. 16; Vasil'eva and Kisliakov, "Voprosy Sem'i i Byta," p. 10; Tolstova, "The Kara-Kalpaks of Fergana," pp. 50–51; "Consumer Goods in Central Asia," *Central Asian Review*, VII (1959), 145; Pipes, "Muslims of Soviet Central Asia," pp. 157–158.

12. Tolstov *et al.*, *Narody Srednei Azii*, I, 292–304; Vasil'eva and Kisliakov, "Voprosy Sem'i i Byta," pp. 8, 10–11; Tolstova, "The Kara-Kalpaks of Fergana," p. 51; "The Peoples of Central Asia: Cultural Development," *Central Asian Review*, VII (1959), 218; Sir Fitzroy MacLean, "My Visit to Central Asia, 1958," *Royal Central Asian Journal*, XLVI (1959), 139.

13. Tolstov *et al.*, *Narody Srednei Azii*, I, 196, 244–245, 573–580; Castagné, "Les Organisations soviétiques," pp. 225–226; A. V. Bakushinsky, "Folk Arts and Crafts," in *The U.S.S.R. Speaks for Itself* (London: Lawrence & Wishart, 1943), pp. 324–325; "Art," *Central Asian Review*, VI (1958), 318; "Consumer Goods in Central Asia," p. 147; Downton, "Soviet Central Asia," p. 136; MacLean, "My Visit to Central Asia, 1958," p. 139.

14. Downton, "Soviet Central Asia," pp. 134–135; MacLean, "My Visit to Central Asia, 1958," p. 139; G. P. Snesarev, "The Survival of Religious and Social Customs in Uzbekistan," *Central Asian Review*, VI (1958), 13–14; "Consumer Goods in Central Asia," pp. 145–151; Tolstov *et al.*, *Narody Srednei Azii*, I, 256; "The People Maintain Public Order," *Central Asian Review*, IX (1961), 276; "Private Property Tendencies," pp. 151–153; Tolstova, "The Kara-Kalpaks of Fergana," p. 50.

15. "The Peoples of Central Asia: Cultural Development," pp. 216–217; Bikzhanova, *Sem'ia v Kolkhozakh Uzbekistana*, pp. 18–23; Snesarev, "The Survival of Religious and Social Customs," p. 11; Tolstov *et al.*, *Narody Srednei Azii*, I, 323–324.

16. Tolstov *et al.*, *Narody Srednei Azii*, I, 326–329; Pipes, "Muslims of Soviet Central Asia," pp. 157–158, 300; Tolstova, "The Kara-Kalpaks of Fergana," p. 52; Sukhareva, *Islam v Uzbekistane*, pp. 82–83; Abramson, "Otrazhenie Protsessa Sblizheniia Natsii," pp. 19–21, 24–25; Vasil'eva and Kisliakov, "Voprosy Sem'i i Byta," pp. 13–14; B. X. Karmysheva, "Raboty Sredneaziatskoi Etnograficheskoi Ekspeditsii (1957–1961)," *Sovetskaia Etnografiia* (1962), No. 2, pp. 137–138; *Kommunist Tajikistana*, May 7, 1963, in *Central Asian Review*, XI (1963), 225; "The Peoples of Central Asia: Social Customs," p. 215; "Crime and the Courts in Tadzhikistan," *Central Asian Review*, XII (1964), 194–195.

17. Pintner, "Initial Problems in the Soviet Economic Development of Central Asia," p. 286; "Some Statistics on Higher Education," p. 234.

18. Tolstova, "The Kara-Kalpaks of Fergana," p. 52.

19. Castagné, "Les Majorités musulmanes," pp. 172, 174–176; Tol-

stov *et al., Narody Srednei Azii,* I, 197, 326–327, 348; Vasil'eva and Kisliakov, "Voprosy Sem'i i Byta," pp. 8–9; Tolstova, "The Kara-Kalpaks of Fergana," pp. 51–52; Bennigsen, "The Muslim Peoples of Soviet Russia and the Soviets," pp. 28–29; *Kommunist Tajikistana,* May 31, 1959, in *Central Asian Review,* VII (1959), 276; "Party Affairs," *Central Asian Review,* XI (1963), 400; Snesarev, "The Survival of Religious and Social Customs," p. 9.

20. Tolstov *et al., Narody Srednei Azii,* I, 317; Karmysheva, "Raboty Sredneaziatskoi Etnograficheskoi Ekspeditsii (1957–1961)," p. 137; Snesarev, "The Survival of Religious and Social Customs," pp. 10–15.

21. Egon Erwin Kisch, *Changing Asia* (New York: A. A. Knopf, 1935), pp. 177–178; Hélène Carrère d'Encausse, "Islam in the USSR," *Central Asian Review,* IX (1961), 335–351; Pipes, "Muslims of Soviet Central Asia," pp. 148–151; Tolstov *et al., Narody Srednei Azii,* I, 322–323; Parker, "My Impression of the Soviet Middle East," p. 350; MacLean, "My Visit to Central Asia, 1958," pp. 137–138.

22. Bennigsen, "The Muslim Peoples of Soviet Russia," p. 28; Snesarev, "The Survival of Religious and Social Customs," p. 7.

23. Philip K. Hitti, *History of the Arabs* (3rd ed.; London: Macmillan and Co., 1946), p. 130.

24. Pipes, "Muslims of Soviet Central Asia," pp. 130, 151; Mac-Lean, "My Visit to Central Asia, 1958," pp. 137–138; Tolstov *et al., Narody Srednei Azii,* I, 322–323; Sukhareva, *Islam v Uzbekistane,* pp. 19–20, 81; Bennigsen, "The Muslim Peoples of Soviet Russia," pp. 26, 28; *Izvestiia,* May 23, 1963, in *Central Asian Review,* XI (1963), 285.

25. Snesarev, "The Survival of Religious and Social Customs," p. 7.

26. Sukhareva, *Islam v Uzbekistane,* pp. 20–21, 81; Tolstov *et al., Narody Srednei Azii,* I, 330; Pipes, "Muslims of Soviet Central Asia," p. 153.

27. Pipes, "Muslims of Soviet Central Asia," p. 151–152.

28. Tolstov *et al., Narody Srednei Azii,* I, 322–323; Snesarev, "The Survival of Religious and Social Customs," p. 6; Bennigsen, "The Muslim Peoples of Soviet Russia," p. 28; Mirkhasilov, "Kul'turnoe Razvitie," p. 14.

29. Sukhareva, *Islam v Uzbekistane,* pp. 82–85; Tolstov *et al., Narody Srednei Azii,* I, 300, 312–313, 316, 323, 329–330; Snesarev, "The Survival of Religious and Social Customs," pp. 6–10; Pipes, "Muslims of Soviet Central Asia," pp. 152, 156–157; Carrère d'Encausse, "Islam in the USSR," p. 343; Bikzhanova, *Sem'ia v Kolkhozakh Uzbekistana,* p. 18.

30. Carrère d'Encausse, "Islam in the USSR," pp. 341–343; Sukha-

reva, *Islam v Uzbekistane,* pp. 84–85; Pipes, "Muslims of Soviet Central Asia," pp. 153–154.

31. Carrère d'Encausse, "Islam in the USSR," pp. 341–343; Snesarev, "The Survival of Religious and Social Customs," pp. 8–9; Sukhareva, *Islam v Uzbekistane,* pp. 44–51.

32. Tolstov *et al., Narody Srednei Azii,* I, 329–331, 342; Sukhareva, *Islam v Uzbekistane,* p. 82; *Kazakhstanskaia Pravda,* March 6, 1962, in *Central Asian Review,* XII (1964), 122; "Moscow Steps up Drive on Religion; New Rites Seek to Supplant Traditional Observances," *New York Times,* June 7, 1964, p. 5; Mirkhasilov, "Kul'turnoe Razvitie," p. 14.

33. Bennigsen, "The Muslim Peoples of Soviet Russia," pp. 30–31; Mirkhasilov, "Kul'turnoe Razvitie," p. 13; "Medical Services in Central Asia and Kazakhstan," pp. 39–40; Tolstov *et al., Narody Srednei Azii,* I, 333–336.

34. Tolstov *et al., Narody Srednei Azii,* I, 310–311; "The People Maintain Public Order," p. 275; "Food Trade and Public Catering," p. 155; Mirkhasilov, "Kul'turnoe Razvitie," p. 14; "Medical Services in Central Asia and Kazakhstan," p. 119.

35. Tolstov *et al., Narody Srednei Azii,* I, 338–339; Troitskaia, "Ferganskaia Teatral'naia Ekspeditsiia," pp. 163–164; A. L. Troitskaia, "Iz Istorii Narodnogo Teatra i Tsirka v Uzbekistane," *Sovetskaia Etnografiia* (1948), No. 3, pp. 71–72; Downton, "Soviet Central Asia," p. 135; Lt. Colonel G. E. Wheeler, "Cultural Developments in Soviet Central Asia," *Royal Central Asian Journal,* XLI (1954), 184; "Pesni za Nalichnie," *Pravda Vostoka,* October 30, 1960, translated as "Paying the Piper," *Central Asian Review,* IX (1961), 182–184; "Agitprop. Some Details of Agitation and Propaganda in the Muslim Republics," *Central Asian Review,* VIII (1960), 382.

36. Tolstov *et al., Narody Srednei Azii,* I, 272, 375–378, 386.

37. Tolstov *et al., Narody Srednei Azii,* I, 340–344.

38. *Kommunist Tajikistana,* August 28, 1963, in *Central Asian Review,* XI (1963), 401–402; *Kommunist Tajikistana,* January· 26, 1962, in *Central Asian Review,* VIII (1960), 386; Mirkhasilov, "Kul'turnoe Razvitie," pp. 9–10, 13.

39. "Trends in Education in Central Asia," *Central Asian Review,* VII (1959), 18; "Reorganization of Education," *Central Asian Review,* IX (1961), 25–26; Theodore Shabad, "Soviet Schooling Cut to 10 Years," *New York Times,* August 13, 1964; Mirkhasilov, "Kul'turnoe Razvitie," pp. 10–11.

Chapter VII

1. Stefan Wurm, *The Turkic Languages of Central Asia: Problems of Culture Contact,* Appendix I (Oxford: Central Asian Research Centre, 1960), p. 50.

2. Paul B. Henze, "Politics and Alphabets in Inner Asia," *Royal Central Asian Journal,* XLIII (1956), 30.

3. Henze, "Politics and Alphabets in Inner Asia," p. 31; Thomas Winner, *Oral Art and Literature,* pp. 23, 109.

4. Henze, "Politics and Alphabets in Inner Asia," pp. 32–33.

5. Henze, "Politics and Alphabets in Inner Asia," pp. 34–35.

6. Paul B. Henze, "Alphabet Changes in Soviet Central Asia and Communist China," *Royal Central Asian Journal,* XLIV (1957), 125–126; Sir Olaf Caroe, "The Heritage of Chaghatai. Language in Russian Central Asia," *Royal Central Asian Journal,* XL (1953), 82–83.

7. "The Russification of the Tadzhik Language," *Central Asian Review,* VI (1958), 25–33.

8. N. Dzhandil'din, "Problems of the Development of National Culture," *Kommunist Kazakhstana* (1957), No. 7, translated in *Central Asian Review,* VI (1958), 22.

9. N. A. Baskakov, "The Turkic Peoples of the USSR: the Development of their Languages and Writing," *Voprosy Yazykoznaniia,* June 1952, translated as *The Turkic Languages of Central Asia: Problems of Planned Culture Contact* (Oxford: Central Asian Research Centre, 1960), with notes and comments by Stefan Wurm; Dulling, *An Introduction to the Turkmen Language.*

10. "Recent Literature in Central Asia and Kazakhstan," *Central Asian Review,* X (1962), 353–362.

Chapter VIII

1. Pierce, *Mission to Turkestan,* p. 2.

2. Alexandre Bennigsen, "The Muslim Peoples of the Soviet Union and the Soviets," *The Islamic Review,* XLIII (1955), No. 7, p. 33.

3. Bennigsen, "The Muslim Peoples of the Soviet Union," No. 6, pp. 14–18.

4. Bennigsen, "The Muslim Peoples of the Soviet Union," No. 7, pp. 29–31.

5. Bennigsen, "The Muslim Peoples of the Soviet Union," No. 5,

p. 14; "Recent Literature in Central Asia and Kazakhstan," pp. 353–362.

6. Bennigsen, "The Muslim Peoples of the Soviet Union," No. 5, p. 14; No. 7, p. 34; Dzhandil'din, "Problems of the Development of National Culture," pp. 20–22; Dzhandil'din, "Some Problems of International Education," p. 339; "The Russification of the Tadzhik Language," pp. 25–33; *Sovetskaia Kirgiziia*, October 13, 1963, in *Central Asian Review*, XII (1964), 56.

7. Pipes, "Muslims of Soviet Central Asia," pp. 306–307; Bennigsen, "The Muslim Peoples of the Soviet Union," No. 5, p. 9; No. 7, p. 30.

8. Schuyler, *Turkistan*, I, 84; Olufsen, *The Emir of Bokhara*, pp. 390, 520; Gardanov *et al.*, "Osnovnye Napravleniia Etnicheskikh Protessov," pp. 27–28; Pipes, "Muslims of Soviet Central Asia," pp. 298–301.

9. Abramson, "Otrazhenie Protsessa Sblizheniia Natsii," pp. 18–34; Mambetali'eva, *Byt i Kul'tura*, pp. 119–120; Zhdanko, "Byt Kolkhoznikov Rybolovetskikh Arteley," pp. 206–213; Pipes, "Muslims of Soviet Central Asia," p. 300; Bennigsen, "The Muslim Peoples of the Soviet Union," No. 7, p. 33.

Bibliography

This bibliography includes only works cited in the notes. Because primary sources and specialized studies were given preference in such citations, many general works on Central Asia have been omitted.

Abramson, S. M. "Otrazhenie Protsessa Sblizheniia Natsii na Semeino-bytovom Uklade Narodov Srednei Azii i Kazakhstana," *Sovetskaia Etnografiia* (1962), No. 3, pp. 18–34.

——. "Preobrazovaniia v Khoziaistve i Kul'ture Kazakhov za Gody Sotsialisticheskogo Stroitel'stva," *Sovetskaia Etnografiia* (1961), No. 1, pp. 54–71.

"Agitprop. Some Details of Agitation and Propaganda in the Muslim Republics," *Central Asian Review*, VIII (1960), 376–386.

Altay, Azamat. "Kirgiziya During the Great Purge," *Central Asian Review*, XII (1964), 97–107.

Andrianov, B. V. "Ak-Dzhagyz (k Istorii Formirovaniia Sovremennoi Etnicheskoi Territorii Karakalpakov v Nizov'e Amu-Dar'i)," in *Arkheologicheskie i Etnograficheskie Raboty Khorezmskoi Ekspeditsii 1945–1948*, ed. S. P. Tolstov and T. A. Zhdanko. ("Trudy Khorezmskoi Arkheologo-etnograficheskoi Ekspeditsii, Vol. I.) Moscow: Akademiia Nauk SSSR, Institut Etnografii imeni N. N. Miklukho-Maklaia, 1952.

——. "Etnicheskaia Territoriia Karakalpakov v Severnom Khorezme (XVIII–XIX vv.)," in *Materialy i Issledovaniia po Etnografii Karakalpakov*, ed. T. A. Zhdanko. ("Trudy Khorezmskoi Arkheologo-etnograficheskoi Ekspeditsii," Vol. III.) Moscow: Akademiia Nauk SSSR, Institut Etnografii imeni N. N. Miklukho-Maklaia, 1958.

Andrianov, B. V., and A. S. Melkov. "Obraztsy Karakalpakskogo Narodnogo Ornamenta," in *Materialy i Issledovaniia po Etnografii Karakal-*

pakov, ed. T. A. Zhdanko. ("Trudy Khorezmskoi Arkheologo-etnograficheskoi Ekspeditsii," Vol. III.) Moscow: Akademiia Nauk SSSR, Institut Etnografii imeni N. N. Miklukho-Maklaia, 1958.

Annaklychev, Shikhberdy. *Byt Rabochikh-neftianikoe Nebit-Daga i Kum-Daga (Istoriko-etnograficheskii Ocherk).* Ashkhabad, 1961. Reviewed by V. Krupianskaia in *Sovetskaia Etnografiia* (1962), No. 1, pp. 115–117.

——. "Nekotorie Storony Byta Rabochikh-neftianikov Nebit-Daga,' *Sovetskaia Etnografiia* (1959), No. 1, pp. 53–68.

Aristov, N. A. "Opyt Viiasneniia Etnicheskogo Sostava Kirgiz-Kazakov Bolshoi Ordy i Karakirgizov na Osnovanii Rodoslovnykh Skazanii i Svedenii o Sushchestvuiushchikh Rodovykh Deleniiakh i o Rodovykh Tamgakh, a takzhe Istoricheskikh Dannykh i Nachinaiushchikhsia Antropologicheskikh Izsledovanii," *Zhivaia Starina*, Vyp. III–IV, Vol. 4 (St. Petersburg, 1894), 391–486.

"Art," *Central Asian Review*, VI (1958), 318–319.

Asfendiarov, S. J. *Istoriia Kazakstana (s Drevneishikh Vremen).* Alma Ata: Kazakstanskoe Kraevoe Izdatel'stvo, 1935.

Atkinson, Thomas Witlam. *Oriental and Western Siberia. A Narrative of Seven Years' Explorations and Adventures in Siberia, Mongolia, the Kirghiz Steppes, Chinese Tartary, and Part of Central Asia.* New York: Harper & Brothers, 1858.

Babur. *The Babur-nama in English (Memoirs of Babur)*, by Zahiru'd-din Muhammad Babur Padshah. Translated by Annette Susannah Beveridge. 2 vols. London: Luzac & Co., 1921.

Bacon, Elizabeth E. *Obok. A Study of Social Structure in Eurasia.* ("Viking Fund Publications in Anthropology," No. 25.) New York: Wenner-Gren Foundation for Anthropological Research, 1958.

——. "Soviet Policy in Turkestan," *The Middle East Journal,* I (1947), 386–400.

Bakushinsky, A. V. "Folk Arts and Crafts," in *The U.S.S.R. Speaks for Itself.* London: Lawrence & Wishart, 1943.

Barthold, W. (Bartol'd, V. V.) *Histoire des Turcs d'Asie Centrale.* Translated by Mme M. Donskis. Paris: Librairie d'Amérique et d'Orient, 1945.

——. *A History of the Turkman People.* ("Four Studies on the History of Central Asia," translated by V. and T. Minorsky, Vol. III.) Leiden: E. J. Brill, 1962.

——. *Istoriia Turetsko-mongolskikh Narodov.* Tashkent: Izdanie Kazakskogo Vysshogo Pedagogicheskogo Instituta, 1928.

——. "Kazak," *Encyclopaedia of Islam* (1st ed.; Leiden: E. J. Brill, 1927), II, 836.

——. "Kirgiz," *Encyclopaedia of Islam* (1st ed.; Leiden: E. J. Brill, 1927), II, 1025–1026.

——. *A Short History of Turkestan.* ("Four Studies on the History of Central Asia," translated by V. and T. Minorsky, Vol. I.) Leiden: E. J. Brill, 1956.

——. *Ulugh-Beg.* ("Four Studies on the History of Central Asia," translated by V. and T. Minorsky, Vol. II.) Leiden: E. J. Brill, 1958.

Baskakov, N. A. "The Turkic Peoples of the USSR: The Development of their Languages and Writing," *Voprosy Yazykoznaniia* (June 1952). Translated as *The Turkic Languages of Central Asia: Problems of Planned Culture Contact*, with notes and comments by Stefan Wurm. Oxford: Central Asian Research Centre, 1960.

"The Basmachis: The Central Asian Resistance Movement, 1918–24," *Central Asian Review*, VII (1959), 236–250.

Bennigsen, Alexandre. "The Muslim Peoples of Soviet Russia and the Soviets," *The Islamic Review*, XLIII (1955), No. 4, pp. 25–31.

——. "The Muslim Peoples of the Soviet Union and the Soviets," *The Islamic Review*, XLIII (1955), No. 5, pp. 8–15; No. 6, pp. 13–18; No. 7, pp. 27–35.

Bennigsen, Alexandre, and Chantal Quelquejay. *Les Mouvements nationaux chez les musulmans de Russie.* Paris and The Hague: Mouton & Co., 1960.

——. "Le problème linguistique et l'évolution des nationalités musulmanes en U.R.S.S.," *Cahiers du monde russe et soviétique*, III (1960), 418–465.

Bergmann, Benjamin von. *Voyage de Benjamin Bergmann chez les Kalmuks.* Translated by M. Moris. Chatillon-sur-Seine: C. Cornillac, 1825.

Bikzhanova, M. A. *Sem'ia v Kolkhozakh Uzbekistana.* Tashkent, 1959. Summarized in "Family Life in the Kolkhozes of Uzbekistan," *Central Asian Review*, IX (1961), 16–23.

Bourlière, François *et al. The Land and Wildlife of Eurasia.* ("Life Nature Library.") New York: Time Incorporated, 1964.

Burnes, Alexander. *Travels into Bokhara; being the Account of a Journey from India to Cabool, Tartary, and Persia in the Years 1831, 1832, and 1833.* 3 vols. London: J. Murray, 1834.

Capus, Guillaume. *À travers le royaume de Tamerlan (Asie Centrale): Voyage dans la Sibérie occidentale, le Turkestan, la Boukharie, aux bords de l'Amou-Daria, à Khiva, et dans l'Oust-Ourt.* Paris: A. Hennuyer, 1892.

Caroe, Sir Olaf. "The Heritage of Chaghatai: Language in Russian Central Asia," *Royal Central Asian Journal,* XL (1953), 82–92.

Carrère d'Encausse, Hélène. "Islam in the USSR," *Central Asian Review,* IX (1961), 335–351.

——. "La Politique culturelle du pouvoir tsariste au Turkestan (1867–1917)," *Cahiers du monde russe et soviétique,* III (1962), 374–407.

——. "Tsarist Educational Policy in Turkestan, 1867–1917," *Central Asian Review,* XI (1963), 374–394.

Castagné, Joseph. *Les Basmatchis: Le Mouvement national des indigènes d'Asie Centrale depuis la Révolution d'Octobre 1917 jusqu'en Octobre 1924.* Paris: E. Leroux, 1925.

——. "Magie et exorcisme chez les Kazak-Kirghizes et autres peuples turks orientaux," *Revue des études islamiques,* IV (1930), 53–156.

——. "Les Majorités musulmanes et la politique des Soviets en Asie Centrale," *Revue du monde musulman,* LIX (1925), 147–211.

——. "Les Organisations soviétiques de la Russie musulmane," *Revue du monde musulman,* LI (October, 1922), vii–xvii, 1–248.

——. "Le Turkestan depuis la révolution russe (1917–1921)," *Revue du monde musulman,* L (June, 1922), 28–71.

"Christian Churches and Sects in Central Asia and Kazakhstan," *Central Asian Review,* XI (1963), 343–354.

Clavijo. *Embassy to Tamerlane 1403–1406.* Translated by Guy Le Strange. New York: Harper & Brothers, 1928.

"The Collectivization Campaign in Uzbekistan," *Central Asian Review,* XII (1964), 40–52.

"Consumer Goods in Central Asia," *Central Asian Review,* VII (1959), 145–152.

"Crime and the Courts in Tadzhikistan," *Central Asian Review,* XII (1964), 185–197.

"Crimes against Women in the 1961 Turkmen Criminal Code," *Central Asian Review,* XIII (1965), 227–231.

Curtis, William Eleroy. *Turkestan: "The Heart of Asia."* New York: Hodder & Stoughton, 1911.

"The Development of Kara-Kalpakia after Union with Russia," *Central Asian Review,* VI (1958), 34–45.

Dimand, Dr. Maurice S. *Peasant and Nomad Rugs of Asia.* New York: Asia House Gallery, 1961.

"Domestic Housing," *Central Asian Review,* IX (1961), 359–370.

Downton, Eric. "Soviet Central Asia," *Royal Central Asian Journal*, XLII (1955), 128–137.

Dulling, G. K. *An Introduction to the Turkmen Language*. St. Anthony's College (Oxford): Central Asian Research Centre, 1960.

Dyrenkova, N. I. "Polychenie Shamanskogo Dara po Vozzreniiam Turetskikh Plemen," in *Sbornik Muzeia Antropologii i Etnografii*, IX (Leningrad: Akademiia Nauk SSSR, 1930), pp. 267–291.

Dzhandil'din, N. "Problems of the Development of National Culture," *Kommunist Kazakhstana* (1957), No. 7, translated in *Central Asian Review*, VI (1958), 16–24.

——. "Some Problems of International Education," *Kommunist* (1959), No. 13. Translated in *Central Asian Review*, VII (1959), 335–340.

"Dzhunaid-Khan, 'King of the Karakum Desert,'" *Central Asian Review*, XIII (1965), 216–226.

Fell, Edward Nelson. *Russian and Nomad: Tales of the Kirghiz Steppe*. New York: Duffield and Company, 1916.

Fiel'strup, F. A. "Molochnye Produkty Turkov-kochevnikov," in *Kazaki: Sbornik Statei Antropologicheskogo Otriada Kazakstanskoi Ekspeditsii Akademii Nauk SSSR, Issledovanie 1927 g.*, pp. 263–301. ("Materialy Komissii Ekspeditsionnykh Issledovanii," Vol. XV, Seriia Kazakstana) Leningrad: Akademiia Nauk SSSR, 1930.

"Fine and Applied Arts in Central Asia," *Central Asian Review*, IX (1961), 261–271.

Fischel, Walter J. "Israel in Iran (A Survey of Judeo-Persian Literature," in *The Jews: Their History, Culture, and Religion*, ed. Louis Finkelstein, pp. 1149–1190. 3rd ed.; New York: Harper & Brothers, 1960.

——. "The Leaders of the Jews of Bokhara," in *Jewish Leaders 1750–1940)*, ed. Leo Jung, pp. 533–547. New York: Bloch Publishing Company, 1953.

"Food Trade and Public Catering in Central Asia," *Central Asian Review*, VIII (1960), 151–159.

Gardanov, V. K., B. O. Dolgikh, and T. A. Zhdanko. "Osnovnye Napravleniia Etnicheskikh Protsessov u Narodov SSSR," *Sovetskaia Etnografiia* (1961), No. 4, pp. 9–29.

Ghirshman, R. *Iran: From the Earliest Times to the Islamic Conquest*. Baltimore, Md.: Penguin Books, 1954.

Grigorief, V. "The Russian Policy regarding Central Asia: An Historical Sketch," Appendix IV in Eugene Schuyler, *Turkistan*, II, 391–415.

Grodekov, N. I. *Kirgizy i Karakirgizy Syr'-Dar'inskoi Oblasti: Iuridicheskii Byt'*. Tashkent: S. I. Lakhtin, 1889.

Hans, Nicholas A. and Sergius Hessen. *Educational Policy in Soviet Russia*. London: P. S. King & Son, 1930.

Henze, Paul B. "Alphabet Changes in Soviet Central Asia and Communist China," *Royal Central Asian Journal*, XLIV (1957), 124–136.

——. "Politics and Alphabets in Inner Asia," *Royal Central Asian Journal*, XLIII (1956), 29–51.

Herodotus. *The Histories*. Translated by Aubrey de Sélincourt. Baltimore, Md.: Penguin Books, 1954.

Hitti, Philip K. *History of the Arabs*. 3rd ed. London: Macmillan and Co., 1946.

Hudson, Alfred E. *Kazak Social Structure*. ("Yale University Publications in Anthropology," No. 20.) New Haven: Yale University Press, 1938.

"Irrigation in Central Asia," *Central Asian Review*, VIII (1960), 44–51, 138–150.

"Irrigation: Progress since 1960," *Central Asian Review*, XI (1963), 138–154.

Izvestiia (Moscow), May 23, 1963, in *Central Asian Review*, XI (1963), 285.

Jochelson, W. *Peoples of Asiatic Russia*. New York: American Museum of Natural History, 1928.

Kamalov, S. "Narodno–osvoboditel'naia Bor'ba Karakalpakov protiv Khivinskikh Khanov v XIX v.," in *Materialy i Issledovaniia po Etnografii Karakalpakov*, ed. T. A. Zhdanko, pp. 133–206. ("Trudy Khorezmskoi Arkheologo-etnograficheskoi Ekspeditsii," Vol. III.) Moscow: Akademiia Nauk SSSR, Institut Etnografii imeni N. N. Miklukho-Maklaia, 1958.

Karmysheva, B. X. "Raboty Sredneaziatskoi Etnograficheskoi Ekspeditsii (1957–1961)," *Sovetskaia Etnografiia* (1962), No. 2, pp. 137–140.

Karryiev, A., and A. Rosliakov. *Kratkii Ocherk Istorii Turkmenistana 1868–1917)*. Ashkhabad, 1956. Summarized as "Turkmenistan 1868–1917," *Central Asian Review*, VI (1958), 125–142.

Karutz, Richard. *Unter Kirgisen und Turkmenen: Aus dem Leben der Steppe*. Leipzig: Klinkhardt & Biermann, 1911. Reissued as *Unter Kirgisen und Turkmenen* (Berlin: Im Verlag Ullstein, n.d.).

Kazakhstanskaia Pravda (Alma-Ata), March 6, 1962, in *Central Asian Review*, XII (1964), 122; August 20, 1962, in *Central Asian Review*, X (1962), 364; October 13, 1962, in *Central Asian Review*, XI (1963), 45.

Kharuzin, A. N. *Kirgizy Bukeevskoi Ordy: Antropologo-etnologicheskii Ocherk.* ("Izvestiia Obshchestva Liubitelei Estestvosnaniia, Antropologii i Etnografii pri Moskovskoe Universitets," Vol. LXIII.) Moscow, 1889.

Kisch, Egon Erwin. *Changing Asia.* New York: A. A. Knopf, 1935.

Klimovich, Professor L. "What an Atheist Should Know about the Quran," *Central Asian Review,* VI (1958), 368–377.

Klodta, E. A. *Kazakhskii Narodnyi Ornament.* Moscow: Iskusstvo, 1939.

Kommunist Tajikistana (Dushanbe), May 31, 1959, in *Central Asian Review,* VII (1959), 276; January 26, 1962, in *Central Asian Review,* VIII (1960), 386; July 12, 13, 1962, in *Central Asian Review,* X (1962), 381; May 7, 1963, in *Central Asian Review,* XI (1963), 225; August 28, 1963, in *Central Asian Review,* XI (1963), 401–402.

Komsomolskaia Pravda (Moscow), January 12, 1961, in *Central Asian Review,* X (1962), 155.

Korbe, O. A. "Kul'tura i Byt Kazakhskogo Kolkhoznogo Aula," *Sovetskaia Etnografiia* (1950), No. 4, 67–91.

Krist, Gustav. *Alone through the Forbidden Land: Journeys in Disguise through Soviet Central Asia.* Translated by E. O. Lorimer. New York: Harcourt, Brace and Company, 1938.

Krivtsov, S. S., ed. *Kazakstan i Kirgiziia.* ("Nash Soiuz.") Moscow: Moskovskoi Oblastnoe Otdelenie Gosizdat RSFSR, 1930.

Kshibekov, D. *O Feodal'no Bayskikh Perezhitkakh i ikh Preodolenii.* Alma Ata, 1957.

Kuftin, B. A. *Kirgiz-Kazaki: Kul'tura i Byt.* ("Etnologicheskie Ocherki," No. 2.) Moscow: Tsentral'nogo Muzeia Narodovedeniia, 1926.

Kuliyev, Nedir. *Anti-nauchnaia Sushchnost' Islama i Zadachi Ateisticheskogo Vospitaniia Trudiashchikhsia v Usloviiakh Sovetskogo Turkmenistana.* Ashkhabad: Akademiia Nauk Turkmenskoi SSR, 1960. Summarized in *Central Asian Review,* X (1962), 105–111.

Lansdell, Henry. *Russian Central Asia, including Kuldja, Bokhara, Khiva and Merv.* 2 vols. Boston: Houghton, Mifflin, and Company, 1885.

Laufer, Berthold. *The Decorative Art of the Amur Tribes.* ("Publications of the Jesup North Pacific Expedition," Vol. I; "Memoirs of the American Museum of Natural History," Vol. VII.) New York: The Museum, 1902.

Levshin, Alexis. *Déscription des hordes et des steppes des Kirghiz-Kazaks ou Kirghiz-Kaissaks.* Translated by Ferry de Pigny. Paris: Imprimerie Royale, 1840.

BIBLIOGRAPHY

Loewenthal, Rudolph. *The Judeo-Muslim Marranos of Bukhara.* ("Central Asian Collectanea," No. 1.) Washington, D.C., 1958.

MacLean, Sir Fitzroy. "My Visit to Central Asia, 1958," *Royal Central Asian Journal,* XLVI (1959), 130–140.

Mambetali'eva, K. *Byt i Kul'tura Shakhterov-kirgizov Kamennougal'noi Promyshlennosti Kirgizii.* Frunze, 1963. Summarized in "The Life of the Kirgiz Miner," *Central Asian Review,* XII (1964), 114–122.

Margulanov, A. M. "Naimany," in *Kazaki: Sbornik Statei Antropologicheskogo Otriada Kazakstanskoi Ekspeditsii Akademii Nauk SSSR, Issledovanie 1927 g.,* pp. 329–334. ("Materialy Komissii Ekspeditsionnykh Issledovanii," Vol. XV, Seriia Kazakstanskaia.) Leningrad: Akademiia Nauk SSSR, 1930.

Masanov, E. A. "Usloviia Truda i Bytovoi Uklad Kazakhskikh Remeslennikov (Vtoraia Polovina XIX i Nachalo XX v.)," *Izvestiia Akademii Nauk Kazakhskoi SSR,* I (XV). Alma Ata, 1961. Summarized in *Central Asian Review,* X (1962), 343–349.

Meakin, Annette M. B. *In Russian Turkestan: A Garden of Asia and Its People.* London: George Allen & Unwin, 1903.

"Medical Services in Central Asia and Kazakhstan," *Central Asian Review,* XI (1963), 30–45, 114–129.

Meyendorff, G. *Voyage d'Orenbourg à Boukhara, fait en 1820.* Paris: Dondey–Dupré, 1826.

Mirkhasilov, S. M. "Kul'turnoe Razvitie Uzbekskogo Kishlaka Niiazbashi," *Sovetskaia Etnografiia* (1962), No. 1, pp. 8–16.

Montgomerie, Major T. G. "Report of 'The Mirza's' Exploration from Caubal to Kashgar," *Journal of the Royal Geographical Society,* XLI (1871), 132–193.

Morgan, E. Delmar. "Recent Geography of Central Asia; From Russian Sources," *Royal Geographical Society: Supplementary Papers,* I (1882), 203–263.

"Moscow Steps up Drive on Religion; New Rites Seek to Supplant Traditional Observances," *New York Times,* June 7, 1964, p. 5.

Moser, Henri. *À travers l'Asie Centrale: La steppe Kirghize, le Turkestan russe, Boukhara, Khiva, le pays des Turcomans et la Perse: Impressions de voyage.* Paris: Librairie Plon, 1885.

"New Settlements in Central Asia and Kazakhstan," *Central Asian Review,* XI (1963), 234–245.

O'Donovan, Edmond. *The Merv Oasis: Travels and Adventures East of the Caspian during the Years 1879–80–81 including Five Months' Residence among the Tekkés of Merv.* 2 vols. London: Smith, Elder, & Co., 1882.

252

Olufsen, O. *The Emir of Bokhara and his Country: Journeys and Studies in Bokhara.* London: William Heinemann, 1911.

——. *Through the Unknown Pamirs: The Second Danish Pamir Expedition 1898–99.* London: William Heinemann, 1904.

Pallas, P. S. *Voyages de m. P. S. Pallas, en différentes provinces de l'empire de Russie, et dans l'Asie septentrionale.* Translated by Gauthier de la Peyronie. 5 vols. Paris: Maradan, 1789–1793.

Parker, John. "Impressions of the Soviet Middle East," *Royal Central Asian Journal,* XXXIII (1946), 341–356.

"Party Affairs," *Central Asian Review,* XI (1963), 400–401.

"The People Maintain Public Order," *Central Asian Review,* IX (1961), 272–280.

"The Peoples of Central Asia," *Central Asian Review,* VII (1959), 109–116, 213–220, 312–321; VIII (1960), 5–13.

"Pesni za Nalichniie," *Pravda Vostoka,* October 30, 1960. Translated as "Paying the Piper," *Central Asian Review,* IX (1961), 182–184.

Pierce, Richard A. *Russian Central Asia, 1867–1917: A Study in Colonial Rule.* Berkeley and Los Angeles: University of California Press, 1960.

——, ed. *Mission to Turkestan: Being the Memoirs of Count K. K. Pahlen 1908–1909.* Translated by N. J. Couriss. London: Oxford University Press, 1964.

Pintner, Walter McKenzie. "Initial Problems in the Soviet Economic Development of Central Asia," *Royal Central Asian Journal,* XL (1953), 284–297.

Pipes, Richard. "Muslims of Soviet Central Asia: Trends and Prospects," *The Middle East Journal,* IX (1955), 147–162, 295–308.

Pravda (Moscow), June 12, 1961, in *Central Asian Review,* IX (1961), 388; May 24, 1962, in *Central Asian Review,* X (1962), 248; May 25, 1962, in *Central Asian Review,* X (1962), 266.

Pravda Vostoka (Tashkent), November 1 and December 12, 1962, in *Central Asian Review,* XI (1963), 45, 59.

"Private Property Tendencies in Central Asia and Kazakhstan," *Central Asian Review,* X (1962), 147–156.

Radloff, Wilhelm. (Radlov, V. V.) *Aus Sibirien.* 2 vols. 2nd ed. Leipzig: T. O. Weigel Nachfolger, 1893.

——. "Die Hausthiere der Kirgisen," *Zeitschrift für Ethnologie,* III (1871), 285–313.

——. *Opyt Slovaria Tiurkskikh Narechi (Versuch eines Wörterbuches der Türk-Dialecte).* 4 vols. St. Petersburg, 1893–1911.

BIBLIOGRAPHY

"Recent Literature in Central Asia and Kazakhstan," *Central Asian Review*, X (1962), 350–364.

"Reorganization of Education," *Central Asian Review*, IX (1961), 24–44.

Rezzakov, I. R. Speech translated in "Conference of Kirgiz Intelligentsia," *Central Asian Review*, VIII (1960), 289–291.

Rudenko, S. I. "Ocherk Byta Severo-vostochnykh Kazakov," in *Kazaki: Sbornik Statei Anthropologicheskogo Otriada Kazakstanskoi Ekspeditsii Akademii Nauk SSSR, Issledovanie 1927 g.,* pp. 1–72 ("Materialy Komissii Ekspeditsionnykh Issledovanii," Vol. XV, Seriia Kazakstanskaia.) Leningrad: Akademiia Nauk SSSR, 1930.

Russia (1923–U.S.S.R.) Tsentral'noe Statisticheskoe Upravlenie. *The National Economy of the USSR in 1960; Statistical Yearbook.* Washington, D.C.: U.S. Joint Publications Research Service, 1962.

"The Russification of the Tadzhik Language," *Central Asian Review*, VI (1958), 25–33.

Sabitov, N. S. "Obshchestvennaia Zhizn' i Semeinyi Byt Kazakhov-kolkhoznikov (Po Materialam Alma-Atinskoi i Dzhambulskoi Oblasti)," *Trudy Instituta Istorii, Arkheologii i Etnografii,* III, *Etnografiia,* pp. 190–230. Alma Ata: Akademiia Nauk Kazakhskoi SSR, 1956.

Samoilovich, A. N. "Kazaki Koshagachskogo Aimaka Oïratskoi Avtonomnoi Oblasti," in *Kazaki: Sbornik Statei Antropologicheskogo Otriada Kazakstanskoi Ekspeditsii Akademii Nauk SSSR, Issledovanie 1927 g.,* pp. 303–327. ("Materialy Komissii Ekspeditsionnykh Issledovanii," Vol. XV, Seriia Kazakstanskaia.) Leningrad: Akademiia Nauk SSSR, 1930.

——. "O Slove 'Kazak,' " in *Kazaki: Antropologicheskie Ocherki*, pp. 5–16. ("Materialy Osobogo Komiteta po Issledovaniiu Soiuznykh i Avtonomnykh Respublik," Vol. XI.) Leningrad; Akademiia Nauk SSSR, 1927.

——. "Zapretnie Slova v Iazyke Kazak-kirgizskoi Zamuzhnei Zhenshchiny," *Zhivaia Starina*, XXVI (1915), 161–168.

Schomberg, Col. R. C. F. *Peaks and Plains of Central Asia.* London: M. Hopkinson, 1933.

Schuyler, Eugene. *Turkistan: Notes of a Journey in Russian Turkistan, Khokand, Bukhara, and Kuldja.* 2 vols. 3rd ed. New York: Charles Scribner's Sons, 1885.

Seager, G. Wilfrid. "Oriental Carpets Today," *Royal Central Asian Journal*, LI (1964), 120–126.

Shabad, Theodore. "Moscow, Reversing Policy, Will Spur Private Farming," *New York Times,* Nov. 7, 1964.

———. "Soviet Schooling Cut to 10 Years," *New York Times,* August 13, 1964.

Shakhmatov, V. G. "The Basic Characteristics of the Kazakh Patriarchal Feudal State Organization," *Central Asian Review,* IX (1961), 126–132.

Shalekenov, U. "Byt Karakalpakskogo Krest'ianstva Chimbaiskogo Raiona v Proshlom i Nastoiashchem," in *Materialy i Issledovaniia po Etnografii Karakalpakov,* ed. T. A. Zhdanko, pp. 269–370. ("Trudy khorezmskoi Arkheologo-etnograficheskoi Ekspeditsii," Vol. III.) Moscow: Akademiia Nauk SSSR, Institut Etnografii imeni N. N. Miklukho-Maklaia, 1958.

Shneider, E. R. "Kazakskaia Ornamentika," in *Kazaki: Antropologicheskie Ocherki,* pp. 137–171. ("Materialy Osobogo Komiteta po Issledovaniiu Soiuzniykh i Avtonomnykh Respublik," Vol. XI, Seriia Kazakstanskaia.) Leningrad: Akademiia Nauk SSSR, 1927.

"The Size of the German Population in Kazakhstan and Central Asia," *Central Asian Review,* X (1962), 372–373.

Skrine, Francis Henry and Ross, Edward Denison. *The Heart of Asia: A History of Russian Turkestan and the Central Asian Khanates from the Earliest Times.* London: Methuen & Co., 1899.

Snesarev, G. P. "The Survival of Religious and Social Customs in Uzbekistan," *Central Asian Review,* VI (1958), 5–15.

"The Social, Economic and Political Effects of Russian Influence in Kirgizia (1855–1917)," *Central Asian Review,* V (1957), 235–246.

"Some Statistics on Higher Education in the Muslim Republics," *Central Asian Review,* X (1962), 229–241.

Sovetskaia Kirgiziia (Frunze), September 19, 1961, in *Central Asian Review,* XI (1963), 225; October 1, 1961, in *Central Asian Review,* X (1962), 60; December 22, 1962, in *Central Asian Review,* XI (1963), 45; July 3, 1963, in *Central Asian Review,* XI (1963), 397; October 13, 1963, in *Central Asian Review,* XII (1964), 57.

"Stabilization of the Nomads," *Central Asian Review,* VII (1959), 221–229.

Stamp, L. Dudley. *Asia: A Regional and Economic Geography.* 9th ed. London: Methuen & Co., 1957.

Sukhareva, O. A. *Islam v Uzbekistane.* Tashkent: Akademiia Nauk Uzbekskoi SSR, 1960.

"The Tashkent Oblast," *Central Asian Review,* VI (1958), 46–58.

BIBLIOGRAPHY

Tolstov, S. P., T. A. Zhdanko, S. M. Abramson, and N. A. Kisliakova, eds. *Narody Srednei Azii i Kazakhstana.* ("Narody Mira. Etnograficheskie Ocherki.") 2 vols. Moscow: Akademiia Nauk SSSR, 1962, 1963.

Tolstova, L. S. "The Kara-Kalpaks of Fergana," *Central Asian Review,* IX (1961), 45–52.

"Town Planning," *Central Asian Review,* X (1962), 269–270.

"Trends in Education in Central Asia," *Central Asian Review,* VII (1959), 14–20.

Troitskaia, A. L. "Ferganskaia Teatral'naia Ekspeditsiia," *Sovetskaia Etnografiia* (1937), No. 1, pp. 163–164.

———. "Iz Istorii Narodnogo Teatra i Tsirka v Uzbekistane," *Sovetskaia Etnografiia* (1948), No. 3, pp. 71–87.

"Tsarist Policy towards Islam: The Soviet Version," *Central Asian Review,* VI (1958), 242–252.

Tsentral'noe Statisticheskoe Upravlenie pri Sovete Ministrov SSSR. *Chislennost' Skota v SSSR: Statisticheskii Sbornik.* Moscow, 1957

———. *Chislennost', Sostav i Razmeshchenie Naseleniia SSSR: Kratkie Itogi Vsesoiuznoi Perepisi Naseleniia 1959 Goda.* Moscow: Gosstatizdat, 1961.

Turkmenskaia Iskra (Ashkhabad), November 21, 1963, in *Central Asian Review,* XII (1964), 39.

Ujfalvy de Mezö-Kövesd, Ch. E. de. *Expédition scientifique française en Russie, en Sibérie, et dans le Turkestan.* 5 vols. Paris: E. Leroux, 1879.

Usenbaev, K. "K Voprosu o Prisoedinenii Iuzhnoi Kirgizii k Rossii," in *Trudy Instituta Istorii* I (Frunze: Akademiia Nauk Kirgizskoi SSR, 1955), pp. 39–63.

Vambéry, Arminius. *Sketches of Central Asia.* London: W. H. Allen, 1868.

———. *Travels in Central Asia: Being the Account of a Journey from Teheran across the Turkoman Desert on the Eastern Shore of the Caspian to Khiva, Bokhara, and Samarkand Performed in the Year 1863.* New York: Harper & Brothers, 1865.

Vans-Agnew, Olivia Fell. "A British Family in the Kazakh Steppe," *Central Asian Review,* X (1962), 5–11.

Vasil'eva, G. P. "Itogi Raboty Turkmenskogo Otriada Khorezmskoi Ekspeditsii za 1948 g.," in *Arkheologicheskie i Etnograficheskie Raboty Khorezmskoi Ekspeditsii 1945–1948,* ed. S. P. Tolstov and T. A. Zhdanko, pp. 427–460. ("Trudy Khorezmskoi Arkheologo-etnograficheskoi Ekspeditsii," Vol. I.) Moscow: Akademiia Nauk SSSR, 1952.

——. "Turkmeny-nokhurli," in *Sredneaziatskii Etnograficheskii Sbornik,* I, 82–215. ("Trudy Instituta Etnografii im. N. N. Miklukho-Maklaia," Novaia Seriia Vol. XXI.) Moscow: Akademiia Nauk SSSR, 1954.

Vasil'eva, G. P. and N. A. Kisliakov. "Voprosy Sem'i i Byta u Narodov Srednei Azii i Kazakhstana v Period Stroitel'stva Sotsializma i Kommunisma," *Sovetskaia Etnografiia* (1962), No. 6, pp. 3–16.

Vinnikov, IA. R. "Rodo-plemennoi Sostav i Rasselenie Kirgizov na Territorii Iuzhnoi Kirgizii," in *Trudy Kirgizskoi Arkheologoetnograficheskoi Ekspeditsii,* ed. G. F. Debets, I, 136–181. Moscow: Institut Etnografii im. N. N. Miklukho-Maklaia, Institut Istorii Ma terial'noi Kul'tury, i Institut Istorii Akademii Nauk Kirgizskoi SSR, 1956.

——. "Sotsialisticheskoe Pereustroistvo Khoziaistva i Byta Daikhan Maryiskoi Oblasti Turkmenskoi SSR," in *Sredneaziatskii Etnograficheskii Sbornik,* I, 3–81. ("Trudy Instituta Etnografii im. N. N. Miklukho-Maklaia," Novaia Seriia, Vol. XXI.) Moscow: Akademiia Nauk SSSR, 1954.

Vostrov, V. V. "Kazakhi Dzhanybekskogo Raiona Zapadno-kazakhstanskoi Oblasti (Istoriko-etnograficheskii Ocherk)," in *Trudy Instituta Istorii, Arkheologii i Etnografii, III Etnografiia,* 5–104. Alma Ata: Akademiia Nauk Kazakhskoi SSR, 1956.

——. "Nekotorye Voprosy Etnografii Kazakhov Kzyl-ordinskoi Oblasti," in *Materialy i Issledovaniia po Etnografii Kazakhskogo Naroda,* pp. 30–50. ("Trudy Instituta Istorii, Arkheologii i Etnografii im. Ch. Ch. Valikhanova," Vol. XVIII.) Alma Ata: Akademiia Nauk Kazakhskoi SSR, 1963.

Vreeland, Herbert Harold, III. *Mongol Community and Kinship Structure.* ("Behavior Science Monographs.") New Haven: Human Relations Area Files, 1954.

Wardell, John W. "An Account of the Happenings at Spasskiy in Kazakhstan between 1914 and 1919," *Central Asian Review,* XII (1964), 109–113.

Wheeler, Lt. Colonel Geoffrey E. "Cultural Developments in Soviet Central Asia," *Royal Central Asian Journal,* XLI (1954), 179–189.

——. "Race Relations in Soviet Muslim Asia," *Royal Central Asian Journal,* XLVII (1960), 93–105.

——. *Racial Problems in Soviet Muslim Asia.* 2nd ed. London: Oxford University Press, 1962.

Weiner, Thomas G. *See* Winner, Thomas G.

Winner, Irene. "Some Problems of Nomadism and Social Organization among the Recently Settled Kazakhs," *Central Asian Review*, XI (1963), 355–373.

Winner, Thomas G. "The Kazak Heroic Epos," *Royal Central Asian Journal*, XXXVIII (1951), 280–291.

——. *The Oral Art and Literature of the Kazakhs of Russian Central Asia*, Durham, N.C.: Duke University Press, 1958.

Woeikof, A. (Voeikov, A.) *Le Turkestan russe*. Paris: Librairie Armand Colin, 1914.

Wolff, Rev. Joseph. *Narrative of a Mission to Bokhara in the Years 1843–1845 to Ascertain the Fate of Colonel Stoddart and Captain Conolly*. 6th ed. Edinburgh: William Blackwood & Sons, 1852.

Wood, Captain John. *A Journey to the Source of the River Oxus*, ed. Alexander Wood. 2nd ed. London: John Murray, 1872.

Wurm, Stefan. *The Turkic Languages of Central Asia: Problems of Planned Culture Contact*, Appendix I. Oxford: Central Asian Research Centre, 1960.

——. *Turkic Peoples of the USSR: Their Historical Background, their Languages and the Development of Soviet Linguistic Policy*. London: Central Asian Research Centre, 1954.

Zakharova, I. V. "Material'naia Kul'tura Kazakhov-kolkhoznikov Iugovostochnogo Kazakhstana (Po Materialam Alma-Atinskoi i Dzhambulskoi Oblastei)," in *Trudy Instituta Istorii Arkheologii i Etnografii*, III, *Etnografiia*, 105–189. Alma Ata: Akademiia Nauk Kazakhskoi SSR, 1956.

Zakharova, I. V. and R. D. Khodzhaeva. "Muzhskaia i Zhenskaia Odezhda Kazakhov XIX-Nachala XX Vekov," in *Materialy i Issledovania po Etnografii Kazakhskogo Naroda*, pp. 51–86. ("Trudy Instituta Istorii, Arkheologii i Etnografii im. Ch. Ch. Valikhanova," Vol. XVIII.) Alma Ata: Akademiia Nauk Kazakhskoi SSR, 1963.

Zaleskie, Bronislas. *La Vie des steppes kirghizes*. Paris: J.-B. Vasseur, 1865.

Zhdanko, T. A. "Byt Kolkhoznikov Rybolovetskikh Arteley na Ostravakh Iuzhnogo Arala," *Sovetskaia Etnografiia* (1961), No. 5. Translated as "The Fishermen of the Southern Aral," *Central Asian Review*, X (1962), 206–213.

——. "Karakalpaki Khorezmskogo Oazisa," in *Arkheologicheskie i Etnograficheskie Raboty Khorezmskoi Ekspeditsii 1945–1948*, ed. S. P. Tolstov and T. A. Zhdanko, pp. 461–566. ("Trudy Khorezmskoi Arkheologo-etnograficheskoi Ekspeditsii," Vol. I.) Moscow: Akademiia

Nauk SSSR, Institut Etnografii imeni N. N. Miklukho-Maklaia, 1952.

———. "Narodnoe Ornamental'noe Iskusstvo Karakalpakov (k Publikatsii Materialov Karakalpakskogo Etnograficheskogo Otriada Khorezmskoi Arkheologo-etnograficheskoi Ekspeditsii v Etnograficheskoi Ekspeditsii ob-va po Izucheniiu Kazakhstana," in *Materialy i Issledovaniia po Etnografii Karakalpakov,* ed. T. A. Zhdanko, pp. 373–410. ("Trudy Khorezmskoi Arkheologo-etnograficheskoi Ekspeditsii," Vol. III.) Moscow: Akademiia Nauk SSSR, Institut Etnografii imeni N. N. Miklukho-Maklaia, 1958.

———. *Ocherki Istoricheskoi Etnografii Karakalpakov. Rodo-plemennaia Struktura i Rasselenie v XIX-Nachale XX veka.* ("Trudy Instituta Etnografii imeni N. N. Miklukho-Maklaia," Novaia Seriia, Vol. IX.) Moscow: Akademiia Nauk SSSR, 1950.

———. "Problema Polyosedlogo Naseleniia v Istorii Srednei Azii i Kazakhstana," *Sovetskaia Etnografiia* (1961), No. 2, pp. 53–62.

Index

INDEX

Automobile, 167, 184, 213
Avicenna, 196
Azerbaijan, 190
Azerbaijani: troupes, 185, 209; Turks, 19, 26

Babur, 5
Bacha, 88; *see also* Dancing boys
Bactria, 3, 4
Bactrian camels, 30, 47
Baghdad, 39
Bahadur, 53
Baïga, 55, 86, 181
Baitursun, Ahmad, 103, 144
Balkh, 3
Balkhash, Lake, 11, 12, 13, 126, 127
Baluchi, 25
Baqshi, 44, 141–142
Bards, 46, 55, 85, 102, 104
Barley, 47, 51, 57, 59
Barthold, W., 22, 48
Barynta, 29
Bashkirs, 117
Basmachi revolt, 152, 171
Batum, 112
Batur, 53
Batyr, 41
Bazaars, 23, 59, 60, 65–66, 67, 71, 81, 87, 110, 166–167, 184
Betting, 87
Bibi Seshambeh, 79
Bicycle, 168
Bii, 38, 47, 97, 98, 99
Bilingualism, 22, 23, 27
Birthday celebrations, 181
"Black bone," 39
Black earth belt, 9, 12
Black Sea, 3
Blacksmiths, 34, 48, 126, 134, 136
"Black water," 11
Blood feuds, 29
Bogarnyi, 126, 127, 128, 158; *see also* Dry farming
Bolshevik revolution, 117
Bombay, 112
Bonfire, 69, 80, 82; *see also* Zoroastrian fire cult

Boundaries of Central Asia, 8–9
Bread, 48, 51, 58, 129, 130, 159, 160, 161, 203, 210
Brick: kiln-fired, 60, 61, 111, 162; sun-dried, 60, 162
Bride price (*kalym, qalyn*), 40, 54, 68–69, 71, 72, 80, 95, 139–141, 155, 168, 169–170, 205, 215
Bride service, 40
Bukeev (Bukey) Orda, 36, 100, 125, 126
Bukhara, 87; religious center, 42, 76, 77, 79, 83, 112, 113, 114, 115; trade center, 13, 25, 65, 73, 75, 110, 167, 184
Bukhara, Emirate of, 21, 22, 23, 50, 72, 75, 83, 105–106
Bukhara, Emirs of, 24, 86, 88, 110
Bukharan Jews, 22; *see also* Jews
Bukharan rugs, 62, 89
Buran, 10
Buza, 89

Cairo, 112
Calendar: lunar, 82; solar, 82
Camels, 2, 30, 31, 33, 47, 50, 51, 58, 126, 167, 168; numbers, 122–123
Caravan routes, 2, 13, 25, 58, 67, 89, 95, 168
Caravansarais, 25, 66, 73
Carpenters, 49, 126, 129, 133–134
Carts, two-wheeled, 48, 58; *see also* *Arba*
Carving, 47, 89, 90, 166
Caspian Sea, 5, 7, 8, 9, 11, 12, 13, 21, 36, 50, 52, 53, 79, 92, 100
Catherine II, 24, 41–42
Cattle, 2, 30, 47, 48, 97, 126, 127, 128; numbers, 122
Chaghataian literature, 28
Chahar Kitab, 83
Chaikhane, 65, 71, 86, 183; *see also* Teahouse
Chalas, 22
Changaraq, 32
Chapan, 34–35, 96, 131, 132
Charcoal brazier, see *Sandal*

INDEX